DISCARD

Revolution in the Social Sciences

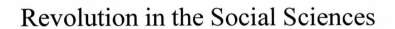

Revolution in the Social Sciences

Beyond Control Freaks, Conformity, and Tunnel Vision

Bernard Phillips and David Christner

LEXINGTON BOOKS
Lanham • Boulder • New York • Toronto • Plymouth, UK

Published by Lexington Books
A wholly owned subsidiary of The Rowman & Littlefield Publishing Group, Inc.
4501 Forbes Boulevard, Suite 200, Lanham, Maryland 20706
www.lexingtonbooks.com

Estover Road, Plymouth PL6 7PY, United Kingdom

British Library Cataloguing in Publication Information Available

Library of Congress Cataloging-in-Publication Data

Phillips, Bernard S.
Revolutions in the social sciences : beyond control freaks, conformity, and tunnel vision / Bernard
Phillips and David Christner.
p. cm.
Includes bibliographical references and index.
ISBN 978-0-7391-7199-8 (cloth : alk. paper) -- ISBN 978-0-7391-7200-1 (electronic)
1. Human behavior. 2. Social interaction. 3. Sociology. 4. Evolution. I. Christner, David. II. Title.
HM1033.P495 2012
302--dc23
2011039368

Printed in the United States of America

Contents

Preface

Is it actually possible that personal and world problems that we presently remain unable to solve have taught us that we are quite limited creatures when in fact our potential for continuing to develop is unbounded? Have the present patterns of organizing society that we have learned to conform to yielded a situation that increasingly threatens the very existence of the human race? However, is there indeed a direction that we can learn to take that will enable us to solve our threatening problems? Does that direction point us toward both the personal evolution of the individual and the evolution of society?

We answer all of these questions with a resounding "Yes!" based not on any gloom-and-doom scenario nor on any utopian dream but rather on realistic optimism derived from our integration of social science knowledge. Just as physicians and engineers solve physical and biological problems on the basis of knowledge from the biophysical sciences, so can we all learn to solve personal and world problems on the basis of knowledge from the social sciences. That knowledge presently exists in bits and pieces that are scattered throughout our libraries. Following Edna St. Vincent Millay's poem "This Gifted Age" that knowledge is indeed "wisdom enough to leach us of our ill," waiting to be integrated so that we can penetrate the complexity of human problems.

Our use in this book of poets like Millay illustrates what we see as an essential direction for such integration: following in the footsteps of Francis Bacon, the founder of the scientific method. Bacon claimed, "I have taken all knowledge to be my province." Together with others in the Sociological Imagination Group that we founded in 2000, our seven previous published books have moved us—one step at a time—toward our present insights within this book. We can now state unequivocally— while giving full recognition to enormous and increasing present-day problems—that we human beings are indeed creatures with unlimited potential not only for solving current problems but also for continuing evolution beyond our wildest dreams.

It is human language that is our greatest invention and our most powerful tool for penetrating the enormous complexity of human behavior and enabling us to solve our problems, and then to go on from there. And it is the extraordinary language of the social sciences—as illustrated by the concepts within the table of contents—that can enable us to increase enormously the power of our linguistic tools. Following part II, language can help us learn to develop not only intellectually with respect to "head" but also emotionally and in our problem-solving ability, relating to "heart" and "hand." It is also that language, following part III, that can help us to change the institutions of society from their present patterns limiting our development to patterns that follow the dream of John Dewey: "the supreme test of all political institutions and industrial arrangements shall be the contribution they make to the all-around growth of every member of society." We have come to see that growth—which has in the past been limited—as potentially unlimited once we learn to make use of the extraordinary language of the social sciences.

It is indeed the case that the social sciences—sociology, psychology, anthropology, political science, economics and history—have as yet failed to yield a clear direction for progress on the fundamental problems threatening contemporary society. And it is also the case that this has yielded widespread discouragement about this possibility not only throughout society but even among social scientists. Yet we are convinced that such assessments do not take into account the enormous complexity of human behavior. And neither do they take into account a human potential that has yet to be fulfilled and that follows the requirements of the scientific method: the integration of our knowledge of human behavior. It is exactly that integration that we have emphasized in this book. It is a direction that Mills called "the promise of sociology" and that we call the promise of the social sciences.

We deeply appreciate the advice and encouragement of Louis C. Johnston, who shares our own vision of human possibilities. And we are equally grateful to J. David Knottnerus for his most insightful comments and enthusiasm. Dean Birkenkamp, Michael Sisskin, Julie Kirsch, and Jana Hodges-Kluck's belief in our contribution has proved to be most helpful. And we would also like to acknowledge the support and feedback we've received from Christian Flores-Cariguan, Robert W. Fuller, Thomas J. Scheff, S. M. Miller, Timothy Chester, and Carl Slawski. Most important, however, we are deeply indebted to all those individuals on whose shoulders we stand and who have filled the pages of our bibliography.

Introduction

In his *The Structure of Scientific Revolutions* (1962), Thomas S. Kuhn—a historian and philosopher of science—saw the continuing development of the physical and biological sciences as largely based on changes in fundamental assumptions or "scientific paradigms." For example, the acceptance of Albert Einstein's Special Theory of Relativity in place of Isaac Newton's laws of motion depended on three things: (1) raising to the surface Newton's basic assumptions and show how they yielded data that were contradicted by evidence; (2) developing alternative assumptions that promised to resolve those contradictions; and (3) evidence for those alternative assumptions. Thus, it was not just (3) such evidence that was essential. It was also dealing with Newton's and Einstein's fundamental assumptions—or (1) and (2)—that was required.

More specifically, Einstein's basic assumptions included the idea that light travels at the same speed in any direction, contradicting Newton's assumption that light can travel at different speeds, depending on circumstances. Yet Newton's assumptions were contradicted by very clear evidence, such as experiments on the speed of light by two engineers, Michelson and Morley, and thus Einstein was able to accomplish (1). As for (2), Einstein developed the alternative assumption that light travels at the same speed in any direction, following the results of the experiments by Michelson and Morley. That assumption helped Einstein to construct his Special Theory of Relativity. As for (3) that third leg of Einstein's achievement, research over time confirmed that theory, such as Einstein's idea that light should bend due to the force of gravitation. This change from the acceptance by physicists of a change from Newton's laws of motion to Einstein's Special Theory of Relativity was no easy matter, given their commitment to those laws for centuries. It required them (1) to face up to the problems posed by their own long-buried assumptions, and (2) to learn to accept the possibility that alternative assumptions might resolve those problems.

Kuhn realized that his theory of how basic changes in science have occurred could be applied to the social sciences no less than the physical and biological sciences. It is that very application to human behavior that is the basis for this book, as indicated by our own title: *Revolution in the Social Sciences*. Just as Kuhn's analysis indicates, such a revolution requires (1) raising to the surface the long-buried assumptions of social scientists about the nature of human behavior and confronting basic problems posed by those assumptions. A revolution in the social sciences also requires (2) alternative assumptions—which might be labeled as a "cultural paradigm, "worldview" or "metaphysical stance"—that promise to solve those problems. Still further, such a revolution requires (3) evidence that supports the theory that is based on those alternative assumptions or that cultural paradigm, worldview or metaphysical stance. Given the deep commitment of social scientists to their present worldview or cultural paradigm, such a revolution will prove to be no easy matter. Yet we are convinced of the enormous importance of that change, given existing and growing problems throughout the world.

Our subtitle—*Beyond Control Freaks, Conformity, and Tunnel Vision*—suggests the problematic nature of our present basic assumptions about human behavior. "Control freaks" and "conformity" suggest patterns of dominance and subservience or hierarchy within all of our institutions. In these ways, where we have learned to bow down to those in authority and supposed experts, we limit our own patterns of interaction with others along with our ability to learn from experiences. And we develop a very limited view of our potentials as individuals coupled with a highly exaggerated view of the abilities of authority figures and so-called experts. Our limited learning in turn suggests our "tunnel vision"—shared by those above us in our hierarchies—where we all fail to see the forest for the trees in our efforts to understand ourselves and our world. In other words, enormous ignorance of how to solve our problems prevails. Yet our subtitle is most optimistic about our possibilities. We can learn (1) to raise to the surface the fundamental assumptions that limit our understanding, assumptions held by social scientists no less than the rest of us.

As for (2), we can build on our democratic ideals that point us away from hierarchies and toward our incredible potential as human beings. We all can learn to move away from our hierarchical way of life and learn to interact with one another in an egalitarian way and thus learn from our experiences in one scene after another. That interaction is an alternative to the relative isolation fostered by our present basic assumptions, cultural paradigm, worldview or metaphysical stance. The result can be not only our continuing to expand our understanding or intellectual development—by contrast with our present tunnel vision—but also our continuing development or evolution as individuals. Indeed, the original title of this book was "Personal Evolution." For our movement away from (1) and toward (2) promises nothing less than the continuing development of our intellect ("head"), our ability to express our emotions ("heart"), and our problem-solving ability ("hand"). Given our tunnel or highly specialized vision, we humans have failed to understand our incredible possibilities.

With respect to (3), our theoretical approach is based on the integration of existing knowledge primarily from the social sciences, an integration that defies the narrow specialization existing throughout the academic world. For example, there are no less than forty-five Sections of the American Sociological Association with very limited contact with one another, and this situation is paralleled throughout the social sciences. Our own emphasis on the integration of knowledge in this book builds on the work of the Sociological Imagination Group that we founded with the help of others in 2000. That work includes these seven books: *Beyond Sociology's Tower of Babel* (Phillips, 2001), *Toward a Sociological Imagination* (Phillips, Kincaid, and Scheff, eds., 2002), *The Invisible Crisis of Contemporary Society* (Phillips and Johnston 2007), *Understanding Terrorism* (Phillips, ed., 2007), *Armageddon or Evolution?* (Phillips, ed., 2009), *Bureaucratic Culture and Escalating Problems* (Knottnerus and Phillips, eds., 2009), and our just-published *Saving Society* (Phillips, 2011).

The Sociological Imagination Group chose its name from the title of the most well-known book written by the American sociologist C. Wright Mills: *The Sociological Imagination* (1959). That book was voted by the members of the International Sociological Association as the second most influential book for sociologists written during the entire 20th century; the most influential one was written early in the century by a major founder of the discipline. Mills's breadth of vision that we are building on in this book is illustrated by this quote from his well-known book:

> The sociological imagination ... is the capacity to shift from one perspective to another—from the political to the psychological; from examination of a single family to comparative assessment of the national budgets of the world; from the theological school to the military establishment; from considerations of an oil industry to studies of contemporary poetry. It is the capacity to range from the most impersonal and remote transformations to the most intimate features of the human self—and to see the relations between the two (1959: 7).

Given the enormous complexity of human behavior, such breadth is essential if we are to understand the pressing problems of contemporary societies and learn to confront them ever more effectively. Mills' vision extended beyond professional sociologists or social scientists to include the rest of us. Indeed, democratic ideals call for a population that is sufficiently educated as to the nature of their problems for them to make intelligent decision about the policies required to confront those problems effectively. Mills' vision, then, suggests the kind of broad education that we all must experience in contemporary society in our effort to achieve a genuine democracy. In our view, that education must point us toward nothing less than our own "personal evolution."

In order to understand the meaning and significance of our concept of "personal evolution," it is essential that we go very far back in time, even to the very origins of the universe some fourteen billion years ago. For we have argued in chapter 1 of this book that the very nature of our universe is interactive, including the interaction among physical phenomena. And we have also argued in that chapter that such interaction is fundamental to the nature of biological evolution. It is such interaction that, over the billions of years of biological evolution, has yielded the development of us humans with our extraordinary tool for interaction that can enable us to learn with no limit whatsoever: language. As claimed by Stephen Jay Gould, our eminent and popular biologist, "We are, in a more than meta-phorical sense, permanent children. . .small face, vaulted cranium and large brain in relation to body size, unrotated big toe, foramen magnum under the skull for correct orientation of the head in upright posture, primary distribution of hair on head, armpits and pubic areas. . . . Hu-mans are learning animals" (Gould, 1981: 333-334). This is not merely the situation of some of us: Gould was writing about every single human being.

Moving much closer to modern times, the American and the French revolutions in the eighteenth century—which built on worldwide devel-opments such as the achievements of ancient Greece and Rome coupled with the European Renaissance that rested on scholarship within Islamic civilization—emphasized democratic ideals with their glorification of the potential of every individual. It is those revolutions, coupled with our continuing scientific and technological revolutions that they helped to spawn, that have yielded what Miller and Savoie have called our contin-uing "respect revolution" (2002, 8-12). That revolution includes a variety of social movements throughout the twentieth century, illustrated by what has occurred in the United States. There has been the civil rights movement, the women's movement, the gay, lesbian and transgender movement, the senior movement, and the disability movement. These movements are continuing into our present century, for the "respect rev-olution"—just like our technological revolution—is a revolution that has not yet ended, as is well-illustrated by what is occuring throughout the Middle East. All of these changes focus on the potential not of only some of us but rather of all of us.

In order to move from the respect revolution to the idea of personal or individual evolution, it is essential that we move toward a still deeper democratic idea—the idea of the intellectual potential of every single one of us—given our present assumptions about the supposed hierarchy of intelligence or capacity to learn. Just as Gould claimed, we are all "learn-ing animals," and we all possess the features of children that he de-scribed. It is in chapter 3 that we discuss studies by Bowles and Gintis, Shenk, Nisbett, and Rosenthal that throw cold water on our assumptions that the individual's intelligence is limited by some number. Indeed, our overall emphasis throughout this book on the importance of "heart" no less than "head" and "hand"—coupled with the gross failures of our intellectual elites to cope with contemporary escalating problems throughout the world—should be enough to shred those assumptions. The result is our idea that every single one of us—regardless of our past achievements or lack of achievement—possesses nothing less than the extraordinary potential not just for further development but rather for continuing personal evolution. To believe otherwise, in our view, is to become our own worst enemies, especially in these times when we must learn to become our own best friends.

Although it will take this entire book to describe and document the breakthrough in the social sciences that results from the integration of social science knowledge—and that is the basis for personal evolution—we can at least provide here some hints about our overall argument. It is human language that is our greatest invention and our most powerful tool for penetrating the enormous complexity of human behavior and enabling us to solve our problems, and then to go on from there. And it is the technical or extraordinary language of the social sciences—as illustrated by the concepts within the table of contents—that can enable us to increase enormously the power of our linguistic tool. Just as the technical languages of the biophysical sciences have been the basis for increasingly effective biophysical technologies, so can the technical language of the social sciences become the basis for increasingly effective personal and social problem-solving technologies.

In part one we shall expand on the ideas in this brief introduction, yielding the framework we require to present that technical or extraordinary language of the social sciences in part two. As discussed in part two, that language can help us learn to develop not only intellectually with respect to "head" but also emotionally and in our problem-solving ability, relating to "heart" and "hand." It is also that language, following part three, that can help us to change the institutions of society from their present patterns limiting our development to patterns that follow the dream of John Dewey: "the supreme test of all political institutions and industrial arrangements shall be the contribution they make to the all-around growth of every member of society." We have come to see that growth—which has in the past been limited—as potentially unlimited once we learn to make use of the technical or extraordinary language of the social sciences

The title of a book by Britain's Astronomer Royal suggests the nature of our present situation: *Our Final Hour: A Scientist's Warning: How Terror, Error, and Environmental Disaster Threaten Humankind's Future in This Century—On Earth and Beyond.* In that book Martin Rees claimed that "The 'downside' from twenty-first century [biological and chemical] technology could be graver and more intractable than the threat of nuclear devastation that we have faced for decades" (2003: vii). We agree with his assessment as to the enormous and increasing threats to our survival. Our present way of life continues to yield wars without end, ever more effective weapons of mass destruction and the means to deliver them, and a wide range of world and personal problems that we cope with only to a very limited extent.

We remain realistic about these problems. However, we are realistic optimists, following our convictions about a revolution in the social sciences based on the integration of social science knowledge, and following our belief in the individual's potential for continuing evolution. This book is by no means a recipe that will enable the individual, after reading the last page, to fulfill unrealized potentials and confront personal and world problems ever more effectively. Yet we do claim, following the vision of the Dutch sociologist Fred Polak, that an image of the future can become the most powerful force we humans can develop for actually creating the future, providing that it is backed up by concrete procedures for moving toward that image. We have put forward our own extremely general image of the future on the website of the Sociological Imagination Group (www.sociological-imagination.org). And we believe that our argument in this book can yield the basic ideas that are essential for making progress toward that vision. We have a dream that:

> There will be a future for our children, our grandchildren, our great-grandchildren, and their great-grandchildren.
>
> One day we will all learn to see ourselves as children who are only just beginning to understand ourselves and our world, and we will also learn to dream about our infinite possibilities and move toward those visions one step at a time.
>
> One day we will all learn to pay close attention to the accomplishments of all peoples throughout history as well as to our own personal accomplishments, and we will also learn to pay close attention to the failures of the human race and to our own personal failures.
>
> One day we will be able to bring to the surface and reduce our stratified emotions like fear, shame, guilt, hate, envy, and greed, and we will learn to express ever more our evolutionary emotions like confidence, enthusiasm, happiness, joy, love, and empathy.
>
> One day we will see peace on earth and fellowship among all humans.
>
> One day we will no longer look down on any other human being.
>
> One day we all will learn to be poets, philosophers, and scientists.

I

Strategy: Learning from History

It is the complex language—more than any other feature—that we humans have created over thousands of years that sharply distinguishes us from all other forms of life and that is the basis for the evolution of the individual and society. It has been basic for helping us to solve problems great and small and enabling us to pass along that knowledge from one generation to the next. It is written language that has been the foundation for the cumulative development of knowledge within science. Isaac Newton claimed, "If I have seen further it is by standing on the shoulders of giants." And it is science that has succeeded in shaping our entire way of life.

Yet human language along with science have proven to be two-edged swords. For example, in chapter 1 we shall learn how we have failed to take advantage of the incredible potentials that language offers to every single one of us. It is a failure illustrated within the most outstanding minds of any given generation—our heroes, our Nobel Prize winners, our leaders in all walks of life—no less than within the minds of the rest of us. It is also in chapter 1 that we shall learn how the social sciences have failed us, as illustrated by this excerpt from Edna St. Vincent Millay's and Norma Millay Ellis's "Upon this age, that never speaks its mind," 1939, 1967 (reprinted by permission of Holly Peppe, Literary Executor, The Millay Society):

> Upon this gifted age, in its dark hour,
> Rains from the sky a meteoric shower
> Of facts . . . they lie unquestioned, uncombined.
> Wisdom enough to leech us of our ill
> Is daily spun; but there exists no loom
> To weave it into fabric .

However, just as language and the scientific method have been much of the basis for the shaping of our world by the physical and biological sciences, so can those tools become much of the basis for the shaping of our world by the social sciences. Social scientists can learn to get their act together. Although presently there are no less than forty-five distinct sections of the American Sociological Association—a situation paralleled within the other social sciences—sociologists can learn to integrate those bits and pieces of knowledge, and other social scientists can follow suit. The "fabric" that they develop can be used to confront our "dark hour" and "to leech us of our ill." And far beyond the solution of our most threatening problems, we humans can continue to evolve, creating the kind of world that we can scarcely imagine.

It is in chapter 2 that we discuss a breakthrough in social science knowledge yielding a "loom" or scientific method broad enough to follow in the footsteps of Francis Bacon. We have been guided here by the words of the sociologist C. Wright Mills: "The sociological imagination . . . is the capacity to shift from one perspective to another—from the political to the psychological; from examination of a single family to comparative assessment of the national budgets of the world; from the theological school to the military establishment; from considerations of an oil industry to studies of contemporary poetry." Mills has been the guiding spirit for our work.

ONE

Problems: "A Little Learning Is a Dangerous Thing"

Edwin A. Abbott's *Flatland: A Romance of Many Dimensions* (1884/1952) is one of the earliest science fiction stories ever written. Flatland is a two-dimensional world inhabited by triangles, squares, polygons and circles, with the number of one's sides determining one's status in society. A square, the narrator, is visited by a three-dimensional sphere who takes him up into space and shows him the wonders of Spaceland, our three-dimensional world. But when the Square returns and attempts to explain his fantastic journey to his countrymen, he is imprisoned for life for his seditious remarks about the supposed existence of a third dimension.

We Spacelanders would not imprison someone for talking about the existence of a fourth dimension of time. Indeed, we freely speak about the past and the future. Yet just how frequently do we think about our millions of past experiences as well as those of society as a whole, and just how far back in the past do we generally travel? Further, how often do we think about the many possible futures that we might construct along with the specific behavior that would take us toward them? Apparently we are creatures of Spaceland rather than Timeland, for we find ways to avoid entering the time dimension more than occasionally. We resist entering Timeland much like the Circles who imprisoned the Square resisted entering Spaceland.

Our failure to move decisively from Spaceland toward Timeland joins us with lower forms of life that are almost completely dominated by the requirements of the momentary external scene. Thus, we continue to largely ignore our own past experiences and those of society, and we continue to largely ignore our future possibilities. Indeed, it is an "outward" orientation to the momentary scene with little awareness of our "inward" past experiences and future possibilities. In other words, we

3

fail to achieve interaction between who we are, based on our past experiences and future possibilities, and our present external experiences. Similar to lower forms of life with no complex language and very limited memory, we humans—with our complex language that gives us memory and future orientations—also point toward an outward orientation. And that outward orientation works against our achieving genuine inward-outward interaction with others. For we must travel inward toward our unique personal experiences in order to achieve such interaction. Instead, our limited inward orientation leaves us largely isolated from our unique selves.

The subtitle of this book illustrates this isolation from our own unique selves with its resulting lack of deep interaction with others. For example, a "control freak" is oriented to making another "conform" to his or her bidding, yet they are both oriented outward rather than both inward and outward. Sociologists have a concept for this: "social stratification," which is the persistence of hierarchy. The control freak is at the top of the hierarchy and the conformist is at the bottom. Their lack of genuine or deep interaction carries over into the lack of genuine interaction among ideas, which is the very nature of "tunnel vision." This is what Edna St. Vincent Millay was writing about when she referred to "a meteoric shower of facts" which "lie unquestioned, uncombined." And it is illustrated as well by the division of the social sciences into hundreds of specialized fields that generally fail to communicate with one another. Given the complexity of human behavior, that lack of the integration of knowledge works against a crucial ideal of the scientific method: that the scientist should be open to all phenomena relevant to the problem under investigation.

We are convinced, then, that we must learn to enter Timeland far more frequently, just as it is essential to take time very seriously if we wish to understand what has happened in the past that has caused our present problems, and if we wish to change our future behavior so as to solve those problems. Presently we continue to swim on the surface of the ocean of time, rarely going far below to explore where we have come from. And if the sky represents the future, we continue to remain on that surface rather than learn to fly. We begin this chapter by journeying billions of years back in time to the development of our physical universe as well as to the evolution of life. We then continue by focusing on the past five centuries of our continuing scientific and technological revolutions. Finally, we take a second look at those centuries, centering on a fundamental and increasing problem: the growing gap between aspirations and their fulfillment. And we discover, following Alexander Pope—an eighteenth-century English poet—that "A little learning is a dangerous thing."

THE PHYSICAL UNIVERSE AND BIOLOGICAL EVOLUTION

The American poet Robert Frost helps us to develop insight into the very nature of our physical universe along with the process of biological evolution in his "Mending Wall":

> Something there is that doesn't love a wall,
> That sends the frozen-ground-swell under it,
> And spills the upper boulders in the sun,
> And makes gaps even two can pass abreast. . .
> I let my neighbor know beyond the hill;
> And on a day we meet to walk the line
> And set the wall between us once again,
> We keep the wall between us as we go. . .
> Before I built a wall I'd ask to know
> What I was walling in or walling out. . . .;
> He moves in darkness as it seems to me,
> Not of woods only and the shade of trees.
> He will not go behind his father's saying. . .
> He says again, "Good fences make good neighbors."

Just as Frost describes the interaction of the frozen ground on the wall's boulders, so is the interaction of all phenomena fundamental to the nature of the universe as a whole. Efforts to wall in and wall out phenomena are doomed to failure in the long run, just as are the human being's efforts to limit his or her full interaction with external phenomena by staying within Spaceland rather than moving into Timeland. No complete isolation of phenomena is physically possible within our universe, for a given phenomenon's container will be affected by what goes on outside of the container and, as a result, will have an impact on what goes on inside the container. And the reverse occurs as well. Interaction among phenomena is thus the name of the game throughout our universe, even if that interaction is quite indirect. Frost's neighbor "moves in darkness" when he says that "good fences make good neighbors," for he is directly opposing the very nature of the universe. He is pointing toward a way of life that requires a narrow "head" orientation, a "heart" oriented to emotional repression, and a "hand" that is relatively ineffective.

If interaction is part of the very nature of our physical universe, then it is no less part of the very nature of our billions of years of biological evolution. For it is the interaction between organisms and their environments that determines whether or not a given species is better adapted to its environment than a species competing with it. Thus, for example, long-necked giraffes would be better adapted to an environment of tall trees than short-necked giraffes. And their progeny would have a better chance of surviving than the progeny of short-necked giraffes, leading to the continuing evolution of the former and the extinction of the latter.

Once again, then, it is interaction—this time between organisms and their environments—that is the fundamental process that is involved. It is interaction by contrast with isolation that is not only fundamental to the very nature of our physical universe. Interaction is equally fundamental to the process of biological evolution. And once again this foreshadows the present-day importance of interaction versus isolation for us humans, for we can choose to move toward isolation by remaining in Spaceland or to move toward interaction by shifting toward Timeland.

Unfortunately, however, our commitment to Spaceland versus Timeland—along with its limitations with respect to our utilization of "head," "heart" and "hand"—parallels the commitment of Abbott's Flatlanders to Flatland rather than Spaceland. Just as the Flatlanders resisted the possibility of a third dimension and thus doomed themselves to a very limited way of life, so do we Spacelanders avoid entering Timeland and thus fail to understand and cope with escalating problems throughout the world. For example, our dominant approach to the nature of the physical universe is to look outward in an effort to discover other intelligent forms of life. At the same time, we continue to largely ignore the possibility of an inward journey, where we would learn about the nature of human behavior and human problems. For example, the specialized knowledge of the physical universe that we humans have developed has failed to see interaction as absolutely fundamental to its nature and has failed to see us human beings—with our complex languages—as by far the most interactive phenomena throughout the known universe. Further, that specialized knowledge fails to detect the barriers we have constructed to fulfill ever more of our interactive potential, such as our commitment to Spaceland rather than Timeland. Thus, our focus on exploring outer space takes away from our possibilities for fulfilling our human potential for understanding increasing problems and confronting them effectively.

This failure to understand the nature of our physical universe and its implications for our situation at this time in history is paralleled by our failure to understand the nature and implications of biological evolution. Charles Darwin's fantastic achievement of unearthing the essential nature of biological evolution in his *The Origin of Species* (1859/1964) shook the world. And biological research during the past century and a half has worked to support and extend his almost unparalleled scientific achievement. Yet our near-universal commitment to our outward-oriented Spaceland rather than an inward-outward oriented Timeland has worked against a profound understanding of the implications of Darwin's findings for human behavior and human problems. Darwin proceeded to enter Timeland with a theory that looked back at nothing less than billions of years of the origins of species from the lowly one-celled organism to the present-day human being. Yet this sweeping approach to the fourth dimension of time goes against the grain of us Spaceland creatures, for our focus is on our own momentary situation, much like the focus of organisms without our complex languages.

More specifically, much of the initial interpretation of Darwin's work applied his explanation of the biological evolution of non-linguistic species to us humans with our complex languages and our ability to learn from experience. Thus, for example, those people with some physical defect or handicap, those with mental problems, those seen as low in intelligence, those who had committed a crime, those addicted to alcohol or drugs, and those who remained in poverty came to be seen as "unfit" within what Darwin had called the competitive "struggle for life." And it is best that they should die in order to make way for the development of "superior" human beings and the progress of society as a whole. This interpretation of Darwin's ideas about the evolution of non-linguistic organisms as applying to human beings strengthened racist ideas, such as those of the Ku Klux Klan in the United States and Adolph Hitler in Nazi Germany, ideas that yielded a rationale for the extermination of the "unfit" as being unworthy of life.

It is this elitist view of Darwin's evolutionary ideas that colors even today any effort to apply the idea of evolution to human behavior. Yet our own vision of personal evolution is not just democratic: it is exceedingly democratic because of its orientation to the potential of personal evolution for every single one of us human beings. We might think of the possibilities of personal evolution as depicted by a stairway to the stars with extremely wide steps, by contrast with a see-saw where the individual can only move up to a limited extent and only at the price of someone else moving downward. Our world at present is a combination of both the see-saw and the stairway, with its areas of business competition coupled with limited human development and its areas of stairways, as illustrated to an extent by the institution of education. Yet both business and education — along with other institutions as well — can be transformed in a more democratic direction, as suggested by John Dewey, the American philosopher and educator:

> Government, business, art, religion, all social institutions have a meaning, a purpose. That purpose is to set free and to develop the capacities of human individuals without respect to race, sex, class, or economic status. And this is all one with saying that the test of their value is the extent to which they educate every individual into the full stature of his possibility. Democracy has many meanings, but if it has a moral meaning, it is found in resolving that the supreme test of all political institutions and industrial arrangements shall be the contribution they make to the all-around growth of every member of society. (Dewey 1920/ 1948: 186)

Dewey presents here a most radical vision of how all of our institutions should be completely transformed from their present directions toward a focus on the continuing development of every individual with whom they come into contact. His effort to "educate every individual into the full stature of his possibility" meshes closely with our own focus on the potential of every individual to continue to evolve with respect to "head," "heart" and "hand." Jane Addams, a well-known American social worker writing in *Democracy and Social Ethics*, shares our own vision of democracy:

> A conception of Democracy not merely as a sentiment which desires the well-being of all men, nor yet as a creed which believes in the essential dignity and equality of all men, but as that which affords a rule of living as well as a test of faith. (quoted in Knowles, 2004: 3)

"Sentiment" has to do with "heart," "creed" with "head," and "a rule of living" with "hand." From this perspective the ideal of democracy becomes broad enough to include the ideas, feelings and actions of the individual. Addams also wrote that "the cure for the ills of Democracy is more Democracy." By so doing she gave recognition to the limitations of present-day political systems of democracy that fail to engage the active and continuing commitment and participation of the individual in the democratic process from one day to the next, rather than simply voting infrequently. She pointed toward the development of nothing less than a democratic way of life for the individual and society, directly opposing patterns of an outward orientation, emotional repression and ineffective actions that generally characterize present-day democracies.

These ideas of democracy build on a most fundamental idea of Darwin's approach to the evolution of species, the idea of interaction, which is equally fundamental to the nature of our physical universe. For it is those organisms that are able to interact more successfully with their environments that survive to yield the progeny that also survive. And it is those organisms that fail to interact successfully with their environments—such as the short-necked giraffe within an environment of tall trees—that become extinct. The idea of democracy also stresses the idea of interaction, for voting—by contrast with having no voice in determining the leaders of society—is an example of interaction between leaders and those who are led. Jane Addams's view of democracy carries still further this idea of interaction, for she sees democracy as creating nothing less than "a rule of living" that yields continuing interaction between leaders and the led. This view of Darwinian theory with its emphasis on interaction is a far cry from the notion of "the survival of the fittest," where the supposedly unfit are left to die rather than encouraged to interact with others in society.

By contrast, an interpretation of Darwin's significance for human behavior that focuses on the survival of the fittest points toward a see-saw world that fails to emphasize interaction and instead focuses on the isolation of individuals. For there is quite limited interaction when hierarchies of individuals are central to society. To illustrate with reference to a stairway world, assuming that the stairway's steps are sufficiently wide, one person's ascent does not get in the way of another person's ascent. Indeed, to the extent that individuals in the process of climbing the stairway interact with one another, they can gain understanding about how to climb the stairway, for the experiences of each individual are at least somewhat unique. However, if the climbers avoided such interaction and centered instead on patterns of hierarchy, they would be able to learn little from one another, and their understanding of how to continue to climb would thus become limited. A more extreme interpretation of Darwin's theory as illustrating hierarchy could result in active opposition among the climbers to one another, yielding more of a see-saw situation than a stairway situation.

The importance of our focus on interaction in interpreting the significance of Darwin's theory for understanding human evolution cannot be understood without direct attention to the nature of language. For it is our complex language that sharply divides us from lower forms of life, and it is language that is the basis for our interaction with one another. Whatever else language helps us to achieve, it is our learning as a result of interaction that is absolutely fundamental. We can use language to learn how to climb that stairway when we interact with others who are also climbing it. Without our complex language, by contrast, our ability to learn from such interaction would be drastically limited. Language enables us to move beyond the momentary Spaceland situation and enter Timeland, exploring people's past experiences of succeeding and failing to climb as well as their plans for attempting to climb in the future. Instead of leaving the poor, the handicapped, the lawbreakers, the addicted and those with mental problems to die within a competitive struggle where only the elite survive, the "unfit" can learn to solve their problems as a result of interacting with our incredibly powerful tool of language. And the result can yield a society that moves ever closer toward Jane Addams's vision of an active democracy that invokes everyone's "head," "heart" and "hand."

Yet if language is indeed such a powerful tool for learning, and if indeed we are all attempting to climb that stairway, how can we explain our failure to develop the kind of active democracy that Addams envisioned? Ludwig Wittgenstein, an eminent twentieth-century philosopher, can help us here, for he claimed, "The limits of my language mean the limits of my world." Somehow we have limited our usage of language, failing to take advantage of its incredible potentials for helping us to learn how to develop ourselves and solve personal and world problems. To probe more fully the nature of language's potentials, we might distinguish among the languages of social science, biophysical science,

and arts that include literature, film, drama, painting, sculpture and music. We might see these languages as emphasizing, respectively, three
capacities of language: dichotomy, gradation or number, and figurative
language, imagery or metaphor.

More specifically the social sciences have emphasized dichotomies,
such as the distinction between equality and hierarchy or conformity and
deviance. This goes back to the fundamental nature of all languages: their
division of the world into two categories. There is the phenomena de-
noted by a given word, on the one hand, and all other phenomena, on the
other hand. The biophysical sciences, by contrast, have emphasized the
gradational component of language. Here, we see things as matters of
degree, such as degree of force and amount of atomic weight, and we can
proceed to assign numbers to those degrees. The use of mathematics has
been essential in the development of the biophysical sciences. The arts, by
contrast, emphasize metaphor, imagery or figures of speech, using language, painting, sculpture or music to represent sense experiences. This
includes taking us back to biological or perceptual experiences that pre-
cede the development of language. Images from the arts are, potentially,
powerful means of communication. They can help us to understand what
we have learned, and they can also help us to communicate knowledge.

This overriding emphasis of the social sciences on dichotomy, the
biophysical sciences on gradation, and the arts on images or metaphors is
a species of a failure to continue to move toward interaction, as illustrated by Frost's neighbor who believes that "good fences make good neighbors." For each of these fields of knowledge within the academic world
has built a linguistic fence separating it from the other fields of knowledge. This is the kind of failure that is nearly universal both inside of the
academic world and outside of it. It was illustrated above by our failure
to enter Timeland and thus interact with past occurrences and future
possibilities. Edna St. Vincent Millay's poem presented the example of a
meteoric shower of uncombined facts. We noted the existence of forty-
five sections of the American Sociological Association with limited communication among them, a situation paralleled throughout the social sciences. And we might also note the enormous chasm between the academic world and the world inhabited by everyone else, with both academics
and lay people generally failing to cross that chasm and interact with one
another.

This failure of us humans to build on the very nature of the universe
and the very nature of biological evolution with their focus on interaction
is paralleled by our failure to learn how to understand our growing problems and move toward solving them. For example, we continue to develop ever more powerful weapons of mass destruction along with ever
more effective means to deliver them. Yet we fail to learn how to halt that
production as well as how to motivate people to avoid using such weapons. We continue to move toward the exploration of outer space, yet we

fail to emphasize what we require most at this time in history: the exploration of inner space. We continue to be plagued by social problems. For example, there is a growing gap between the rich and the poor throughout the world; there are widespread patterns of addiction to alcohol, drugs and other obsessive patterns of behavior; there is equally widespread physical and mental abuse between individuals inside of and outside of families; and there is the continuing inability of leaders and our specialized "experts" to make significant progress on these and a wide range of other problems throughout society.

Yet despite the apparent hopelessness of our current situation, there is indeed a way out. Just as the ideals of the scientific method call for "standing on the shoulders of giants"—based on written language's ability to communicate what those giants have discovered—so can those ideals point toward a genuinely interactive academic world as well as the world outside of academia. If interaction is indeed the name of the game of both our physical universe and the process of biological evolution, then we should also be able to learn—by following scientific ideals—how to make interaction the name of the game of our world, including the interaction among ideas as well as individuals. And just as interaction has yielded an evolutionary history resulting in the emergence of the human being, so can a scientific method that emphasizes interaction enable us humans to continue that evolutionary journey so that we can not only solve our current problems but also move far beyond them.

As for the nature of such an incredibly broad scientific method—yet one that follows scientific ideals—that is a task that will be addressed by this book as a whole. Before that, however, we can at least provide a hint of our vision of this kind of scientific method, based on an image of a pendulum that can swing in ever-widening arcs. The first paragraph of the introduction to part I illustrates the significance of this metaphor. That paragraph invokes the ability of our complex language to help us solve our problems, corresponding to optimism about solving the problems suggested by Millay, such as our "dark hour" and our shower of uncombined facts. Such optimism suggests that we can in fact learn to solve problems with the aid of the scientific method. For example, we can build on the power of the biophysical and social sciences along with the humanities by making use of all three of language's major potentials: gradational, dichotomous and metaphorical. It is exactly here that the extraordinary or technical language of the social sciences can help us by reconstructing it so as to open up to all three of language's major potentials. By so doing, that extraordinary language moves us away from the tunnel vision of specialization with limited communication. And that technical language moves us toward fulfilling the broad ideals of the scientific method.

Given that initial optimistic assumption of our potential for solving problems with a scientific method, we are in a position to swing our pendulum of the scientific method to the left, where we learn to become aware of a given problem and become committed to making progress on it, as illustrated in the second paragraph with its attention to what Millay called our "dark hour" and our "meteoric shower" of "uncombined" facts. That awareness and commitment in turn becomes the basis for a swing to the right—illustrated by our third paragraph—where we can learn to make actual progress on the problem. That progress in turn becomes the motivation or momentum for a swing even further back to the left, followed by a swing even further to the right, and so on. We might note the close relationship between the pendulum metaphor for the scientific method and movement from Spaceland into Timeland. For it is in Timeland that we open up to personal and world phenomena throughout the past as well as within possible futures. And it is essential for a scientific method that hopes to uncover the complexities of human behavior to deal with that full range of phenomena.

This pendulum metaphor for the scientific method is thus nothing less than a vision of continuing interaction: between awareness of and commitment to solving a given problem, on the one hand, and progress on that problem, on the other hand. This is interaction that begins with optimism that problems that are put forward can in fact be solved. Given that optimism, which we may see as an initial assumption as to the possibilities of the scientific method, the scientist can then move back and forth from awareness and commitment to a problem, represented by a swing of the pendulum to the left, and progress on that problem, represented by a swing to the right. And it is such interaction that can continue indefinitely if the problem is sufficiently difficult—as is the case for fundamental problems of human behavior—so as to require a very long period of effort in making progress on the problem. Thus, the pendulum metaphor for the scientific method carries forward the idea of interaction that is so central to the nature of the universe as well as the process of biological evolution.

In the section to follow, "The Continuing Scientific and Technological Revolutions," we shall make use of this pendulum metaphor that conveys both our ideals for the scientific method as well as a pattern of interaction that is so fundamental to the nature of the universe, the process of biological evolution and the ideal of democracy. As we shall see, scientific ideals along with ideals for interaction have been only partially illustrated by the history of the past five centuries. And it is that very limitation which is much of the basis for our present situation of escalating problems throughout the world. Yet we can indeed move toward fulfilling our ideals for the scientific method by opening up to the full complexities of language. And we can accomplish this with the aid of the extraordinary or technical language of the social sciences.

THE CONTINUING SCIENTIFIC AND TECHNOLOGICAL
REVOLUTIONS

As we continue to present our ideas within part I, "On the History of the Human Race," we are well aware of how audacious we must appear to many readers who are aware of the thousands of existing books on social change, biological evolution, the nature of democracy and the scientific method. Yet we believe that our own approach—building on our seven books published over this past decade—is unique. We combine a deep commitment to confronting escalating world problems—with that escalation documented in *The Invisible Crisis of Contemporary Society*—with an extremely broad focus on understanding and confronting those problems. That focus is based on an emphasis on interaction because of its centrality to the nature of our universe, to biological evolution, to our ideals for democracy and to the very nature of the scientific method. Such breadth is not to be found elsewhere.

For a summary of the ideas within this book as a whole, we recommend the three items on the website of the Sociological Imagination Group, www.sociological-imagination.org The thirty-two-page "Guide to Personal Evolution: Confronting Limited Self-Image, Negative Emotions, and Isolation" focuses on our basic argument within chapters 3, 4 and 5. The very short home page provides information on the origin, past work and future goals of the Sociological Imagination Group, including e-mail addresses. And the ten-page biography of C. Wright Mills yields some insight into the work of the man who continues to inspire all of our efforts. Yet given the complexity of human behavior coupled with the powerful forces arrayed against our ability to understand—let alone solve—our fundamental problems, such materials can do little more than start us on a path leading toward solutions.

We shall proceed to skip over most of human history to begin by touching on the last five centuries, granting the many achievements of us humans over those many thousands of years. Those achievements, such as the invention of written language, the university and the printing press—along with a great many other inventions—made possible our scientific and technological revolutions that are continuing to shape the world. In particular, we shall have very little to say about almost everything that has taken place over the past five hundred years except for a very few ideas that have formed the basis for (1) the development of scientific ideals, (2) the development of biophysical technologies and (3) the development of forces that have opposed the continuing development of science and technology. Our focus will continue to emphasize what we have found to be so important in the previous section on the physical universe and biological evolution, namely, the idea of interaction versus isolation. It is an idea that we also see as central to the problem of achieving the continuing evolution of the individual and society.

The Development of Scientific Ideals

There is just one individual who is more responsible than any other for founding the American philosophy of pragmatism, which is arguably the most profound framework for scientific ideals: Charles Sanders Peirce. Peirce's 1877 essay, "The Fixation of Belief," presents a fundamental step within the scientific method:

> The irritation of doubt is the only immediate motive for the struggle to attain belief. . . . With the doubt, therefore, the struggle begins, and with the cessation of doubt it ends. . . . Some philosophers have imagined that to start an inquiry it was only necessary to utter a question whether orally or by setting it down upon paper, and have even recommended us to begin our studies with questioning everything! But the mere putting of a proposition into the interrogative form does not stimulate the mind to any struggle after belief. "There must be a real and living doubt, and without this all discussion is idle." (10–11)

Recalling the pendulum metaphor for the scientific method. Peirce's idea about "the irritation of doubt" has to do with a swing of the pendulum to the left where one becomes aware of and committed to making progress on a problem, given an initial assumption as to the potential and power of the scientific method. Peirce was invoking nothing less than the overriding importance of the scientist's deep commitment to making such progress. For this kind of motivation is crucial for enabling the scientist to confront the problem with everything that he or she has to offer. And it is equally crucial to enable the investigator to continue with efforts that may involve the work of a great many years.

Phillips's mentor at Columbia, the sociologist C. Wright Mills, was—among all of the teachers and professional social scientists that he ever encountered—the individual most committed "to find out" the solution to the problems he investigated. Mills revealed that commitment in whatever he did: in his roaring tone of voice in the classroom, in the muscular language he used in his books, in his sharp critiques of many of his colleagues and in his powerful indictment of those whom he believed were responsible for society's problems.

In Mills's *The Sociological Imagination* (1959), rated by the members of the International Sociological Association as the second most influential book for sociologists published throughout the twentieth century, Mills illustrated his ability to express his emotions with these words:

> I do not know the answer to the question of political irresponsibility in our time . . . But is it not clear that no answers will be found unless these problems [achieving reason and freedom in modern society] are at least confronted? Is it not obvious that the ones to confront them,

above all others, are the social scientists of the rich societies? That many of them do not now do so is surely the greatest human default being committed by privileged men in our times. (176)

It is exactly this kind of deep commitment "to find out" that powers the scientific method, giving the pendulum the momentum it requires to swing back and forth in ever widening arcs so as to yield interaction between awareness of and commitment to a problem, on the one hand, and progress on that problem, on the other hand. It is that kind of commitment that can enable the social scientist to continue to make progress on a fundamental social problem in all of its complexity—such as the problems of war and terrorism—throughout his or her lifetime. And it is that kind of commitment which is, unfortunately, much too rare throughout the scientific world. Yet we can well understand that rarity once we come to the realization of the existence of powerful forces throughout society pointing toward isolation, as illustrated by our near-universal focus on Spaceland by contrast with Timeland.

Peirce also described further steps of the scientific method in addition to the necessity for one's deep emotional commitment to a given problem. He believed that the following rule "deserves to be inscribed upon every wall in the city of philosophy: Do not block the way of inquiry" (1896/1955: 54). Metaphorically, this rule indicates the importance for that pendulum to swing back and forth in ever-widening arcs until the problem is solved, that is, the importance of continuing interaction between awareness and commitment to the problem and progress on the problem. Peirce described several common ways in which scientists contradict this rule and thus avoid such continuing interaction. For example, they may assert that we already know the answer to the problem, or that we can never learn the answer because the problem is unsolvable. Peirce's rule of not blocking the way of inquiry is particularly relevant for the social sciences, where even a lifetime of inquiry may prove to be insufficient to solve fundamental problems of human behavior. There, the scientist's deep commitment to solving the problem at hand must somehow be sufficient for that extended period of time.

Another of Peirce's ideas that is central to our own work has to do with the field of philosophy known as "metaphysics," which involves one's absolutely fundamental assumptions as to the nature of reality. Social scientists generally dismiss this field as much like considering questions about angels who dance on the head of a pin. Yet as a result they fail to recognize the impact of their own deepest yet unrecognized assumptions on their own scientific work as well as on their own everyday behavior. Peirce claimed that this field of knowledge "is in a deplorably backward condition" (1898/1955: 310), and we completely agree. It is the contrast between interaction and isolation that we see as alternative metaphysical views as to the very nature of reality. And we see the metaphysical idea of interaction as central to the nature of the physical universe, of the process of biological evolution, of democratic ideals and of the nature of the scientific method.

Social scientists generally limit their interaction with specialists in neighboring fields of social science, failing to be aware that by so doing they are violating the metaphysical idea of interaction as well as the ideals of the scientific method itself. And they also frequently violate the metaphysical assumption as to the centrality of interaction by a lack of the kind of deep commitment to a problem that is sufficient to motivate them to go back and forth with that same problem—from increasing awareness of and commitment to it to making progress on it—for a very long time. By contrast, they frequently jump from one problem to another, and thus make little progress as a result, given the complexity of problems of human behavior. By so doing they also violate Peirce's idea of not blocking the way of inquiry.

The Development of Scientific Technology

It is one thing to develop scientific ideas within the academic world, yet it is quite another thing to use those ideas to develop products for the marketplace. Scientific technology makes use of the scientific method just as does the science that is practiced throughout the academic world, but its focus is on the application of that knowledge to satisfy the desires of consumers rather than on the further development of scientific knowledge. Institutions of society other than the institution of science must become involved in order for this to happen. A major finding of Max Weber, one of the founders of sociology, is that the institution of religion—and, in particular, Protestantism—helped to make this happen for the early scientific findings in the physical and biological sciences, granting the involvement of other institutions as well. The result has been our continuing technological revolution tied to our continuing scientific revolution, with each supporting the other: the development of technology encouraged the development of science, and vice-versa.

More specifically, Weber's *The Protestant Ethic and the Spirit of Capitalism* (1905/1958) described the development of a powerful work ethic originally tied to the desires of Protestants with respect to their afterlives. They came to see hard work along with the accumulation of wealth as an indication that they would be saved for afterlives in Heaven rather than eternal afterlives in hell. It is difficult to imagine what could be more motivating for the development of technology than this. And even after this early religious idea faded, that work ethic has continued in force and currently works to power the continuing technological revolution, granting that there are other forces that can encourage an emphasis on the importance of work.

Weber quoted Benjamin Franklin's *Necessary Hints to Those That Would Be Rich* to illustrate the enormous power of the work ethic:

> Remember that time is money. He that can earn ten shillings a day by his labour, and goes abroad, or sits idle one half of that day, though he spends but sixpence during his diversion or idleness, ought not to reckon that the only expense; he has really spent, or rather thrown away, five shillings besides. . . .
>
> The most trifling actions that affect a man's credit are to be regarded. The sound of your hammer at five in the morning, or eight at night, heard by a creditor, makes him easy six months longer; but if he sees you at a billiard-table, or hears your voice at a tavern, when you should be at work, he sends for his money the next day; demands it, before he can receive it, in a lump. (48–49)

Following Weber, what creditors want to hear and see is their borrowers' economic health, as illustrated by long-term interactions with their environments so as to yield products that can be sold and thus repay a debt. They want to see borrowers who are highly motivated to pay back their loans. By contrast, idleness yields no such interaction and suggests no such motivation. We might note here the importance of emotional repression within the work ethic. For going abroad, sitting idle, playing billiards or going to a tavern comes to be seen as wasting or throwing away money. The emotional expression that might be linked to leisure activities is viewed negatively by Franklin along with the multitudes of others who became committed to the work ethic.

We can thus come to see the scientific technology that Weber illustrated by quoting from Frankln's book as an illustration of interaction—paralleling the pendulum metaphor for the scientific method—but a narrow interaction that excludes a range of human emotions. For what is involved is the same kind of deep commitment to one's efforts that Peirce emphasized as essential to the scientific method when he wrote about the importance of "the irritation of doubt." The commitment to hard work is indeed a commitment to a lifetime of interaction with one's environment so as to yield the accumulation of wealth. Thus, once again we can see the power of interaction—this time motivated not by an effort "to find out" but by an effort to reach heaven—to make progress on a given problem as well as to shape the world by fostering our continuing technological revolution. Interaction thus appears to be a basis not only for the nature of the physical universe, for biological evolution, for the ideals of democracy and for the development of the scientific method, but also for the development of scientific technologies that build on the knowledge developed within the physical and biological sciences.

Yet Weber was well aware of the human losses as well as the gains resulting from the kind of interaction centering on the accumulation of wealth. At the end of his monumental *The Protestant Ethic and the Spirit of Capitalism* he wrote these words:

> In Baxter's view the care for external goods should only lie on the shoulders of the "saint like a light cloak, which can be thrown aside at any moment." But fate decreed that the cloak should become an iron cage. . . . No one knows who will live in this cage in the future. . . . For of the last stage of this cultural development, it might well be truly said: "Specialists without spirit, sensualists without heart; this nullity imagines that it has attained a level of civilization never before achieved." (182)

Granting the incredible power of the interaction that has powered our continuing technological revolution and shaped our world—together with our continuing scientific revolution—over the past five centuries, Weber sees us as having paid a huge price for these developments. We have learned to live in an "iron cage," having become "specialists without spirit, sensualists without heart." In other words, we have learned to repress the human emotions that give us the broad "spirit" and "heart" that is the basis for our continuing emotional development. And the iron cage we find ourselves in is the cage of a bureaucratic way of life. In his later works Weber saw no way out of that cage, for he came to believe that modern bureaucracy is the best way we have to develop modern societies that can solve their problems.

In our own view, however, there is indeed a way out that points us toward the development of the social sciences, thus avoiding a one-sided materialistic civilization. For we consumers have learned to "shop until we drop" to satisfy our addiction to material goods. And although producers of those goods no longer believe that their accumulation of wealth will yield a ticket to heaven, they still remain in their iron cages of bureaucracy and still continue with their work ethic, for in common with Weber they see no alternative to that way of life. Yet the alternative of social science development is a way out that invokes a broader approach to interaction than that developed within the biophysical sciences along with their technologies. It is an approach to interaction that leads to an understanding of how to express the full range of our emotions rather than to repress much of that range. And it is thus an approach that points the individual inward as well as outward toward the solution of external problems. Still further, it is an approach that can address the escalating problems in society that the narrow approach to the scientific and technological revolutions have yielded.

Yet before we proceed to examine the nature of this alternative in chapter 2, it is essential that we learn more about the nature of our iron cage, the forces that have yielded our patterns of emotional repression and the nature of our escalating problems. We will once again go back over the past five centuries. Only this time our focus will not be on the incredible achievements of our continuing scientific and technological revolutions. For those revolutions have been a two-edged sword. Instead, our focus will be on the other edge of that sword: the problems that have resulted from our journey into the iron cage of a bureaucratic way of life with its focus on isolation by contrast with interaction.

THE GROWING ASPIRATIONS-FULFILLMENT GAP AND EMOTIONAL REPRESSION

Alexander Pope, an eighteenth–century English poet, helps us to understand why "a little learning is a dangerous thing":

> A little learning is a dangerous thing;
> Drink deep, or taste not the Pierian spring:
> There shallow draughts intoxicate the brain,
> And drinking largely sobers us again.(1711/2004)

In Greek mythology the Pierian Spring of Macedonia was believed to be a fountain of knowledge, located as it was near Mount Olympus, thought to be the seat of the gods of the arts and sciences. Pope believed that a "shallow draught" from existing knowledge—by contrast with a deep draught that yields genuine wisdom—can prove to be most dangerous. This is indeed what we have discovered in the case of the development of the physical and biological sciences coupled with the limited development of the social sciences. For example, we've developed societies where children can turn AK-47 automatic rifles on their classmates, yet where we do not understand how to teach them to love their fellow students. However, we are convinced that we can indeed learn to "drink deep" from the Pierian spring, as illustrated by the analysis in this section of a fundamental problem that has been developing over the past five centuries.

The Grocer and the Chief

In order to probe the origin and nature of the major problems blocking the evolution of the individual and society, we turn to an international study of the change from pre-industrial to modern society. Directed in the 1950s by Daniel Lerner, a political scientist, results were published in 1958 in *The Passing of Traditional Society*. Part of the study centered on the tiny farming village of Balgat, just outside of Turkey's capital city of Ankara. In the spring of 1950 an interviewer named Tosun B, who lived in Ankara, drove over a dirt road for two hours, finally arriving at Balgat. Tosun started by seeking out the village chief, a sixty-three-year-old man whom Tosun later described as "the absolute dictator of this little village." Tosun asked the chief how satisfied he was with life, and he replied, "What could be asked more? God has brought me to this mature age without much pain, has given me sons and daughters, has put me at the head of my village, and has given me strength of brain and body at this age. Thanks be to Him." Tosun then asked the chief what he would do if he were president of Turkey. Responding, he would seek "help of money and seed for some of our farmers." Tosun then asked, "If you could not live in Turkey, where would you want to live?" The chief responded, "I was born here, grew old here, and hope God will permit me to die here."

Tosun later searched out the village grocer and asked how satisfied he was with life. "I have told you I want better things. I would have liked to have a bigger grocery shop in the city, have a nice house there, dress nice civilian clothes." He had visited Ankara many times and had seen a different way of life, but he was also well aware of his limitations: "I am born a grocer and probably die that way. I have not the possibility in myself to get the things I want. They only bother me." The village grocer was, according to Tosun, "the only unfarming person and the only merchant in the village . . . he is considered by the villagers even less than the least farmer." In the eyes of the villagers, he had rejected not only the worth of the community but even the supreme authority of Allah. Tosun asked the grocer what he would do as president of Turkey: "I would make roads for the villagers to come to towns to see the world and would not let them stay in their holes all their life." Where would he want to live if he could not live in Turkey? He replied, "America, because I have heard that it is a nice country and with possibilities to be rich even for the simplest persons."

This contrast between the chief and the grocer is also a contrast between pre-industrial and modern society. The chief is satisfied with his life ("What could be asked more?"), but the grocer wants a great deal more out of life ("I have told you I want better things"). The chief had a very limited view of what he might do as president of Turkey (he would seek "help of money and seed for some of our farmers") as distinct from the grocer ("I would make roads for the villagers and would not let them stay in their holes all their life"). The chief could not imagine living outside of Turkey ("I . . . hope God will permit me to die here"), but the grocer's imagination was not so limited ("America, because I have heard that it is a nice country and with possibilities to be rich even for the simplest persons"). The chief still was a farmer, but the grocer was not. The chief remained in Balgat, but the grocer traveled frequently to Ankara.

Harlan Cleveland, an American governmental official, coined a phrase that can help us to understand the forces that have yielded the great change from a pre-industrial to a technological way of life: "the revolution of rising expectations." The chief's expectations or aspirations are most limited by comparison with those of the grocer, illustrating that revolution. This "revolution of rising expectations" that we moderns have experienced and are continuing to experience had its origins perhaps five centuries ago with the onset of the scientific and industrial revolutions originating in Western society. It was those revolutions that increasingly yielded the way of life that the grocer had experienced in Ankara and that had raised his aspirations far beyond those of the chief.

The grocer's aspirations were by no means limited to materialistic goals: "I would make roads for the villagers to come to towns to see the world and would not let them stay in their holes all their life." For the scientific and technological revolutions were joined by political revolutions over the past two-plus centuries, such as the American and French revolutions, the American civil rights movement, the women's movement, the gray panther's movement, and the gay and lesbian movement. We have learned to want not only more and more things, but also more and more equality, freedom, democracy and respect for the ultimate worth of every single individual.

Yet as a result of our revolution of rising expectations coupled with our limited ability to learn how to fulfill those expectations, we are all presently experiencing an increasing aspirations-fulfillment gap over the full range of our aspirations or values. In other words, no longer are we like the chief of Balgat, who stated, "What could be asked more?" Instead, we have become much like the grocer of Balgat, who said, "I have told you I want better things." The resulting problem for all of us is absolutely fundamental, as stated by the grocer: "I have not the possibility in myself to get the things I want. They only bother me." We are one with the grocer. The fulfillment of our basic aspirations or values is fundamental for our satisfaction with life, our sense of well-being, our moment-to-moment feelings about our own self-worth. Yet a five-century-long train of events has yielded a barrier to our ability to attain what matters to us and thus gain a sense of well-being and personal fulfillment.

"Substantial evidence" was presented supporting the hypothesis that "the gap between aspirations and their fulfillment is in fact increasing in contemporary society" in Phillips and Louis C. Johnston's *The Invisible Crisis of Contemporary Society* (2007: 234-235). In that book they also found "substantial evidence" supporting this hypothesis: "To the degree that a worldview or metaphysical stance is stratified [calls for persistently hierarchical relationships] versus interactive, there will be a large gap between aspirations and their fulfillment" (234–235). The significance of the increasing gap between aspirations and their fulfillment is not to be taken lightly. It was the basis for their calling their book *The Invisible Crisis*. What is at stake is nothing less than the frustration of the full range of the deepest desires of the individual as well as society as a whole. We are accustomed to examining specific social problems like nuclear proliferation or global warming, but what the aspirations-fulfillment gap points to is our whole range of problems.

The impact of our increasing aspirations-fulfillment gap may be illustrated by the Great Recession of 2008–2009. For example, individuals with limited incomes were encouraged by banks and other lenders to buy houses requiring mortgage payments that would easily become beyond their means, given any personal emergency, and housing foreclosures soon followed. Investment bankers, on their own part, were also following the American dream of gaining increasing wealth by packaging these mortgage agreements in complex "derivatives" and selling them so as to reap huge profits. On its part, the federal government kept its hands off of these financial schemes, assuming that governmental interference in the working of the free market poses a threat to our economic system. At the same time, individuals felt free to invest their savings in the stock market, anticipating increasing wealth year after year without understanding the risk involved in those investments.

Overall, what we experienced when the stock market crashed, when unemployment and housing foreclosures increased, and when consumers limited their consumption, was a large and growing gap between people's aspirations for wealth, for housing, for employment, for the ability to retire from work and for health care, on the one hand, and their ability to fulfill those aspirations, on the other hand. It was an experience based on the American dream of an ever higher standard of living largely due to continuing technological developments over a period of five centuries, that is, a revolution of rising expectations.

We can see this same huge aspirations-fulfillment gap on the current political scene, as described in the *Sarasota Herald-Tribune* on November 9, 2010:

> With their victory in the midterm elections, Republicans now share more than power with Democrats. They share the exact same problem that felled House Democrats. It isn't just a policy problem, though—not the deficit, taxes or even the economy. Instead, it is a deeper, more profound, structural political problem: the problem of constantly rising—and unfulfilled—expectations. . . .Politicians have an unfortunate habit of raising people's expectations with cheap and easy promises. Unfortunately for both parties, theirs is a recipe for failure, frustration and continued turmoil. (Parker and Allen, 2010: 9A)

Our continuing revolution of rising expectations—along with our large and growing aspirations-fulfillment gap—encompasses far more than our standard of living, as illustrated by a cover of the *New Yorker* magazine dated April 6, 2009. A series of cartoons are portrayed with captions advertising products catering to our incredible aspirations: "Amazing sex every time forever," "Turn back the clock with Dr. Nesbit's face cream made with our patented 'essence of youth' oil," "Vitamins that make you smarter," "Finally: a candy bar that burns 500 calories as you eat it!" "Turn your kids into domestic help," "Mind-reading hat picks up hidden neuro-transmissions!" "Build muscles, learn a foreign language, earn big bucks while you sleep" and "Lucky quarter, only a few left in stock." Similar offers, although not quite so outrageous," appear as e-mail spam that users of computers receive every day.

We can understand why this phenomenon of an increasing aspirations-fulfillment gap has remained almost invisible not only to the public at large but also to professional social scientists. For example, what is involved is a historical span of no less than five centuries, while social science research—following a Spaceland rather than a Timeland perspective—almost invariably focuses on tiny spans of time. Also, that gap includes the full range of our values, by contrast with prevailing patterns of research that generally neglect values entirely or at most deal with only one value. Still further, studies rarely combine attention to both values and their fulfillment, given the narrow specialization among the social sciences as well as within each of them. In other words, what we have in social science is highly specialized research that fails to encompass the wide range of phenomena that is required to penetrate the complexity of human behavior. And what we also have are social scientists who have become far too specialized to understand the importance of communicating whatever they have learned to the general public, especially in ways that would make sense to the public. Also, it is a rare journalist with the understanding that Parker and Allen illustrate in the above quote.

But there is yet another powerful force that works to hide our escalating aspirations-fulfillment gap from us. It is a force that operates not just in the United States and Europe but also throughout the world. It is a force that affects all human behavior, for it has to do with how we all have learned to handle our emotions. Just as emotional commitment is so fundamental to our continuing scientific and technological revolutions, so is emotional repression—the opposite of emotional commitment—so fundamental to fostering the escalating aspirations-fulfillment gap that has resulted from those revolutions.

To address that widening gap we equally need emotional commitment, but not by physical and biological scientists who know little about human emotions, and not by highly specialized social scientists who are in much the same boat. But by social scientists who have learned the importance of taking into account the interaction among all three of the major components of human behavior: metaphorically, "head," "heart" and "hand." We may recall that this breadth is exactly what Jane Addams had in mind in her vision of democracy. Given what we see as the enormous power of emotional repression, we believe in the overriding importance of attention to "heart" no less than "head" and "hand" if indeed we humans are to learn how to solve our escalating problems and move toward personal evolution. Yet in order to accomplish this, we must examine the forces that yield emotional repression and learn how to turn them aside so as to make way for emotional expression.

Emotional Repression

Arthur J. Vidich and Joseph Bensman, two American sociologists oriented to the importance of social psychology, collaborated on a study in the late 1950s of "Springdale," a town in upper New York State, publishing their results as *Small Town in Mass Society: Class, Power and Religion in a Rural Community* (1960). Springdale township had a population of only about 3,000 when Vidich and Bensman did their study. Economically, the central village—with a population of about 1,000—served as a farm trading center, with retail establishments having farm merchandise and with the presence of a milk collecting plant. Lumber was the chief economic resource of the community, with a commercial sawmill operated by two families. Vidich and Bensman saw their study as "an attempt to explore the foundations of social life in a community which lacks the power to control the institutions that regulate and determine its existence" (1960: x).

One overall hypothesis we are advancing is that there exists an increasing gap within modern society between aspirations or expectations and their fulfillment. It is that problem which, in our view, is the basis for an invisible crisis in modern society. To the extent that a large gap generally exists for the Springdalers, how are they able to function with such a gap? This problem, according to our hypothesis, affects all of us moderns. Vidich and Bensman focus in their last chapter on four phenomena, all of which illustrate a gap between aspirations or expectations and their fulfillment:

1. The small-town resident assumes the role of the warm, friendly, sociable, helpful good neighbor and friend. However, the forms of social competition and the struggle for individual success . . . [tend] to devalue his neighbors' success.
2. The goal of success as a major value and meaning in life stands in contrast to the inaccessibility of the means to achieving success . . . [which] are not equally available to all groups.
3. The illusion of democratic control over his own affairs given by the formal structure of government stands in sharp contrast to the actual basis of local politics. . . .
4. The belief and illusion of local independence and self-determination prevent a recognition of the central place of national and state institutions in local affairs. (291–292).

Given such fundamental gaps between aspirations and their fulfillment, how do Springdalers manage to cope with them? Vidich and Bensman analyze the "major modes of adjustment" to those four gaps. They include two patterns of emotional repression of those gaps, both of which achieve the isolation of the individual from the problem posed by those gaps, by contrast with interaction with them through awareness of their nature and efforts to solve that problem by narrowing those gaps. Thus, instead of a scientific approach to their problem based on awareness of and commitment to solving the problem—swinging their pendulum to the left—they repress their problems and thus avoid any effort to solve it. Vidich and Bensman proceed to describe the impact of these patterns of the failure of Springdalers to achieve their goals:

> All these explicit mentions of community dependence are made in the context of highly specific detailed cases . . . so that individuals are not explicitly aware of the total amount of their dependence. Particularizations prevent the realization of the total impression. *The technique of particularization* is one of the most pervasive ways of avoiding reality. It operates to make possible not only the failure to recognize dependence but also the avoidance of the realities of social class and inequalities.
>
> The realization of lack of fulfillment of aspiration and ambition might pose an unsolvable personal problem if *the falsification of memory* did not occur, and if the hopes and ambitions of a past decade or two remained salient in the present perspective. But the individual, as he passes through time, does not live in spans of decades or years. Rather, he lives in terms of seasons, days and hours and the focus of his attention is turned to immediate pressures, pleasures and events. . . .As [hopes and aspirations] are in process of disappearing, other thoughts of a more concrete and specific nature occupy the individual's attention, and new goals are unconsciously substituted for those that are being abandoned. . . . As a consequence, his present self, instead of entertaining the youthful dream of a 500–acre farm, entertains the plan to buy a home freezer by the fall. (299, 303; italics ours)

The technique of particularization and the falsification of memory both involve Spaceland rather than Timeland behavior, proceeding unscientifically to narrow the individual's consciousness. And both illustrate emotional repression. Yet why do the Springdalers proceed in this way? Why do they resort to techniques that illustrate emotional repression rather than procedures enabling them to confront those problems? In our view such repression results from an inability to solve the problems posed by those four fundamental contradictions in their lives standing in the way of their ability to fulfill their goals, as described above. They lack the scientific tools, as illustrated by the pendulum metaphor, that would enable them to begin with the optimistic assumption that they can solve their problems if they would only confront rather than repress them. Those tools would enable them, for example, to gain insight into their own values and patterns of behavior, and to gradually work to change their way of life so as to narrow their aspirations-fulfillment gap by swinging their pendulum back and forth in widening arcs.

Vidich and Bensman go on to describe different aspects of the Springdalers' patterns of behavior that further illustrate their techniques of particularization and falsification of memory. For example, they emphasize hard work, and that outward orientation helps them to avoid examining themselves. Similarly, they actively pursue religious activities such as suppers, choirs and fund raising, all of which involve a great deal of physical and social effort, and all of which continue their self-avoidance. As a result, following Vidich and Bensman, their procedures that yield emotional repression nevertheless enable them to survive. For example, suppers, choirs and fund raising involve a great deal of physical and social effort, and thus support the process of continuous externalization.

However, Vidish and Bensmen suggest that such externalization has at least some merit.

> But the people of Springdale are unwilling to recognize the defeat of their values, their personal impotence in the face of larger events and any failure in their way of life. By techniques of self-avoidance and self-deception, they strive to avoid facing issues which, if recognized, would threaten the total fabric of their personal and social existence. . . . Because they do not recognize their defeat, they are not defeated. The compromises, the self-deception and the self-avoidance are mechanisms which work; for, in operating on the basis of contradictory, illogical and conflicting assumptions, they are able to cope in their day-to-day lives with their immediate problems in a way that permits some degree of satisfaction, recognition and achievement. (311–320)

We believe that Vidich and Bensman succeed in describing not just the lives of the Springdalers in the late 1960s but also the lives of almost all of us living today in contemporary societies. They are able to succeed in illustrating our own emotional repression with our "system of illusions," "self-avoidance," "self-deception," "techniques of particularization," "falsification of memory" and "contradictory, illogical and conflicting assumptions." At the same time they are able to account for such behavior as yielding a measure of satisfaction not only for the Springdalers but also for the rest of us, at least in the short run. For those procedures enable the Springdalers—and the rest of us— "to cope in their day-to-day lives with their immediate problems in a way that permits some degree of satisfaction, recognition and achievement."

In the long run, however, we appear to be heading for nothing less than disaster, resulting from our widening aspirations-fulfillment gap coupled with our failure to confront it effectively. We illustrated this above with our analysis of the Great Recession of 2008 and 2009, with its stock market crash, unemployment and housing foreclosures. And we also illustrated it with a brief view of the political situation of the United

States following the elections of 2010, where both Democrats and Republicans have raised aspirations so far as to create wide aspirations-fulfillment gaps, yielding political paralysis rather than effective efforts to solve basic problems. Yet this is not to suggest that both parties are equally at fault.

Given the absolutely fundamental importance of such patterns of emotional repression for the future of the world, and given their relatively invisible nature, we shall continue in our efforts to understand that nature along with their implications for the future. Yet we should not forget the intimate link between such repression and what we have learned about the power of patterns of interaction to narrow that gap, as discussed in the earlier sections of this chapter, for we need such optimism in order to probe more deeply into our problems. More specifically, our finding of "substantial evidence" that an interactive approach to life—by contrast with the behavior of the Springdalers—yields a narrowing of the aspirations-fulfillment gap was supported by no less than all thirty-three of the individuals discussed in *The Invisible Crisis of Contemporary Society*.

We might proceed to name those thirty-three individuals so as to indicate more fully the nature of that "substantial evidence." There were nineteen social scientists from sociology, psychology and history (Walter Buckley, Lawrence Busch, Emile Durkheim, Erving Goffman, Alvin Gouldner, David Knottnerus, Jack Levin, George Lundberg, Karl Marx, Robert Merton, C. Wright Mills, Thomas Scheff, Georg Simmel, Arthur Vidich, Robin Williams, George Kelly, Milton Rokeach, Robert Sommer and Thomas Kuhn), five novelists (Edwin Abbott, Herman Hesse, Fred Hoyle, George Orwell and A. E. Van Vogt), three philosophers (Abraham Kaplan, Friedrich Nietzsche and Charles Peirce), two educators (Paulo Freire and Ivan Illich), one television producer (John Berger), one psychoanalyst (Karen Horney), one law professor (Amy Chua) and one political leader (Mahatma Gandhi).

For further insight into emotional repression we turn to Karen Horney, an eminent twentieth-century psychoanalyst who succeeded in extending the work of Sigmund Freud by emphasizing the role of culture in the development of mental problems. In her *The Neurotic Personality of Our Time* she describes two major contradictions within contemporary society that affect all of us negatively to a greater or lesser degree:

> The first contradiction to be mentioned is that between competition and success on the one hand, and brotherly love and humility on the other. On the one hand everything is done to spur us toward success, which means that we must be not only assertive but aggressive, able to push others out of the way. On the other hand we are deeply imbued with Christian ideals which declare that it is selfish to want anything for ourselves, that we should be humble, turn the other cheek, be yielding.

> The second contradiction is that between the stimulation of our needs and our factual frustrations in satisfying them. For economic reasons needs are constantly being stimulated in our culture by such means as advertisements, "conspicuous consumption," the ideal of "keeping up with the Joneses." For the great majority, however, the actual fulfillment of these needs is closely restricted. The psychic consequence for the individual is a constant discrepancy between his desires and their fulfillment. (1937: 287–288)

Those contradictions both illustrate an aspirations-fulfillment gap, paralleling the first two gaps faced by the Springdalers, as quoted above. The first one points to values in conflict that prevent the individual from fulfilling both unless that conflict is resolved. In Horney's case it is "between competition and success" and "brotherly love and humility." In the case of the Springdalers it is much the same: between "the role of the warm, friendly, sociable helpful good neighbor and friend" and "the forms of social competition . . .and the struggle for individual success." As for the second contradiction, for Horney it is "between the stimulation of our needs and our factual frustration in satisfying them." For Vidich and Bensman it is between "the goal of success" and "the inaccessibility of the means to achieving success."

Horney claimed that there are only two solutions to her first contradiction: "within the normal range" "to take one of these strivings [competition and success, on the one hand, and brotherly love and humility, on the other hand] seriously and discard the other" or "to take both seriously with the result that the individual is seriously inhibited in both directions." Yet the "normal range" suggests no fundamental changes in society, and what we are claiming in this book is that we must go beyond "the normal range" and develop such fundamental changes if indeed we are to avoid the coming of catastrophe.

We believe that there is indeed another alternative, one that speaks not only to the first and second contradictions of Horney and Vidich and Bensman but also to the range of problems discussed in this chapter. Here we have centered on the forces at work within present-day society. In chapter 2 we move toward outlining a direction for countering the forces that are yielding our escalating problems, such as our growing gap between aspirations and their fulfillment. And in the chapters to follow we shall move toward filling out that outline. As we shall see, it is patterns of interaction that can yield the additional alternative that Horney failed to see. Those patterns have to do not only with the interaction among individuals, and not only with the interaction among ideas, but also with the interaction of "head," "heart" and "hand" within the individual, for our present patterns of emotional repression work to prevent such interaction. More specifically, they work to foster fear and hate (along with shame, guilt, despair and anxiety) versus confidence and love (along with pride, self-acceptance, hope and serenity).

It is also in chapter 2 that we will continue to swing our pendulum of the scientific method further to the left as well as further to the right as it moves in widening arcs. As it moves to the left we will learn about the powerful forces of our "iron cage" that stands in the way of our continuing development or evolution. It is a cage that has existed throughout human history, and it is largely invisible, thus working against any awareness of our imprisonment. Yet we can learn to see that cage and as a result break out of it, swinging our pendulum of the scientific method to the right. Chapter 2 will begin to describe a basic tool we shall use to move out of our prison: the extraordinary language of the social sciences. Just as our complex language is our most powerful tool for solving problems, it is the extraordinary language of the social sciences that can help us to strengthen that tool by enabling us to follow scientific ideals as we penetrate the complexity of present-day personal and world problems.

TWO

Toward Solutions: The Road to Individual Evolution

I celebrate myself, and sing myself,
And what I assume you shall assume,
For every atom belonging to me as good belongs to you. . . .
Divine am I inside and out,
And I make holy whatever I touch or am touch'd from,
The scent of these arm-pits aroma finer than prayer,
This head more than churches, bibles, and all the creeds.
If I worship one thing more than another it shall be the spread of my own body
—Walt Whitman (1892/1983)

In chapter 1 we began to look back at the history of the human race by starting with a view of the physical universe and biological evolution. We discovered there the centrality of the interaction of phenomena, by contrast with their isolation. Proceeding to the past five centuries we discovered both the incredible achievements of the biophysical sciences in shaping our world along with increasing problems linked to a widening aspirations-fulfillment gap. And we also discovered a reaction to that widening gap that enables us to achieve a measure of satisfaction with life in the short run: emotional repression. But in the long run, largely given our continuing failure to confront the escalating yet invisible crisis of an increasing aspirations-fulfillment gap, we are heading for nothing less than disaster.

However, we need not continue to fiddle while Rome burns. There is indeed a way out, given the incredible potentials of every single one of us. Walt Whitman, America's poet of human worth and possibilities, points to the direction that we must take: opening up to ourselves as individuals, to our extraordinary worth and to our unbelievable possibilities. Whitman was a nurse during the American Civil War and saw a great deal of death, yet apparently this helped him to open up to the potentials of life. He somehow learned the importance of celebrating the individual human being, illustrated by the above quote from his "Song of Myself" as well as by his lifelong commitment to writing and revising his *Leaves of Grass* (1892/2004) that includes this poem.

Historically, we can come to see our past five centuries not just as a history of ever more bloody wars but also as a history of ever greater human triumphs, thus following in the footsteps of Whitman. For example, we humans have experienced the development of democracy throughout most of the world, with its orientation to equality along with a belief in the ultimate worth of every single individual. And we've also experienced the positive impacts of science and technology, and not just the negative ones. For example, we have the birth of the scientific method along with the social sciences, giving us a beginning in an effort to learn who we are, what are our potentials and how to move toward them. And of course we humans have to our credit a great many other achievements in all fields of human endeavor.

This chapter, "The Road to Individual Evolution," takes us in its three sections from very general ideas in its first section to more specific ideas in its second section, and then to still more specific ideas in its final section, previewing part II on individual evolution. We begin with "Basic Assumptions: From Isolation toward Interaction," focusing on our most fundamental or metaphysical ideas about the nature of reality. That focus is on the basic idea developed in chapter 1: the centrality of interaction—by contrast with isolation—within the nature of the universe, within biological evolution and also within human history. We discuss what Max Weber called the "iron cage," the cage of a bureaucratic way of life that we believe has been central to our wars without end coupled with the greatest crime in human history: the Holocaust, with its deliberate slaughter of millions of Jews and non-Jews who were seen as "unfit for life." Yet within this first section we also develop a direction for breaking out of the iron cage of bureaucracy. That direction requires us to confront our deepest and largely invisible assumptions and to change them so as to move from our emphasis on isolation toward an emphasis on interaction.

Our second section, "Scientific Method: Breakthrough in the Social Sciences," is based on that movement of our worldview or metaphysical stance from isolation toward interaction. Granting the achievements of the social sciences over the past two centuries despite the great complexity of human behavior, those achievements remain limited by the prevailing bureaucratic scientific method. Thus, the further development of the social sciences requires that we raise that method up to the surface so that we can become aware of its contradictions. And we must then proceed to develop a broader approach to the scientific method in order to follow the scientific ideal of opening up to the full range of factors that are relevant to any given problem, thus dealing with human complexity. This will enable it to be used by all of us in our everyday lives. We might see that method as following the pendulum metaphor for the scientific method with the aid of the technical or extraordinary language of the social sciences. For it is our own reconstruction of that language that will open us up to the full potentials of language: its gradational, dichotomous and metaphorical potentials.

Our third and final section is still more specific: "East–West Strategy: Eastern Situations and Western Structures." It takes up both the West's love-affair with Buddhism and the East's love affair with Western biophysical science. Both Buddhism and Western biophysical science, once they are integrated, can become the basis for strategies for solving problems in our everyday lives that we desperately need at this time in history, thus making use of the breakthrough in the social sciences. Rudyard Kipling wrote these lines:

> Oh, East is East, and West is West, and never the twain shall meet,
> Till Earth and Sky stand presently at God's great Judgement Seat;
> But there is neither East nor West, Border, nor Breed nor Birth,
> When two strong men stand face to face, tho' they come from the ends of earth.

We may remember the first two lines, yet it is the second two that will guide us as we develop an East-West strategy for human behavior. For those two take us away from the separation of East and West and toward their interaction with one another.

BASIC ASSUMPTIONS: FROM ISOLATION TOWARD INTERACTION (METAPHYSICS/WORLDVIEWS)

Charles Peirce, the founder of the philosophy of pragmatism, wrote that "metaphysics is in a deplorably backward condition," as quoted in chapter 1. If this field of knowledge that is so central to the discipline of philosophy is so backward, then the rest of us can hardly be expected to make sense of it. Yet making sense of metaphysics —or the nature of our basic assumptions about reality or our worldview—is absolutely fundamental for achieving a profound understanding of ourselves, our problems and the world. For those assumptions shape the full range of our behavior. Our ignorance of those assumptions is nothing less than appalling, ignorance that itself reflects the impact of submission to a worldview that calls for isolation rather than interaction.

William James, who assisted Peirce in founding pragmatism, suggested the importance of metaphysics in particular and philosophy in general in quoting from an essay by G. K. Chesterton, a twentieth-century English essayist:

> There are some people—and I am one of them—who think that the
> most practical and important thing about a man is still his view of the
> universe. We think that for a landlady considering a lodger, it is impor-
> tant to know his income, but still more important to know his philoso-
> phy. We think that for a general to fight an enemy, it is important to
> know the enemy's numbers, but still more important to know the ene-
> my's philosophy. (1907/1995: 1)

Paralleling this quote, we think that for an individual to know himself it
is important to know his health and wealth, but it is far more important
for him to know his worldview.

In this section we shall begin by returning to Max Weber's metaphor
of the "iron cage," the prison in which us moderns find ourselves as a
result of our continuing scientific and technological revolutions. This is
an excellent metaphor for the nature of our worldview, for it indicates
how much we are prevented from moving out to fulfill our possibilities.
Yet this metaphor is still quite vague, just as is the very general idea of
"isolation" as the nature of our worldview. Granting the importance of
both ideas, we can become more systematic by turning to an idea that
Weber not only developed in his time a century ago but that has proven
to become central to our understanding of modern society: the idea of
bureaucracy. In our treatment of bureaucracy we will not lose sight of its
role as an iron cage. And neither will we lose sight of its role in the
isolation of phenomena. But in addition we shall examine just how our
worldview—which we might call a "bureaucratic worldview"—manages
to achieve its ability to cage the individual and its ability to isolate the
individual and isolate knowledge. We shall begin this section with a
subsection titled "The Iron Cage of Bureaucracy." And we shall conclude
with a subsection called "Breaking Out of the Iron Cage." Weber along
with almost all social scientists have concluded that bureaucracies are
essential in the modern world, granting their problems, and that the best
that we can do is to attempt to minimize those problems. Our own approach is much different. We believe that it is essential for us to learn to
move away from bureaucracies if indeed we wish to solve our basic
problems.

The Iron Cage of Bureaucracy

We may understand a bureaucracy to be a group with an extensive
hierarchy and division of labor that has been deliberately constructed to
solve specific problems. Weber saw modern bureaucracies as illustrating
a most useful change from the generally irrational nature of traditional
organizations to the rationality within modern organizations. He saw
that change as based in part on the development of the institutions of
science and education in modern society. Yet patterns of persisting hierarchy as well as the division of labor—granting their usefulness in con-

temporary bureaucracies by comparison with traditional bureaucracies—pose enormous problems for the effectiveness of these organizations. For one thing, generally they sharply limit the interaction among the individuals working in a bureaucratic organization, thus limiting the development of ideas that can help to solve the problems that the organization is supposed to solve. For another thing, the development of democratic ideals or values in modern society yields conflicts between those egalitarian values or ideals and a bureaucracy's emphasis on hierarchy. And for a third thing, that conflict between values and patterns of hierarchy yields the values-fulfillment gap discussed in chapter 1, a gap that produces emotional repression because the individual remains unable to narrow it.

Unfortunately for all of us, these patterns of behavior as well as problems of large organizations are by no means limited to large organizations, for those organizations influence the rest of us. Patterns of persisting hierarchy—or what sociologists call "social stratification"—are to be found throughout contemporary societies, within tiny groups like families as well as within monster organizations, following the many studies of social scientists. And the value of equality has been increasingly emphasized throughout modern history, as social scientists have also taught us. This is illustrated by the development of social movements like the civil rights movement, the women's movement, the gray panthers and the gay and lesbian movement. Here then is another illustration of the existence of our wide and widening values-fulfillment gap, given the conflict between the value of equality and bureaucracy's focus on persisting hierarchies. In chapter 1 we put forward a broad picture of a revolution of rising expectations, aspirations or values accompanying our scientific and technological revolutions. Here we focus on just one aspiration or value: equality. In both cases the result is the same.

Yet it is not only the persistence of hierarchy that is fostered by our bureaucratic way of life: it is also a division of labor which is to be found not only throughout large organizations but is also to be found throughout contemporary societies. We might recall here the phrase from Max Weber's Protestant Ethic: "Specialists without spirit." And we might also recall our citation of the existence of no less than forty-five distinct sections—and counting—of the American Sociological Association with limited communication among them. And this is in the face of enormous human complexity that demands the integration of knowledge, following the scientific ideal that we must take into account all factors relevant to a given problem and not just a few of them. We might also recall Edna St. Vincent Millay's poem about our meteoric shower of uncombined facts. She did not just refer to the situation of sociologists, for that lack of integration of knowledge is to be found throughout modern society.

Thus, our iron cage of bureaucracy limits the integration of knowledge through both its patterns of persisting hierarchy as well as its division of labor, granting that it is more effective in solving problems than pre-industrial bureaucracies. Yet there is another fundamental problem to be found with our bureaucratic way of life: the repression of emotions, as discussed in chapter 1. There our focus was broadly on the increasing aspirations-fulfillment gap resulting largely from our continuing scientific and technological revolutions. This is a gap that we have learned to repress in order to achieve—following Vidich and Bensman—"some degree of satisfaction, recognition and achievement." Not only does such repression get in the way of our ability to solve external problems, including both the specific problems addressed by a given bureaucratic organization or the fundamental problems of society as a whole. Such repression also gets in the way of the individual's ability to solve personal problems and, more generally, to develop or evolve as a human being. For we are unitary creatures of "head," "heart" and "hand," and emotional repression holds back our "heart" and, thus, the development of our "head" and "hand" as well.

It is such emotional repression linked to persisting patterns of hierarchy along with a narrow division of labor that not only helps us to understand contemporary problems but also can yield insight into past problems. For we can move out of our Spaceland perspective and enter Timeland with its attention to the past no less than the present and the future. For example, here is the description of a scene outside one of Hitler's concentration camps, as described by an SS officer and cited by Niall Ferguson in his *The War of the World*:

> The train arrives. Two hundred Ukrainians fling open the doors and chase people out of the wagons with their leather whips. . . . Then the procession starts to move. They all go along the path with a very pretty girl in front, all naked. . . . They enter the death chambers. . . . The corpses are thrown out wet with sweat and urine, smeared with excrement and menstrual blood on their legs. . . . Two dozen dentists open mouths with hooks and look for gold. . . . Some of the workers check genitals and anus for gold, diamonds and valuables. (2006: 507–508)

Bureaucracies are organizations that are deliberately constructed to solve specific problems. Such problems can include the slaughter of millions of people viewed as unworthy of life as well as the building of a bridge, a plane or a car. The bureaucratic organizations required for solving all of these problems are similar, as illustrated by the work of Germany's highly successful captains of industry to solve the problem of how to kill all of those innocents within a society that had risen to the very heights of cultural achievements. For example, patterns of hierarchy must be highly effective, illustrated by the protests of the Nazi leaders at the Nuremburg trials that they were not responsible for their deeds because they had to follow orders. Yet so have the rest of us learned to follow orders within our own bureaucratic societies: children learn to bow down to the dictates of their teachers just as the rest of us learn at work to conform to our bosses. And such patterns of hierarchy are to be found in families as well, as is illustrated by widespread patters of physical, emotional and mental abuse along with high divorce rates.

Yet in order for our bureaucratic way of life to continue—given its increasing contradiction with the value of equality, its profound problems must remain largely hidden. The universal specialization with limited communication throughout our society illustrates the ease of hiding information within a bureaucratic organization, let alone throughout society as a whole or the world at large. For example, those individuals manning the death camps—chasing their soon-to-be-slaughtered victims out of the wagons and trains, turning on the gas jets of the death chambers, listening to the heart-rending screams of the men, women and children in their death throes, and later hunting for gold and valuables in the mouths and other orifices of those victims—must somehow be immunized against the horrors they were perpetrating so as to be able to perform their tasks efficiently. And the rest of us must also learn to repress our emotions throughout the many negative experiences within our bureaucratic way of life, granting that those of us who kill others in combat frequently later suffer a lifetime of post-traumatic stress disorders.

If all of these problems linked to the iron cage of bureaucracy that are prevalent throughout contemporary societies—and that have existed in the past as well—appear to be insurmountable, and if our growing pessimism about any chance of finding some direction for solving those problems is added to this mix, then our modern situation does indeed appear to be hopeless. And we can well understand the rapid shift of public opinion in the United States from supporting the Democratic party in the 2008 election to supporting the Republican party in the 2010 election, given the inability of political leaders to make substantial progress on growing problems. Further, we can expect the continuation of such shifts in future elections unless political leaders can somehow learn to make substantial progress on problems that are not only increasing but that also pose threats to the future of the human race. Is such learning in fact possible? Is there indeed a way out for the human race, given such increasing threats as those cited by Martin Rees, Britain's Royal Astronomer, in the introduction to this book? Given the growing effectiveness of chemical, biological and nuclear weapons coupled with the means to deliver them, do we have enough time to learn how to counter such dangers and others as well? Can we expect that—following our own dream—"There will be a future for our children, our grandchildren, our great-grandchildren, and their great-grandchildren"?

Breaking Out of the Iron Cage

We have deliberately swung our pendulum of the scientific method very far to the left—where we gain awareness of and commitment to solving a given problem—in order to gain the momentum or motivation that is required to make progress on our vast and apparently unsolvable problems with a swing to the right. What we require most of all at this point is nothing less than the enormous optimism that is linked to the scientific method, a method that has indeed succeeded in shaping our world over the past five centuries. Just as that method has yielded solutions to biophysical problems previously thought to be unsolvable, so can it yield solutions to our present vast problems of human behavior, problems that a great many of us believe can never be solved.

Although most contemporary social scientists go along with Weber's assessment that, for all of its problems, the bureaucratic pattern of organization remains the best way of organizing us humans to solve the problems of modern societies, not all social scientists agree. A substantial amount of research contradicts Weber's belief in the rationality and effectiveness of the modern bureaucracy. One example is the work of Stanley Udy, presented in a 1959 article titled "'Bureaucracy' and 'Rationality' in Weber's Organization Theory." Udy's research built on a 1958 article by Helen Constas, "Max Weber's Two Conceptions of Bureaucracy." Constas and Udy both found that modern bureaucracies consist of both scientific and unscientific patterns of behavior. Their work implies that we would do well to eliminate the unscientific elements and emphasize the scientific elements of bureaucratic organizations if we wish to reduce and perhaps even eliminate their problems, emerging as a result with a different kind of organization.

More specifically, Udy studied 150 organizations producing material goods within 150 societies, based on existing information that had been painstakingly collected by anthropologists and sociologists over many years. Constas had distinguished between those characteristics of bureaucracies emphasizing limited communication or the isolation of information, on the one hand, and those characteristics that encouraged the communication of information or its interaction and integration, on the other hand. For example, Constas saw a steep hierarchy—where those on top are rewarded substantially more than those at lower levels of the hierarchy, coupled with a minute division of labor—as illustrating a nonscientific pattern of organization. By contrast, she saw such features as rewards based on the effectiveness of one's performance rather than the height of one's hierarchical position as illustrating a scientific pattern of organization. What Udy found was that these nonscientific and scientific patterns of organization generally were not to be found within the same organization. Those 150 organizations could be divided into the less scientific or bureaucratic ones, on the one hand, and the more scientific ones, on the other hand.

Udy was not able to go on and attempt to compare the relative effectiveness of these two types of organizations, yet his work, and that of Constas, is highly suggestive. For their division of organizations into those that are relatively more scientific and those relatively less scientific points toward nothing less than our own contrast between two worldviews. There is a bureaucratic worldview with its isolation of phenomena—including both information and people—and an interactive worldview with its emphasis on the interaction of phenomena. For example, giving rewards to individuals based on their positions in hierarchies strengthens an organization's hierarchical nature, thus limiting the flow of information up that hierarchy, for those on top generally will favor their own ideas and will not like being challenged by those below. By contrast, an emphasis on performance coupled with an egalitarian structure will encourage the communication of ideas throughout the organization, for that will prove to be most effective in solving problems. Equally, a minute division of labor will work to prevent the sharing of information, by contrast with a limited division of labor that will yield far more communication and will thus prove to be more effective for solving problems.

Just as Weber saw modern bureaucracies as more rational and effective than pre-industrial bureaucracies largely because of the more scientific orientation of their educated staffs, so can we now see a new type of organization that succeeds in emphasizing the scientific method even more as superior to our present bureaucratic organizations. We might choose to call that new type of organization a "learning group," as indicated in chapter 6's heading: "From the Learning Individual toward the Learning Group, Institution, and Society." It is exactly here that our breakthrough in the social sciences can impact present-day bureaucratic organizations. As outlined in chapter 1, it is indeed possible to move from our present way of life with its barriers to interaction—as illustrated by the bureaucratic organization—toward a way of life that emphasizes interaction. And that breakthrough, with its focus on changing our fundamental assumptions, worldview or metaphysical stance from isolation toward interaction, is what we desperately need. For a change in worldview will impact the full range of our behavior, just as a bureaucratic worldview does the same.

Our scientific breakthrough that can yield a change from our bureaucratic to an interactive worldview calls for, first of all, the optimism that is so basic to scientific ideals: once we define a problem, even an extremely difficult one, we can learn how to solve it one step at a time. The metaphor of a pendulum swinging in ever-widening arcs can help us to visualize what can be involved. We must learn to swing that pendulum ever further to the left, where we face up to the depths of the problem that is involved. And we must also learn to swing ever further to the right, where we continue to make progress on the problem. Further, the full range of our behavior must be involved, for nothing less than that is required if indeed our worldview is at stake. This includes "heart" as well as "head" and "hand," for our bureaucratic worldview has taught us to bury our emotions, and we must now learn to express them. It also includes our relationships with others in groups, institutions, and society as a whole, to be discussed in chapter 6.

In order to understand more specifically just how it is possible to change something so fundamental as our worldview or basic assumptions about the nature of reality, we turn to the work of Thomas Kuhn, a historian as well as a philosopher of science. His focus in his *The Structure of Scientific Revolutions* (1962) was on fundamental changes in scientific theories, such as the change from Newton's laws of motion to Einstein's theories of relativity. Kuhn was concerned with absolutely fundamental changes within science, just as we are concerned with absolutely fundamental changes within society. And Kuhn even suggested the existence of a parallel between scientific revolutions and "political revolutions," granting that he was not able to develop a systematic argument about the nature of that parallel. However, it is exactly that suggestion that we have proceeded to take up, following Kuhn's understanding of how scientific revolutions occur and applying that understanding to cultural revolutions or fundamental changes in our worldview or metaphysical stance.

Kuhn's basic contribution was to introduce the concept of "scientific paradigm," which we may understand to be widely shared and fundamental assumptions—largely invisible—on which any given scientific theory rests. As a result, he influenced social scientists within a variety of disciplines—including Phillips—to pay attention to the "paradigm" or worldview underlying their own theories. Just as Kuhn suggested a parallel between scientific and political revolutions, we see that same parallel between changes in science and changes in culture, granting the much greater breadth of the latter. And just as Kuhn emphasized the importance of developing an alternative scientific paradigm in order to change an existing scientific theory, so do we see the importance of developing an alternative worldview in order to change existing theories about how to solve social problems.

From Kuhn's perspective, evidence supporting a new theory is not enough to convince scientists to abandon a prior theory. For that prior theory is supported by relatively invisible fundamental assumptions, namely, a scientific paradigm. Thus, a new scientific paradigm must accompany that new scientific theory. And that new scientific paradigm together with its new scientific theory must promise to make progress on the problems within the old theory and paradigm. The work of the Sociological Imagination Group over this past decade has followed Kuhn's analysis. For all of the books that the group has developed have not only examined the nature of our existing cultural paradigm but have also put forward an alternative cultural paradigm. This approach is behind our emphasis in this book on the contrast between a bureaucratic and an evolutionary worldview. And we also follow Kuhn in our view of the promise of an evolutionary worldview, for we are convinced that it can succeed in resolving the contradictions within our bureaucratic worldview and way of life.

Yet there is a substantial gap between a scientific paradigm and a specific scientific theory, namely, the nature of the scientific methods that are employed to develop and test that theory, methods that are based on the assumptions within that scientific paradigm. The history of philosophy has filled out that gap in its attention to the field of "epistemology" along with the field of "metaphysics." Epistemology has to do with the procedures that are used to learn about what metaphysics calls for, namely, an understanding of the nature of reality. Thus, before we can get into the specifics of theories that can help us to move from a bureaucratic to an evolutionary way of life we must address the nature of the procedures that we are using to learn how to develop and test those specific theories.

The next subsection, "Scientific Method: Breakthrough in the Social Sciences," centers on the nature of the broad scientific method that we require to move toward changing our worldview or cultural paradigm. We will focus there on the contrast between the present approach to the scientific method that builds on our bureaucratic worldview and an alternative approach that builds on an evolutionary worldview. We see the former as failing to follow the scientific ideal of opening up to the range of phenomena involved within a given problem. Given the complexity of human behavior, we understand how difficult it is to follow that ideal. Yet we are convinced of the importance of doing so despite the difficulties involved. For the partial use of the scientific method by social scientists has been accompanied by escalating problems that remain to be solved.

SCIENTIFIC METHOD: BREAKTHROUGH IN THE SOCIAL SCIENCES (EPISTEMOLOGY)

By contrast with an outward focus emphasized within our bureaucratic worldview, our breakthrough in the scientific method calls for a focus inward no less than outward. The scientist—and the rest of us who use the scientific method—must learn to address the full complexity of any given human scene by seeing self as well as seeing others, for we have an impact that cannot be ignored on external phenomena. For example, if we remain with our bureaucratic worldview and way of life, then we will remain unaware of the fact that we are not facing up to the complexity of anything that we see. Following Peirce's idea that the scientific method depends on the existence of "a real and living doubt" or deep sense of problem in the investigator, that sense of problem will remain limited if it fails to include the actual complexity of the situation under investigation. By contrast, an evolutionary worldview calls for a deep commitment to opening up to that complexity by including one's own impact on the research situation, thus swinging one's pendulum of the scientific method far to the left.

Throughout history individuals in disciplines outside of the sciences—such as philosophers, novelists, poets and religious leaders—have attempted to teach us of the importance of looking inward no less than outward. For example, it was Socrates who claimed that "the unexamined life is not worth living." A passage from St. Luke in the New Testament states, "Physician, heal thyself." We find this question when we go far back to the Upanisheds, the sacred Hindu treatises, "How can the knower be known?" Voltaire, the French philosopher of the Enlightenment era, stated, "We must cultivate our garden." Robert Burns, the Scottish poet, writes, "O wad some Pow'r the giftie gie us To see oursels as others see us!" Albert Camus, the French novelist and dramatist, wrote, "An intellectual is someone whose mind watches itself." Carlos Pecotche, a Brazilian educator, devoted his life to helping students learn to achieve "conscious evolution." Gishin Funakoshi, the father of modern karate, put forward this guiding principle: "First know yourself, then know others." And Walt Kelly's opossum, Pogo—his cartoon character—exclaimed when coming upon litter under a tree, "We have met the enemy and he is us."

Yet despite all of this advice, our continued conformity to a bureaucratic worldview indicates that we are failing to take such advice seriously. This outward orientation applies to the traditional approach to the scientific method as well as to the rest of our behavior. However, this failure to follow the ideal of the scientific method that calls for addressing the range of phenomena affecting a given problem has led to severe limitations to the development of the social sciences, limitations that we can no longer afford as problems continue to escalate. In the following two subsections, we point toward an alternative that invokes an approach within the social sciences that follows scientific ideals. "Toward a Reflexive Way of Life" opens up to the complexity of the human situation and "Beyond Value Neutrality" also calls for reflexivity, focusing in particular on the investigator's emotions and values. Together these sections outline an evolutionary versus bureaucratic scientific method, an outline that will be essential in the chapters to follow.

Toward a Reflexive Way of Life

Although very few social scientists have followed the advice of those historical figures calling for an inward no less than an outward orientation, there are exceptions. One of them was C. Wright Mills, discussed in chapter 1, whose appendix to *The Sociological Imagination* contained these words:

> It is best to begin, I think, by reminding you, the beginning student, that the most admirable thinkers within the scholarly community you have chosen to join do not split their work from their lives. They seem to take both too seriously to allow such dissociation, and they want to use each for the enrichment of the other. Of course, such a split is the prevailing convention among men in general.(1959: 195)

Mills thus encouraged students of sociology to pay attention to human behavior's interactive nature as well as its complexity, contrasting this approach with what generally prevails throughout society. Yet he joins the other figures cited above—Socrates, St. Luke, Voltaire, Burns, Camus, Pecotche, Funakoshi and Kelly—in opposing our extremely powerful bureaucratic worldview pointing us outward rather than both inward and outward, and thus limiting his impact. Yet a decade later another sociologist, Alvin W. Gouldner, carries further Mills's, developing the idea of a "reflexive sociology" in his *The Coming Crisis of Western Sociology*:

> What sociologists now most require from a Reflexive Sociology, however, is not just one more specialization, not just another topic for panel meetings at professional conventions. . . . The historical mission of a Reflexive Sociology as I conceive it, however, would be to transform the sociologist, to penetrate deeply into his daily life and work, enriching them with new sensitivities, and to raise the sociologist's self-awareness to a new historical level. . . . A Reflexive Sociology means that we sociologists must—at the very least—acquire the ingrained habit of viewing our own beliefs as we now view those held by others. (1970: 489)

In that book Gouldner recognized the importance of the "background assumptions" or metaphysical stance that lies behind and shapes one's research methods. And he also gave recognition to the importance of Mills's work. His idea of a "reflexive sociology" opens up to the complexity of human behavior just as Mills did. One achievement of such a broad approach to research would be to communicate more of the forces involved within any research on a given problem, thus following scientific ideals. Just as witnesses in a courtroom must be cross-examined because their own personal commitments or values shape their testimony, so should social scientists at least attempt to communicate those commitments in their publications, since readers can then understand more of the forces that led to a given conclusion. Yet we would find this kind of communication is extremely rare if we proceeded to examine the millions of published social science articles and books.

We should note the interactive nature of a reflexive orientation to sociology, for as a result it meshes with our analysis of physical and biological structures in chapter 1. It is indeed difficult to understand, initially, why a field of knowledge that is oriented to human interaction, as sociology is, has continued to ignore the interaction between an investigator and those whom he or she is studying. Yet once we understand the existence of an outward-oriented worldview or metaphysical stance that we all subscribe to, we can understand this lack of reflexivity among sociologists. For this lack represents conformity to extremely powerful forces, for it is the very nature of a worldview or metaphysical stance to generate such forces.

We might also note Gouldner's vision of the potential of a reflexive sociology "to transform the sociologist, to penetrate deeply into his daily life and work, enriching them with new sensitivities, and to raise the sociologist's self-awareness to a new historical level." Here Gouldner joins us in his interest in the development or evolution of the sociologist. For the vision of sociology's possibilities developed among the classical sociologists emphasized the role of the discipline in solving society's fundamental problems. Yet it is a vision that remains to be fulfilled. Gouldner along with Mills never gave up on the early dream of sociology's possibilities, and we share as well a commitment to fulfilling that dream. We see a reflexive sociology as an important step in that direction.

After the publication of *The Coming Crisis*, Gouldner responded to a review of his book in an article, "The Politics of the Mind: Reflections on Flack's Review of *The Coming Crisis of Western Sociology*," which appeared in Social Policy in 1972:

> The pursuit of . . . understanding, however, cannot promise that men as we now find them, with their everyday language and understanding, will always be capable of further understanding and of liberating themselves. At decisive points the ordinary language and conventional understandings fail and must be transcended. It is essentially the task of the social sciences, more generally, to create new and *"extraordinary" languages*, to help men learn to speak them, and to mediate between the deficient understandings of ordinary language and the different and liberating perspectives of the extraordinary languages of social theory. . . . To say social theorists are concept-creators means that they are not merely in the knowledge-creating business, but also in the language-reform and language-creating business. In other words, they are from the beginning involved in creating a new culture. (Gouldner, 1972: 16; italics ours)

Gouldner continues to express his commitment not only to social science knowledge but also to social technology or solving the problems of society, a stance that we share with him. Yet it is a stance that requires sociologists and other social scientists to integrate their knowledge so that they can confront the complexity of human behavior. Recalling the history of the past five centuries as discussed in chapter 1, it was not just the development of the biological and physical sciences that proceeded to shape the world: it was a combination of biophysical technologies together with biophysical science that yielded enormous changes throughout societies. Correspondingly, we cannot expect the development of the social sciences alone to repair the one-sided materialistic nature of the world that resulted from those five centuries. Individual and social technologies must join with the social sciences to achieve a balanced world, and Gouldner points toward that balance. This invokes changes not only in the sciences but also in the full range of our institutions: in education, the economy, the political institution, religion and the family.

In this quote Gouldner's focus is on the "extraordinary language" of the social sciences as a fundamental tool that scientists must employ in their efforts to solve problems. Such a language parallels the technical languages of the physical and biological sciences, languages that have proven to be essential to the ability of those fields to solve problems. Phillips recalls the importance of those technical languages during his experiences as a pre-medical student at Columbia prior to changing to sociology as a result of the influence of Mills, a time when he was immersed in the fields of physics and chemistry. He learned that key concepts like force and mass in physics as well as valence and the periodic table in chemistry were crucial to understanding the nature of those disciplines. Correspondingly, the "extraordinary language" or technical language of the social sciences is equally important for understanding human behavior. Yet there are literally hundreds of concepts that are emphasized throughout the shattered social sciences, and they remain— following Millay's poem—"uncombined."

Following the necessity of moving from our bureaucratic worldview with its emphasis on isolation, the publications of the Sociological Imagination Group have been moving over the past decade ever closer toward ways of achieving interaction among the central concepts of the social sciences. This is fundamental to achieving a breakthrough in the social sciences. That movement is broad enough to invoke "heart" no less than "head" and "hand." In part II we will introduce and illustrate our selection of those concepts from social science's extraordinary language that we see as most effective for understanding how to move in an evolutionary direction. Chapters 3, 4 and 5 focus on "head," "heart" and "hand," respectively, and that focus will include those elements of the extraordinary or technical language that we believe can yield understanding of those fundamental elements of human behavior.

Yet a breakthrough in the social sciences requires special attention to "heart." Our analysis in chapter 1, with its treatment of our increasing aspirations-fulfillment or values-fulfillment gap, focused attention on the resulting pattern of emotional repression as a device for coping with that gap. Following the pendulum metaphor, the scientific method calls for ever greater commitment to a given problem as the pendulum swings back and forth in increasing arcs. The problem this poses, then, is how to move from emotional repression toward emotional expression. We take this up in the following subsection, "Beyond Value Neutrality," where the principle value neutrality is largely based on patterns of emotional repression.

Beyond Value Neutrality

William Butler Yeats, a twentieth-century Irish poet, wrote these lines after the end of World War I:

> Turning and turning in the widening gyre
> The falcon cannot hear the falconer;
> Things fall apart: the center cannot hold;
> Mere anarchy is loosed upon the world.
> The blood-dimmed tide is loosed, and everywhere
> The ceremony of innocence is drowned:
> The best lack all conviction, while the worst
> Are full of passionate intensity. (1921/2004)

Yeats's image "The falcon cannot hear the falconer" suggests the isolation of phenomena and people that is shaped by our bureaucratic worldview. And his image "Things fall apart: the center cannot hold" suggests the deepening problems of the modern world, as illustrated by our growing values-fulfillment gap. The last two lines suggest the isolation of "head" and "heart" if we assume that the "best" are those with the best understanding of the modern situation while the "worst" have the most limited understanding. Thus, those with the most developed "head" "lack all conviction" ("heart"), and those with the most limited "head" "are full of passionate intensity ("heart"). For an illustration of the "worst" being full of passionate intensity, we might use the rise of Hitler and the Nazi movement in Germany, with the "best" illustrated by the Social Democrats who opposed that movement. It was that very passionate intensity that succeeded in sweeping Hitler into power as the result of a democratic election.

We do not argue here that "passionate intensity" or "emotional expression" is necessarily a direction for solving the fundamental problems of society, as illustrated by the passionate intensity of Hitler as fundamental to the rise of the Nazi movement. For "heart" is combined with "head" and "hand." And if "head" points narrowly toward the isolation of ideas while "hand" points toward emphasizing a hierarchy so pronounced that those at the bottom may be seen as unfit for life, then emotional expression can become exceedingly dangerous, creating enormous problems for the world. Yet the reverse can occur when "head" points toward the interaction of ideas and "hand" points toward democratic and egalitarian ideals. For in this way problems can be solved. And the emotional commitment of individuals is essential to such solutions, just as it is essential to the development of ever greater understanding of human behavior by using the scientific method.

Our focus on the importance of "heart" — granting that it is accompanied by a "head" and "hand" oriented to an interactive and evolutionary worldview — is supported by many statements by individuals throughout history. For example there are ideas about the negative impact of a lack of emotional expression, such as that of the American philosopher and poet, Ralph Waldo Emerson: "Nothing great was ever achieved without enthusiasm." Elie Wiesel, the Auschwitz survivor and Nobel Prize winner, joins Emerson in his views: "The opposite of love is not hate, it's indifference. The opposite of art is not ugliness, it's indifference. The opposite of faith is not heresy, it's indifference. And the opposite of life is not death, it's indifference." We also have a statement by Abraham Cowley, the seventeenth-century English poet and essayist: "Lukewarmness I account a sin, As great in love as in religion."

There are also many quotes about the positive impact of emotional expression. For example, we have the statement by Benjamin Disraeli, the nineteenth-century British statesman and novelist: "Man is only truly great when he acts from the passions." The early nineteenth-century poet William Blake declared, "Exuberance is beauty." Dylan Thomas, the twentieth century Welsh poet whom we quote at greater length in chapter 5, stated, "Do not go gentle into that good night, Old age should burn and rave at close of day, Rage, rage against the dying of the light." E. M. Forster, the twentieth-century English novelist, wrote, "Only connect the prose and the passion, and both will be exalted, and human love will be seen at its height." Also, we have this proverb: "Hope deferred maketh the heart: but when the desire cometh, it is a tree of life." Further, we have this statement from Ice-T, the American rap-musician: "Passion makes the world go round. Love just makes it a safer place."

The idea of the importance of "value neutrality" is generally accepted throughout the social sciences. It points the scientist away from commitment to any values or goals, with the rationale that such a commitment can bias the scientist and thus take away from the truth of his or her conclusions. Yet if the scientist's value commitment is to a broad approach to the scientific method that follows the scientific ideal of attention to evidence versus pre-conceived ideas, then that commitment points away from such bias. And this is especially true when a commitment to scientific ideals is strengthened by a commitment to an interactive or evolutionary worldview. Without these value commitments, however, the social scientist is more open to arriving at biased results. For he or she may remain unaware of just how much the research has been distorted by personal beliefs. Thus, value neutrality would open the way for bias when such neutrality has to do with commitment to scientific ideals.

Our argument for reflexivity within the above subsection points to an alternative to the stance of value neutrality. For a reflexive approach to research will encourage the social scientist to reveal his or her values. And those who read the results of social science research will be able to take the existence of those values into account as they proceed to assess or evaluate the conclusions of the investigation. Of course, this will increase the complexity of such research, for the investigator will be required to investigate his or her own values along with everything else. And the job of the reader will become more complex as well, since the values of the investigator will have to be taken into account. Yet all of that complexity will be simplified to the extent that the investigator learns to become deeply committed to a broad approach to the scientific method as well as an interactive or evolutionary worldview, since those commitments will work to trump other values pointing in biased directions.

A recent collection of the work of eleven contemporary philosophers of science edited by Harold Kincaid and others — *Value-Free Science? Ideals and Illusions* — suggests that arguments for value neutrality are invalid:

> All the chapters in this book raise doubts about the ideal of a value-free science. That ideal takes science to be objective and rational and to tell us about the way things are, but not the way they should be. That ideal has dominated our conception of science for centuries. . . . If the critics of the value-free science ideal are right, then these traditional claims about science not only are ungrounded but also can have pernicious consequences. . . . It means ignoring the value assumptions that go into science and the value implications of scientific results. Important value assumptions will be hidden behind a cloak of neutrality in public debates over policy and morality. If scientific results concerning IQ and race, free markets and growth, or environmental emissions and planetary weather make value assumptions, treating them as entirely neutral is misleading at best. (2007, 3–5)

The authors argue that the present near-universal emphasis on value-neutrality throughout the sciences — including the social sciences — is "misleading at best" and "pernicious" at worst. This is yet another argument for the necessity of fundamental changes in the approach to the scientific method throughout the social sciences. Value neutrality coupled with a lack of reflexivity have resisted change despite their departure from the scientific ideal of opening up to the full range of phenomena that is relevant to a given problem. This resistance is based on the power of the bureaucratic worldview to which our traditional approach to the scientific method is attached. Movement away from that worldview, and away from our bureaucratic scientific method, requires a specific strategy for how to proceed with research in addition to a general approach to reflexivity and value commitment. It must be a strategy that makes use of a technical or extraordinary language of social science that builds on past research. In the final section of this chapter we turn to such a strategy. It is one based on two lines from Kipling quoted above: "But there is neither East nor West, Border, nor Breed nor Birth, When two strong men stand face to face, tho' they come from the ends of earth!"

EAST-WEST STRATEGY: EASTERN SITUATIONS AND WESTERN STRUCTURES (THEORY)

This third and final section of the chapter can be understood metaphorically by returning to the metaphors of Spaceland and Timeland, as discussed at the beginning of chapter 1, where we took up Edwin Abbott's early science-fiction story *Flatland*. Just as the Square remained unable to convince his countrymen about the existence of Spaceland, so do we all have difficulty in moving from Spaceland to Timeland. As suggested in that earlier discussion, we swim on the surface of an ocean, with the past underneath us and the future above us, yet we only rarely dive down or fly up. In this way we behave much like our pets with their focus on the momentary present scene with little attention to the past or the future. Yet our complex language enables us to imagine diving very far down, even to the beginnings of the universe, and language also enables us to imagine flying up to the far-distant future. By so doing we can learn about the vast potentials for changing ourselves and our world, by contrast with our present convictions as to our limitations.

By learning to move from Spaceland toward Timeland, a project that can at least begin as a result of reading this book, we can succeed in tapping those potentials. This will require movement away from our bureaucratic worldview and toward an evolutionary worldview, as discussed in the first section of this chapter. That will equally be a movement away from the isolation fostered by the bureaucratic worldview's focus on persisting hierarchy and a narrow division of labor. Movement toward Timeland will also require not only this very general change in what philosophers call our "metaphysical stance" or our fundamental assumptions, as discussed in the first section of this chapter. It will also require an intermediate change in what philosophers call our "epistemological stance," namely, the bureaucratic scientific method that is almost universally employed, as discussed in the second section of this chapter. Movement toward an evolutionary scientific method can enable us to follow the scientific ideal of opening up to the full complexity of human behavior. That involves a reflexive orientation that can help us move toward emotional expression.

Granting the difficulty of achieving these changes at a general and an intermediate level of breadth, achieving a third change centering on a specific level that is required is no less difficult, and that change is the focus of this third section of chapter 2. Metaphorically, we must prepare

the way for such specific behavior by (1) learning to swim on the surface
while at the same time making use of our imagined experiences of swim-
ming to the bottom of the ocean and flying to the height of the universe.
By so doing we learn to change our basic assumptions, metaphysical
stance or worldview. Also, we must (2) learn to swim on the surface
while at the same time making use of our imagined experience of swim-
ming to an intermediate level of depth and flying to an intermediate
height. Here, we change our approach to the scientific method. This preparation for moving toward Timeland has been the subject of the first and
second sections of this chapter which focused on our worldview and on
the scientific method. In addition, in this third section of the chapter we
must (3) learn to swim on the surface while applying a specific strategy
for guiding our very specific behavior from one moment to the next that
helps us to achieve (1) and (2) as well as (3). Our (1) basic assumptions or
worldview along with our (2) approach to the scientific method are essential if indeed we wish to (3) change our very specific behavior with the
aid of the East-West strategy. This strategy combines Eastern realism
with Western idealism or optimism, yielding an emotional orientation
that we call "realistic optimism." Our first subsection, "The Eastern and
Western Strategies," describes the present-day Eastern and Western strategies for solving problems. Our second subsection, "The East-West Strategy: Situations and Structures," describes our own alternative strategy.
By learning an East-West strategy we are also learning to combine a focus
on the momentary "situation" as well as on long-term "structures." And
we also learn to move toward Timeland and an interactive way of life.
Thus, as a result of practicing (1), (2) and (3) with the aid of the East-West
strategy, we learn to move toward the evolution of the individual and
society.

The Eastern and Western Strategies

The Eastern strategy for solving problems is well illustrated by Buddhist thought, based on the ideas of Gautama Siddartha Sakyamuni, the
original Buddha, who was born some twenty-five hundred years ago (see
Kaplan, 1961). His teaching is based on the Four Noble Truths and the
Eightfold Noble Path. The first Noble Truth has to do with the universal
existence of "dukkha," or pain, sorrow and suffering. More precisely,
however, dukkha suggests the lack of complete fulfillment of all human
pursuits, and thus it is much the same as our aspirations-fulfillment or
values-fulfillment gap. There is, then, always an aspirations-fulfillment
gap. Nothing is ever wholly satisfying, and this is true even for the most
fortunate human beings. This, then, is the first Noble Truth: that dukkha
or an aspirations-fulfillment gap exists for all of us human beings. The
existence of dukkha is the problem that Gautama Siddartha Sakyamuni
addressed, much like the focus of the scientific method on a problem

similar to Charles Peirce's view—quoted in chapter 1—that the scientific method is based on the idea that "There must be a real and living doubt."

The law of causality—like the assumption of modern science—is the second Noble Truth: everything that happens is caused. For example, as we sow, so shall we reap: our own actions will determine our own fate. This is also the Hindu law of "karma" or moral causation: our future is determined by what we have done in the past. Following this law of causality, if we remove the cause of dukkha or our aspirations-fulfillment gap, then dukkha will disappear. Here is a rational or "head" view of how the world works that matches the rationality of Western science. As for the third Noble Truth, it is the renunciation of desire, "thirst" or aspirations, the removal of passions, which will inevitably be frustrated to some degree. The fourth Noble Truth specifies the Eightfold Noble Path as the concrete direction for actually removing dukkha: right views, right aspirations, right speech, right conduct, a right livelihood, right efforts, right thoughts and right contemplation.

What the Buddha achieved was nothing less than a strategy for living that anyone and everyone might adopt, by contrast with an approach to life for an elite group. It was and is a strategy that includes fundamental elements of the scientific method, especially illustrated by the first and second Noble Truths. We might compare this approach to science with the narrow approach taken initially throughout Western Society and now throughout the world. For science is almost universally seen as the business of a highly specialized group of individuals who call themselves scientists, by contrast with the rest of us. Thus, the Buddha would claim that there is every reason why all of us, and not just an elite group of scientists, should learn to use the scientific method in our everyday lives. It is an argument that points away from our highly specialized bureaucratic worldview and way of life. And it points toward the evolution of the individual.

Yet the third and fourth Noble Truths depart from the ideals of the scientific method to an extent. As for the third Noble Truth, it is by no means possible or even desirable to eliminate desire, thirst or aspirations completely, granting that this would eliminate the aspirations-fulfillment gap. For such emotions are fundamental to human behavior. "Heart" goes together with "head" and "hand." To focus on the elimination of emotions is to follow the same problem that Western society has experienced, namely, the repression rather than the expression of emotions. Let us recall here our discussion of "emotional repression" in chapter 1 and of "value neutrality" in this chapter. Following the first Noble Truth, it is essential to focus on dukkha or the aspirations-fulfillment gap as a fundamental problem that we all should focus on. Such commitment to solving a problem requires not "the renunciation of desire, 'thirst' or aspirations"—as indicated in the third Noble Truth—but genuine and deep emotional commitment. And commitment not just by an elite group of scientists, but by the rest of us as well.

However, we do agree with some aspects of the third Noble Truth. We are committed to the removal of the one-sided materialistic passions developed in a world of materialistic products based on the successes of the biophysical sciences. Thus, we go along with the third Noble Truth in seeking to narrow our very wide aspirations-fulfillment gap with respect to materialistic aspirations. Indeed, we believe in the importance of narrowing that gap for the full range of our aspirations, material and non-material. We follow, then, the Buddha's realism in his awareness of how destructive a wide aspirations-fulfillment gap is to the well-being of the individual. It is, then, *unrealistic aspirations* that should be eliminated and replaced by realistic ones, namely, aspirations that we stand a good chance of fulfilling. Indeed, this may well be what the Buddha meant by the Third Noble Truth. We might recall here, from chapter 1, the unrealistic aspirations of home-buyers and lenders that were fundamental to the development of the Great Recession of 2008–2009.

As for the fourth Noble Truth—"right views, right aspirations, right speech, right conduct, a right livelihood, right efforts, right thoughts and right contemplation"—we agree completely with the breadth of the Buddha's approach, which covers "head," "heart" and "hand." This "Eightfold Noble Path" encompasses "head" in its attention to "right views," "right thoughts," "right contemplation"). It deals with "heart" in its inclusion of "right aspirations." And "hand" is included with the listing of "right speech," "right conduct," "a right livelihood" and "right efforts." This enormous breadth contrasts with the relatively narrow approach within Western society, with all of its focus on specialization coupled with limited communication among specialists. We should also note here that aspirations are included rather than eliminated in the Eightfold Noble Path, indicating that all emotion is not renounced within Buddhism, and thus suggesting that our disagreement with the third Noble Truth may not be justified.

Let us emphasize here the focus of the Eightfold Noble Path on the efforts of the individual, by contrast with the actions of a group. Here, the Buddha's remedy for changing the world is much different from that of most Western social scientists or political leaders, and it is a remedy that we agree with. Unless individuals can demonstrate that they can in fact achieve fundamental changes or developments with respect to "head," "heart" and "hand," there is no way on earth for leaders to enable them to achieve such development. And leaders themselves must learn how to achieve such development or evolution in their own lives before they can hope to teach others to do the same. Our own emphasis on personal evolution in this book follows the Buddha's approach. We should note that part II on individual evolution precedes part III on the evolution of society.

By itself, the Eastern approach to solving fundamental human problems takes us a substantial distance toward an evolutionary perspective. It points us in a direction that we all can take versus one to be adopted by only a small elite, thus leading us away from our bureaucratic division of labor. It also alerts us to the problem of dukkha or the aspirations-fulfillment gap as absolutely central to the welfare of humanity, thus raising up to full view this absolutely fundamental yet relatively invisible problem. This is no small achievement, for we cannot confront a problem that we cannot see, one that we have buried using such procedures of emotional repression as the "falsification of memory" and "techniques of "particularization." The Eastern strategy also alerts us to the importance of individuals' learning to use the scientific method in their own lives in order to achieve fundamental changes in themselves and in society. Still further, the Eastern orientation points up the importance of individuals' learning to change the full range of their behavior—including "head," "heart" and "hand"—if they wish to make progress on reducing dukkha, the aspirations-fulfillment gap, which is so central to the fundamental and increasingly threatening problems of contemporary society.

Yet the Eastern approach remains limited, granting its impressive achievements. For example, the Eightfold Noble Path fails to define specifically the nature of "right" or moral behavior. Exactly what are "right thoughts"? What are "right aspirations"? And what is "right conduct"? Granting the scientific basis for Buddhist thought, it does not emphasize the importance of carrying further that scientific orientation so as to include what the human race has learned about human behavior over the past 2500 years. That knowledge comes largely from the social sciences, but it also includes what has been learned in all other fields of human endeavor. And all of that knowledge can help us in gaining understanding of the nature of human behavior as well as how to make progress on our escalating problems. Of course, social scientists themselves, granting their achievements, have failed to integrate their knowledge, making it most difficult for the rest of us to apply their knowledge to our problems.

The Western strategy for problem solving has also achieved a great deal, and that strategy is limited as well. As we have seen in chapter 1, the history of the West includes the triumph of Western science and technology over the past five centuries in its ability to shape the world. Unfortunately, that triumph includes the East as well as the West, thus working against achievements within Eastern thought that conflict with the Western strategy. For example the Eastern orientation of the potential of the individual to continue to develop or evolve as a basis for solving fundamental problems in society—our own focus in this book—has come to be overshadowed. This Western triumph has been based on the development of the scientific method along with its philosophical framework, as illustrated by the work of Charles Peirce and William James. And it also includes the development of scientific technologies throughout society, as illustrated by incredible achievements in medicine and engineering.

It is, then, the scientific method that is in our view the greatest achievement of the Western strategy for problem solving, granting immense achievements in other areas of life. It is a method that we might understand by referring once again to the pendulum metaphor for the scientific method. Granting the West's focus on an elite of professional scientists, it is a method that captures the idealism or optimism to be seen throughout much of the history of Western philosophy. It starts with the optimistic assumption that any problem can be solved scientifically once it is defined. That assumption enables the scientist to swing the pendulum far to the left, opening up to any and every problem. And that swing in turn yields the momentum or motivation required for a swing far to the left, where progress on that problem is developed. And just as Peirce argued, "Do not block the way of inquiry"—that pendulum can continue to swing in ever-widening arcs, making ever more progress on the most difficult problems that might be defined. It has been that very optimism within the scientific method that became the basis for the optimism within technologies that have succeeded in shaping the world

That same optimism, developed further as the result of those achievements in biophysical science and technologies, became the basis for the development of Western social science. If the scientific method could be harnessed to solve physical and biological problems, perhaps it could be harnessed as well to solve the deepest problems of human societies. Based on that optimism together with the use of the scientific method insofar as it was understood, we have the development of the social sciences over the past two centuries. And their achievements in yielding understanding of human behavior have been enormous. Those achievements are particularly impressive when we see them against the background of the incredible complexity of human behavior, a complexity that far exceeds that to be found within physical or even biological phenomena. And those achievements are even more impressive when seen as opposing a worldview or metaphysical stance that points away from the integration of knowledge, an integration fundamental to penetrating human complexity. We can of course come to see the forty-five sections of the American Sociological Association with the limited communication among them in an entirely negative light. Yet we can also see them in a most positive light, for each one has managed to bring forward new understanding of human behavior that we should take into account if indeed we wish to penetrate the complexity of human behavior, understanding that is waiting to be integrated.

The limitations of the Western strategy for problem solving derive largely from the one-sidedness of its accomplishments in the biophysical sciences and their technologies by contrast with accomplishments in the social sciences and their technologies. Despite the achievements of the social sciences, their failures to integrate their knowledge are also failures to develop effective social technologies, which require broad knowledge to penetrate the complexities of human behavior. This results in escalating problems in contemporary societies. For example, we have the invention of weapons of mass destruction and the means to deliver them, based on biophysical technologies, yet we do not have the invention of social technologies that can be effective in preventing the development or use of such weapons. More generally, we have an increasing gap between aspirations and their fulfillment, or dukkha in the language of Buddhism, as documented in *The Invisible Crisis* (Phillips and Johnston, 2007: 234–235).

The good news, however—also documented in *The Invisible Crisis* (234–235) is that there is "substantial evidence" that movement from a bureaucratic worldview and toward an interactive worldview will in fact help to narrow that gap. That movement will in turn work to yield movement from a bureaucratic scientific method toward an evolutionary scientific method that also follows scientific ideals by pointing in a more interactive direction. And these changes in both our bureaucratic worldview and scientific method can be guided by an East-West strategy, combining the strengths of the Eastern strategy and the Western strategy while avoiding their weaknesses.

The East-West Strategy: Situations and Structures

The Eastern strategy is oriented to a realistic approach to the momentary situation. This includes lowering one's aspirations in a particular situation so that one has a better chance of fulfilling them, and also emphasizing what has occurred in the past, with all of its limitations, as a guide for the present. By contrast, the Western strategy emphasizes future possibilities to guide one in the present, often leading to a wide gap between one's aspirations and one's ability to fulfill them. By combining the two strategies within an East-West strategy, however, we are able to move into Timeland, taking into account both past and future as we deal with the present.

This movement into Timeland enables us to focus on both the momentary scene that we are presently in as well as long-term structures that we have developed in the past and would like to change in the future, such as changing from bureaucratic to evolutionary structures. It is behavior in one situation after another after another, over a substantial period of time, that can yield structural change. Once again, it is interaction that is the key to such movement. In this case it is interaction between past, present and future. For a concrete illustration of structural change we turn here to the wartime experience as a paratrooper of Donald M. Murray, a correspondent to *The Boston Globe*:

We didn't just go out and jump from perfectly good airplanes. With in-your-face drill sergeants, we learned discipline, and then we learned skills, one step at a time. . . .We first took that step out onto nothing by stepping out of a mockup of a C-47 on the ground, again and again and yet again. Then we stepped from a tower, and finally when habit made the difficult routine, from a plane. There were no surprises—even once when my chute didn't open.

I realize that is what I do in writing my books. I face a massive rewrite of a manuscript. I don't imagine the pile of pages I must accumulate. Tomorrow morning I will write Updike's three pages, perhaps two, perhaps one. If not a page, a paragraph; if not a paragraph, a sentence; if not a sentence, a line; if not a line, a word. . . .This is also how I face the daily fear of aging, of a new kind of warfare, of all the what-ifs that lie in ambush, just doing what I know how to do one morning at a time. (2001: 11B)

A problem that this approach addresses is being able to focus clearly within a specific present situation on the behavior that will take into account what one has learned in the past, and then acting in the present in such a way as to move toward developing the long-term structures one wishes to develop in the future. For example, learning to become a paratrooper includes the "structure" or the specific skill or habit of learning to parachute out of a plane. With respect to Alcoholics Anonymous, the key structure, skill or habit involved is the avoidance of drinking or doing drugs. With respect to writing a book there are the skills, structures or habits of learning to write sentences, paragraphs, subsections, sections, chapters, parts and the book as a whole. In all of these cases it is movement from Spaceland toward Timeland that can help us to move toward developing the structural changes that we desire.

Yet movement into Timeland is by no means an easy matter, given the enormous power of our bureaucratic worldview to narrow our perspective. For example, Murray points out the importance of "overcoming fear." Timeland encompasses the full range of our past experiences and future possibilities along with the range of alternative actions that we can take in the present. Among all of these experiences our emotions stand out as having special importance, given the forces invoked by a wide aspirations fulfillment gap to bury them, and given their importance for motivating our behavior. How are we to learn how to deal with our fears along with the range of our other emotions in our efforts to develop new structures and change old ones? Murray has given us examples that emphasize repetitive behavior, and this is most important, for structures, habits or skills like jumping out of a plane develop as the result of behavior in one situation after another after another. But what about problems that are far more general than that of jumping out of a plane, like learning to move away from emotional repression—and not just repressing the particular emotion of fear—and toward emotional expression? What about the still more general problem of moving from a bureaucratic way of life to an evolutionary way of life? What behavior can we adopt in one situation after another that will yield such broad structural changes?

It is exactly here that the "extraordinary language" or technical language of social science—outlined in the above section on a breakthrough in the social sciences—comes to play a fundamental role. For each concept from that language is a very broad theme that we can learn to hold in mind. Those concepts are structures that can continue to guide us, whether to understand our movement in a bureaucratic direction or in an evolutionary direction. It is because these concepts are general or abstract that they have the power to encompass many specific instances of behavior. For example, we can learn to see "emotional repression" in more and more of our momentary situations: in our friendships, within our families, on television, and in the newspapers and magazines. Yet we can also come to see emotional repression in relation to the broader theme of a bureaucratic versus an evolutionary way of life. For each of the concepts from the extraordinary language is tied to the others, and all of them are tied to this contrast.

The East-West strategy is our effort to wed key elements of Eastern and Western thought as a basis for making progress on problems. We might understand it to be a scientific method building on those Eastern and Western insights that follow scientific ideals and that we can all use in our everyday lives. More specifically, when we use the East-West strategy we pay close attention to the problems within the momentary situation—coming down from unrealistic aspirations that take us away from those problems—and thus follow Eastern strategy. By so doing, we move toward narrowing our values-fulfillment gap by initially lowering our aspirations. Then we make use of the full power of the scientific method to raise both our aspirations and our ability to fulfill them. In that way we employ the Western orientation to look to the future and to raise aspirations. But we also follow the Eastern orientation of keeping those aspirations close to our ability to fulfill them. And we then continue to raise both our aspirations and our fulfillment of those aspirations, depending on the scientific method to enable us to accomplish this. That method requires us to make full use of the extraordinary or technical language of the social sciences.

In these two chapters within part I we have outlined both fundamental problems within contemporary society and a direction for making progress on them. Yet it remains for us to fill out that outline. For example, what is the nature of the extraordinary or technical language of the social sciences that we shall focus on, versus the hundreds of other technical concepts that social scientists have developed over the past two centuries? More specifically, which technical concepts shall we apply to "head," to "heart" and to "hand"? Can the technical concepts of the social scientists actually help us to change structures as fundamental as our patterns of emotional repression and our bureaucratic worldview? Exactly how do we envision the kind of society that we would move toward with the aid of an evolutionary worldview? Can the individual actually continue to develop or evolve in fundamental ways throughout life? Can we learn, both as individuals and as societies, to narrow our aspirations-fulfillment or values-fulfillment gap? Our approach, following Eastern thought, is to begin by centering on the individual, and then to continue, following Western thought, to center on society. We are convinced that it is nothing less than the evolution of the individual and society that we require if indeed we wish not only to solve our problems but to survive as a human race.

Tactics: Individual Evolution— "Head," "Heart" and "Hand"

The very idea of the evolution of the individual is extremely suspect, given the outward orientation of our bureaucratic worldview, as illustrated by our patterns of emotional repression and value neutrality. Not only is an inward orientation avoided, especially in Western society, but we tend to see it negatively. For example, we have this from Lord Acton, a nineteenth-century British historian: "Power tends to corrupt and absolute power corrupts absolutely." Given our own broad approach to the scientific method in order to address the full complexity of human behavior, we might turn to an example from science fiction—just as we did when we invoked *Flatland*—to communicate more fully by engaging "heart" no less than "head." An episode from the original *Star Trek* television series—"Where No Man Has Gone Before"—illustrates Lord Acton's belief.

In this episode the Enterprise ventures beyond the frontier of Earth's galaxy, and as a result encounters a huge magnetic space storm that severely damages the ship. But Captain Kirk and the crew manage to steer the Enterprise back into our galaxy. However, the storm has deeply affected Lieutenant Commander Gary Mitchell. Sparks had invaded his body, jerking him around like a marionette, and he had fallen unconscious to the deck. He is taken to sick bay, with his eyes having turned from blue into a gleaming metallic silver. Not only was Commander Mitchell recovering rapidly but he was accomplishing amazing feats, feats that were becoming ever more amazing with the passage of time. The story continues:

> Mitchell increased the speed of the viewer's turning pages. An image of the turning pages was showing on Spock's library computer screen. When Kirk joined him, they were turning so quickly that their movement was blurred. Spock said, "He's reading faster with every passing second. . . . "About an hour ago," Scott said, "the bridge controls started going crazy. . .Instrument readings wavered from safety points to danger ones." "And on my monitor screen," Spock said, "I saw the

Commander smile each time it happened. He treated the confusion he caused as though this ship and its crew were toys created for his amusement." . . . Mitchell's powers continued to expand. He changed at will the readings on the medical panels monitoring his body functions from zero, indicating death, to normal readings. . . . He announced, "I am thirsty," and across the room a metal cup on the water dispenser slid under the spigot, water flowed into it, and the filled cup lifted, floated through the air, and settled into Mitchell's outstretched hand. (Blish, 1972: 95, 99)

As Mitchell's powers continued to increase, he struggled with Kirk and Spock, exclaiming, "Soon I will squash you all like crawling insects." Following Lord Acton's view, the degree of his corruption matched the increase in his powers. We need not go into the details of the remainder of the episode, where Kirk and Spock, after a number of narrow escapes, manage to deal with the threats from Mitchell's increasing powers. Yet the distrust of the evolution of the individual in a humanistic direction expressed in this *Star Trek* episode, by Lord Acton and by our bureaucratic worldview, speaks volumes about widespread ideas about individual evolution.

Yet by seeing individual evolution negatively we are turning our backs on the interactive nature of the physical universe and the process of biological evolution, as discussed in chapter 1. The history of the universe has yielded, after fourteen billion years, a creature that is more interactive than any other entity throughout the known universe: the human being. Our interactive potential has been developed much further by our complex language. And the invention of the scientific method has given us a tool that can enable us to continue to fulfill that interactive potential with no limit as to how far we might go, just as there is no limit to how far the scientific method can take us in the pursuit of understanding. The power of our possibilities is well illustrated by the one-sided development of biophysical technologies in medicine and engineering that have finally enabled us to destroy ourselves. Yet we need not share the pessimism of Lord Acton or "Where No Man Has Gone Before." We can learn to move away from our one-sided development of biophysical versus social science so as to change our pessimism to optimism about the possibility of our continuing evolution in a humanistic direction.

The three sections of chapter 2—centering on worldviews or metaphysical stances, the scientific method or epistemology, and the East-West strategy with its attention to both situations and structures—have taken us on a journey from the most general ideas to quite specific ones. The ability to use the scientific method in everyday life is an ability to move back and forth from those very general ideas to those specific ones. By employing that method, broadened so as to follow scientific ideals, we are able to move away from not only a bureaucratic worldview, and not only a bureaucratic scientific method, but also the East or West strategies that have yielded increasing dukkha or a widening aspirations-fulfill-ment gap. Those ideals call for attempting to address the full range of phenomena that impact any research project, just as they have been sug-gested in those three sections of chapter 2.

For example, those phenomena most certainly include the impact of the investigator on the research project, an impact that requires the understanding derived from what Gouldner called a "reflexive sociolo-gy." Emotional repression on the part of the investigator simply will not do, for those emotions must be expressed in order to assess their impact on the research project. And value neutrality also will not do, for the researcher must develop a deep commitment to following the ideals of the scientific method in the search for understanding. That kind of com-mitment is essential if the investigator is to confront the threatening na-ture of the human situation at this time in history coupled with the need for a continuing struggle not only "to find out" but also to help develop the powerful personal and social technologies that are desperately needed.

Yet the idea of the scientific method makes still more demands on all of us. For it moves us away from our bureaucratic view of the expert society, with the scientist as a key expert. By so doing it takes the rest of us toward assuming the responsibility that we should be shouldering for our own fate and the fate of society. The Buddha was very clear about the importance for every single one of us, and not just some elite group, of taking on such responsibilities. And even the most revered scientist has much to learn about how to use the scientific method throughout his or her life. Yet scientists also have much to teach the rest of us about the scientific method, just as Gouldner suggested. Let us recall some of his words, as quoted in chapter 2:

> At decisive points the ordinary language and conventional under-standings fail and must be transcended. It is essentially the task of the social sciences, more generally, to create new and "extraordinary" lan-guages, to help men learn to speak them, and to mediate between the deficient understandings of ordinary language and the different and liberating perspectives of the extraordinary languages of social theory. (1972: 16)

As we proceed to chapters 3, 4 and 5 we shall select from the "extraordi-nary" or technical language of the social sciences particularly broad con-cepts that we see as most helpful for learning to move from a bureaucrat-ic toward an evolutionary way of life. Given their breadth, we might see those technical concepts—referred to in the table of contents—as "um-brella concepts," in that they encompass many more specific technical concepts from the social sciences. They do not substitute for those more specific concepts but rather can help us to understand their more general significance. Those concepts are also essential tools for making use of the

East-West strategy with its attention to both the momentary situation as well as long-term structures. The three sections in each of the three chapters in part II include umbrella concepts dealing with both situations and structures. Following the East-West strategy, basic changes in the individual and society require attention to both situations and structures.

Chapters 3, 4 and 5 emphasize "head," "heart" and "hand," respectively. Yet these are no more than emphases, for interaction among them is essential for understanding human behavior, solving problems and moving toward an evolutionary way of life. Let us recall here the pendulum metaphor for the scientific method. Given the enormous problems that we face as a result of the impact of our bureaucratic worldview — especially our widening aspirations-fulfillment gap — we must begin with the optimism that we require if we are to confront those problems instead of burying them. If we can learn to transfer our optimism about using the scientific method to solve biophysical problems to using it to solve personal and social problems, then we can gain momentum for swinging our pendulum far to the left. And that movement could in turn give us the motivation or momentum for swinging it far to the right. In this way we could learn to continue to make progress on our escalating problems by continuing to swing our pendulum in ever-widening arcs with respect to "head," "heart" and "hand," moving toward personal evolution and the evolution of society. This is our dream, but not only for ourselves. Looking to part III, we see the potential of every single one of us not only to light a little candle but to do nothing less than to change the world.

THREE

"Head": Perception/Thought, Self-Image and Worldview

Our metaphors introducing chapters 3, 4 and 5 follow those in *The Wizard of Oz* as well as in the original *Star Trek* series: "head," "heart" and "hand." Who can forget Ray Bolger as the Scarecrow whose "head" was stuffed with straw, Jack Haley as the Tin Woodman without a "heart," and Bert Lahr as the Cowardly Lion without a "hand" for action in the face of danger? As we have used these terms in part I, they are metaphors for the three basic components of human behavior: thought, emotions and actions. As for *Star Trek*, Spock emphasizes "head," McCoy "heart" and Captain Kirk "hand." Yet it is this very specialization of individuals that illustrates our bureaucratic way of life, by contrast with the focus on the interaction among these three elements of human behavior within an evolutionary way of life.

C. Wright Mills, Phillips's mentor at Columbia, illustrated such interaction while still a freshman at Texas A & M in a letter to the Batallion, the student newspaper. In an earlier letter he had protested the mindless disciplinary oppression undergone by freshmen at the hands of upper-classmen, drawing a rejoinder accusing him of a lack of "guts." He penned these words in a second letter:

> Just who are the men with guts? They are the men who have the ability and the brains to see this institution's faults, who are brittle enough not to adapt themselves to its erroneous order—and plastic enough to change if they are already adapted; the men who have the imagination and the intelligence to formulate their own codes; the men who have the courage and the stamina to live their own lives in spite of social pressure and isolation. These my friends, are the men with "guts." (1935/2009)

We might recall here the quote from Mills's *The Sociological Imagination* in chapter 1 that equally reveals his ability to couple emotional force or "heart" with "head" and "hand." He accused "social scientists of the rich societies" who failed to develop responses to current threats to reason and freedom as revealing "surely the greatest human default being committed by privileged men in our times." We see Mills as a rare example of an individual moving toward individual evolution, a process cut short when he died in his forties in 1962. And we see those whom he criticized throughout his career as much like the rest of us: victims of our own bureaucratic way of life that pushes us to separate "head," "heart" and "hand."

It is in chapter 3 that we begin our focus on the concepts that we have reconstructed from the technical language of social science. That language, just like language in general, is a tool for solving problems. The fundamental problem that we are confronting in this book is how to move from our bureaucracy toward an evolutionary way of life. This breaks down more specifically in chapter 3 to three distinct problems centering on "head." They have to do with our patterns of perception and thought, our self-image and our worldview, thus taking us from a focus on the momentary situation to a focus on our long-term structures. By so doing we are moving from Spaceland to Timeland, with its combination of both a short-term and a long-term view of phenomena. And when we enter Timeland we move toward learning how all phenomena—past, present and future—interact with one another, by contrast with Spaceland's emphasis on the isolation of past and future from the present momentary situation.

It is our present bureaucratic concepts bearing on "head" that stand in the way of our ability to make progress on the fundamental and increasing problems of modern society. "Outward perception and thought" takes us away from our own emotions by contrast with Mills's ability to link "heart" with "head" and "hand." Also, by contrast with Mills's self-image that gave him the confidence that he needed to accomplish so much, a "bureaucratic self image" separates "head" and "hand" from "heart," yielding emotional repression and an emphasis on value neutrality. And as we have seen in part I, a "bureaucratic worldview" with its focus on isolating phenomena stands in the way of both our ability to solve escalating problems as well as our own evolution.

Before plunging into chapter 3, let us recall here what we stated in our preface about the meaning and significance of our concept of "personal evolution." For that idea includes not just our view of an interactive physical universe or our notion of the interactive nature of biological evolution. Not just Stephen Jay Gould's view of ourselves as "permanent children" and "learning animals." Not just the historical revolutions that have spawned our "respect revolution," which encompasses the civil rights movement, the women's movement, the gay, lesbian and transgender movement, the senior movement, and the disability movement. And not just the studies of intelligence to be discussed in this chapter. For our idea of "personal evolution" builds on all of these ideas, taken together, and points toward human possibilities that we are convinced can enable us to confront effectively the escalating problems of our times.

INWARD-OUTWARD VERSUS INWARD OR OUTWARD PERCEPTION/THOUGHT: SITUATIONS

The power of the concepts from the extraordinary language of the social sciences that we have selected as those most helpful for understanding evolution is largely based on their breadth or generality, by contrast with the highly specialized concepts that generally populate that language. For example, our focus in this section is not just on thought, and is not just on perception, but rather is on perception and thought. In this way we are able to enter Timeland by moving far back in the human being's history to our situation as newborns prior to our development of language when we perceived phenomena without the impact of language. Of course, our patterns of perception have been shaped throughout our lives by language. Yet those patterns remain important in themselves, since we perceive phenomena from one moment to the next. Certainly our experiences with language are absolutely fundamental in shaping our behavior, yet this does not imply that we should ignore the importance of perception.

Our contrast between "inward or outward perception and thought" and "inward-outward perception and thought" calls to mind our contrast in chapter 2 between an Eastern or Western strategy for problem solving and an East-West strategy. The Eastern Strategy with its emphasis on the past points inward, granting that the technological successes of the West have shifted most Easterners toward a Western orientation. By contrast, the Western strategy, with its focus on the future, points outward. The East-West strategy combines elements of the East and the West, producing an inward-outward strategy that includes both past and future along with the present. It is, then, a strategy for entering Timeland, with its focus on the interaction of all phenomena, past, present and future.

As an example not just of our orientation to inward or outward perception and thought but also to inward-outward perception and thought, we turn to an allegory or extended metaphor that happens to be the most famous one developed throughout all of Western history. It is Plato's image of us humans as prisoners in a cave—an image that may have been derived from Plato's teacher, Socrates—that he put forward in the fourth century B.C.:

Imagine men to be living in an underground cave-like dwelling place, which has a way up to the light along its whole width, but the entrance is a long way up. The men have been there from childhood, with their neck and legs in fetters, so that they remain in the same place and can only see ahead of them, as their bonds prevent them from turning their heads. Light is provided by a fire burning some way behind and above them. Between the fire and the prisoners . . .there is a path across the cave and along this a low wall has been built, like the screen at a puppet show in front of the performers who show their puppets above it. . . . See then also men carrying along the wall, so that they overtop it, all kinds of artifacts, statues of men, reproductions of other animals. . . .

Do you think, in the first place, that such men could see anything of themselves and each other except the shadows which the fire casts upon the wall of the cave in front of them? . . . Altogether then, I said, such men would believe the truth to be nothing else than the shadows of the artifacts? . . . the men below had praise and honours from each other, and prizes for the men who saw most clearly the shadows that passed before them, and who could best remember which usually came earlier and which later. (Plato, 1974: 168-169)

Following Plato's allegory, we prisoners are unable to see the reality of either ourselves or our external situation. As a philosopher, Plato was much concerned with the nature of the human being's worldview, metaphysical stance or basic assumptions about the nature of reality. He was attempting to communicate the idea that our present worldview is false, and that we must shift to another worldview if indeed we wish to escape from the prison of our present worldview and learn how to fulfill our capacities as human beings. This is exactly our own stance in this book and in our previous work. And we can even add to Plato's allegory to bring it up to date. For example, we might see that fire in the cave as being fanned by forces of human behavior that remain invisible, and it is moving rapidly toward us. This is illustrated by the widening of our values-fulfillment gap, as in the case of the increasingly deadly nature of our weapons of mass destruction and improvements in the means to deliver them. As a result, we have only a limited time within which to change our worldview, break our bands and climb out of our cave.

The power of Plato's allegory is that it communicates most powerfully the general nature of our problem as human beings and therefore points to a very general direction for solving that problem. His optimism about the possibility of solving the fundamental problems of the human being enabled him to swing his pendulum far to the left where lies awareness of problems and the commitment to solving them. More specifically, the problem faced by us prisoners in Plato's cave is that we cannot look either inward or outward to see the nature of reality. We are tied up in such a way that we can neither look at ourselves nor look at our fellow prisoners. Plato spent much of his life in an effort to solve that problem. He founded the Academy in Athens, the first institution of higher learning in the Western world, hoping to teach us humans how to climb out of our cave.

Let us note here the importance of our perception, which includes sight along with our other senses such as hearing, touch, taste and smell. Perception is most influential because it takes place from one moment to the next. Our worldview includes a "view." It is not just thought: it is perception as well. If we are to change our worldview then we must somehow learn to change the way we perceive ourselves and the world from one moment to the next. In order to update Plato's allegory, we should distinguish our images of physical and biological phenomena from our images of human phenomena, with the latter being shadows of reality far more than the former. As physical and biological science continue to progress, we learn to see biophysical phenomena ever more clearly. Yet at the present time our images of human behavior are much like what Plato described: little more than shadows. For example, as discussed in chapter 2, we fail to be reflexive, as illustrated by our patterns of emotional repression. Further, our failure to integrate the bits and pieces of our knowledge of human behavior yields an unrealistic view of other human beings and fails to detect invisible forces like our widening values-fulfillment gap.

Yet the problem that Plato uncovered is more than one of perception: it includes language and thought as well. He stated, "the men below had praise and honours from each other, and prizes for the men who saw most clearly the shadows that passed before them, and who could best remember which usually came earlier and which later." The language they used and the thoughts that they communicated to one another succeeded only in focusing very narrowly on the wall of the cave where the shadows appeared. Their language and thought were not broad or general enough to take into account more of their situation so as to understand the inadequacy of their perceptions. Thus, Plato's allegory points not only to the problem of perception but also to the problem of language and thought. Such basic problems could not be unearthed without attention to our worldview or basic assumptions about the nature of reality.

Contemporary psychological research can help us to understand the forces that prevent us from paying more serious attention to our actual perceptions, pointing us instead to seeing shadows on the cave wall, which are nothing less than figments of our imagination. There is what has been called the phenomenon of "verbal overshadowing," as illustrated by the distortion of people's initial perception of a given face by verbal descriptions of that face (Schooler and Engstier-Schooler, 1990; see also Lehrer, 2010: 52–57). This study sparked the development of numerous other studies, and it has been cited over four hundred times. Although it had previously been believed that verbalization generally improves memory, these studies indicated the reverse. These findings have implications for the history of the human race. For they at least suggest that we humans, with our overriding emphasis on language, have learned to de-emphasize our perceptions. For "verbal overshadowing" succeeds in working against our ability to perceive inward no less than outward.

Plato's uncovering of these two major problems—our patterns of perception and our patterns of thought on the basis of language—also suggests a direction for addressing those problems. Our ability to gain profound insights by turning to worldviews is based on their incredible generality. Given that generality, we are able to see any and every experience that we have had as having something do with isolation and interaction. For example, in chapter 1 we were able to see the very nature of our physical universe as illustrating interaction more than isolation, and we saw the process of biological evolution in the same way. It was the extremely general concept of "worldview" that enabled us to accomplish this. Yet given this direction for making use of very general concepts, this is our key to locating the extraordinary language that we need not only to unearth problems but also to move toward solving them. If language is indeed the most important characteristic separating human beings from all other organisms, and if language is indeed our most powerful tool for solving problems, then we should look to language for unearthing our deepest problems as well as for solving them.

If we turn to the language of the physical sciences, we can come up with examples of the importance of such generality as fundamental to the successes of those sciences. To illustrate, there is no physical body to which we cannot apply the concepts of "atom" and "molecule." Recalling Edna St. Vincent Millay's poem, it is such general concepts that can be applied to all of our behavior that can enable us to integrate our "meteoric shower of facts" that presently lie "uncombined." Looking back to the language that we used in part one, we anticipated this idea of the importance of very general concepts. For example, we emphasized the contrast between the "interaction of phenomena" and the "isolation of phenomena." We brought forward the idea of "worldview," which every human being has regardless of whether or not one is aware of this situation. We also focused on the phenomena of "emotional repression," which we all engage in to somewhat varying degrees. And we emphasized, as a fundamental yet invisible problem that we all have, the aspirations-fulfillment or values-fulfillment gap.

Based on the Eastern and the Western strategies for solving problems, a general concept that we can select from social science's extraordinary language is *inward or outward perception and thought*. In order to emphasize these concepts we will italicize them wherever they appear. Our aim is to use these concepts as tools for moving, one step at a time, from our bureaucratic way of life toward an evolutionary way of life. An initial step is learning to apply a concept from the extraordinary language that we have selected to more and more of our everyday behavior, and thus shaping more and more of one's everyday situations. Phillips provides this example in his unpublished journal:

> I am using a pen to write these words on a sheet of paper while lying down on a rug in my living room. My perception and thought of the pen, the words, the paper, the rug and the living room all illustrate outward perception and thought. By contrast, the ideas in my head that no one can see but that govern what I write illustrate inward perception and thought. And when I depart from my usual Western outward orientation and become aware of an inward orientation as well, then I am moving toward inward-outward perception and thought.

I should note that in this way I am learning to use the scientific method in my everyday life, as illustrated by the pendulum metaphor. I start with the scientific optimism that I will be able to solve a problem once I define it, thus giving me the motivation or momentum I need to address a problem as humongous as changing my own way of life. I can now swing my pendulum far to the left, facing up to my deep involvement in outward perception and thought. Yet I have in mind—based on my efforts to integrate social science knowledge—an alternative: inward-outward perception and thought. Knowing that alternative gives me the motivation or momentum I need to swing my pendulum far to the right, where I make a bit of progress in learning to move toward inward-outward perception and thought.

The other two section headings in chapter 3 reveal additional steps that I should take in order to move toward an evolutionary way of life, with both steps involving my learning to use other concepts from the extraordinary language in my everyday life. I should move from my *bureaucratic self-image* toward an *evolutionary self-image*, and from my *bureaucratic worldview* toward an *evolutionary worldview*. Such movement requires not merely situational change but also structural change, for a self-image and a worldview are more than momentary ideas. They are ideas that stay with me in one scene after another after another, and thus they are structures with their extension within the dimension of time. By taking that first step of moving from *outward perception and thought* toward *inward-outward perception and thought,* I have prepared the way for changing these structures having to do with my self-image and worldview. For I have learned to pay attention to myself and my own possibilities as a prelude to developing my self-image and worldview. Yet my journey toward an *evolutionary way of life* is by no means over, as there are additional steps I should take that will be outlined in chapters 4 and 5. Given the many steps involved in this journey, it is essential that I learn how to continue to swing my pendulum in ever-widening arcs.

By proceeding in this way, an individual is learning to make fuller use of the potentials that our complex language holds out to us, potentials that we presently use only to a limited extent. Let us recall from the very first section of chapter 1 our discussion of the nature of language. There we distinguished three capacities of language: dichotomy, gradation and metaphor. And we stated that the social sciences have emphasized dichotomies with their focus on everyday language; the biophysical sciences have emphasized gradation with their emphasis on mathematics, and the arts have centered on metaphor with their attention to imagery and figures of speech. Yet our bureaucratic world with its emphasis on specialization with limited communication makes it most difficult for the individual to learn to use all three potentials of language along with the concepts developed within these fields of knowledge. For example, biophysical and social scientists learn to stay as far away from metaphor as possible, viewing such language as too vague for scientific use. But as a result they lose out on powerful ways of understanding what they themselves are accomplishing as well as communicating their findings to others. And the rest of us learn to avoid efforts to learn the concepts used by biophysical and social scientists along with their findings, as well as the basic metaphors developed within the arts.

By contrast, our own effort to move toward evolution makes use of all of these three potentials together by selecting very broad concepts from the technical or extraordinary language of the social sciences. For example, we make full use of dichotomies, given their dramatic power and resulting ability to invoke our emotions. Our contrast between *inward or outward perception and thought* and *inward-outward perception and thought* illustrates the remainder of our concepts selected from the extraordinary language, for they are all involved in dichotomies between bureaucratic and evolutionary behavior. As for gradation, we see ourselves on a continuum stretching between *inward or outward perception and thought*, on the one hand, and *inward-outward perception and thought*, on the other hand. Further, metaphors are crucial in our approach to the problem of moving in an evolutionary direction, as illustrated by "head," "heart" and "hand," by the pendulum metaphor, by the Spaceland-Timeland metaphors, by Plato's allegory of the cave and by our quotes from poetry and fiction.

By selecting concepts from social science's technical language that use this broad linguistic approach to human behavior, and by applying those concepts to one's everyday experiences, one can learn over time to see any given experience through the lenses of all of the concepts from our selected concepts. For each of them is so general that it can apply to any instance of human behavior, just as the concepts of "atom" and "molecule" can apply to any instance of the physical universe. As one continues to apply our selection from the extraordinary language to one's experiences in one situation after another, one learns to see more and more of those experiences on a continuum stretching from a bureaucratic toward an *evolutionary way of life*. Given the contradictions between a *bureaucratic way of life* and democratic as well as scientific ideals—and given the promise of an *evolutionary way of life* for resolving those contradictions—this will motivate one to move along that continuum toward that *evolutionary way of life*.

This would result in a reorganization of the hundreds of technical concepts developed by social scientists in sociology, psychology, anthropology, political science, economics and history. Generally they follow the indictment of Edna St. Vincent Millay. They are "a meteoric shower of fact," and "they lie . . . uncombined." Yet all of that specialized knowledge, following Millay, includes "wisdom enough to leech us of our ill" once we succeed in integrating it, and that integration is exactly our own direction. That integration can in turn become the basis for the integration of the thousands of concepts within the ordinary language that the rest of us use.

We are convinced that all of this can and must change if indeed we are to confront effectively our threatening problems at this time in history. Our selection of general concepts from social science's technical language can help us to accomplish this by providing a direction for integrating existing technical and everyday concepts that focus on human behavior. That selection makes full use of language's dichotomous, gradational and metaphorical potentials. We have emerged with the concepts that appear as headings in the sections of chapters 3, 4 and 5. Those extraordinary concepts can help us to organize our shattered ideas about human beings so that we can learn to bring more and more of those ideas to bear on the problems that we are facing. Indeed, this is the promise of human language: that it can enable us to continue to learn how to solve problems, with absolutely no limit as to how far it can take us.

However, we should be aware of the difficulties involved in continuing such movement if indeed we hope to keep moving despite discouraging experiences along the way. For we all have developed a great many structures tied to a *bureaucratic way of life*, as outlined by fully half of the concepts that we have selected from social science's extraordinary language. Those structures are kept in place by our *bureaucratic worldview* and have to do with "head," "heart" and "hand." To illustrate those structures, we turn to George Gurdjieff—an Armenian philosopher who traveled extensively throughout the Middle East, Africa and Central Asia as a young man and later taught in Moscow and St. Petersburg at the turn of the twentieth century. One of his students, P. D. Ouspensky, recorded and explained Gurdjieff's ideas in *The Fourth Way* (1957/1971), ideas that emphasize Eastern thought with its focus on the experiences of the individual.

Ouspensky wrote about the possibilities of the individual together with our failure to fulfill those possibilities in his *The Fourth Way: A Record of Talks and Answers to Questions Based on the Teaching of G. I. Gurdjieff*, possibilities that include our moving away from outward perception or thought:

The chief idea of this system was that we do not use even a small part of our powers and our forces. We have in us, so to speak, a very big and very fine organization, only we do not know how to use it. In this group they employed certain oriental metaphors, and they told me that we have in us a large house full of beautiful furniture, with a library and many other rooms, but we live in the basement and the kitchen and cannot get out of them. If people tell us about what this house has upstairs we do not believe them, or we laugh at them, or we call it superstition or fairy tales or fables. . . .The study of man is closely connected with the idea of the evolution of man. . . .

The human being is a very complicated machine and has to be studied as a machine. We realize that in order to control any kind of machine, such as a motor car or a railway engine, we should first have to learn. We cannot control these machines instinctively, but for some reason we think that ordinary instinct is sufficient to control the human machine, although it is so much more complicated. This is one of the first wrong assumptions: we do not realize that we have to learn, that control is a question of knowledge and skill. (1957/1971: 2, 9)

Gurdjieff and Ouspensky did not have at their disposal the benefit of social science knowledge, yet somehow they were able to develop profound ideas about human possibilities by combining Eastern and Western thought. Their idea that we must "learn" about how to manage ourselves—just like we must learn to manage any complex machine—points us away from our passivity about our own development, as enforced by a *bureaucratic worldview* that points us outward. As for the power of that worldview, Ouspensky had this to say:

If we begin to study ourselves we first of all come up against one word which we use more than any other and that is the word "I". We say "I am doing," "I am sitting," "I feel," "I like," "I dislike" and so on. This is our chief illusion . . . we consider ourselves one . . . when in reality we are divided into hundreds of different "I"s. . . . So in self-observation . . . generally you do not remember yourself . . . because you cannot remember yourself, you cannot concentrate, and . . . you have no will. If you could remember yourself, you would have will and could do what you liked. . . . You may sometimes have will for a short time, but it turns to something else and you forget about it . . . we become too absorbed in things, too lost in things.(Ouspensky: 3–4, 12)

Ouspensky's idea that "we become too absorbed in things, too lost in things" illustrates the Western push toward outward perception and thought. We remain largely glued to perceiving external phenomena within any given momentary scene, failing to enter Timeland and think about our many past experiences and future possibilities. Indeed, such behavior parallels the behavior of our pets, who are largely chained to the momentary situation. Our assumption that we have a unitary "I" in any and every situation hides this fact from us. By contrast, Ouspensky claimed that "this is our chief illusion." Thus, he links our outward orientation to our self-image. And he does not stop there, for the limitations of our self image are tied as well to our "heart" and "hand." Our lack of a unitary "I" results in the situation where "you have no will," that is, we lack will power or motivation, just like the Tin Man without a heart in *The Wizard of Oz* based on a children's book (Baum, 1960). That lack of will power yields our failure to develop "hand" so as to "control the human machine," just as the Cowardly Lion in *The Wizard of Oz* remained frozen, unable to act in the face of the empty threats from the Wizard.

Yet although Ouspensky and Gurdjieff knew little about the social sciences, they nevertheless had somehow developed optimism, paralleling scientific optimism, about the possibilities of the individual for developing "will" or motivation and how one could "learn" to control one's "human machine." Their approach pointed in the same direction as that of Alvin Gouldner with his emphasis on the importance of developing a "reflexive sociology," where the individual sociologists learns to study himself or herself in addition to studying others. But Ouspensky and Gurdjieff, given their immersion within Eastern thought, were more aware—granting their optimism—of the enormous difficulties involved in developing a reflexive orientation. For example, they saw clearly the importance of developing a unitary "I," a self-image much different from what presently exists throughout the world. Such a "head" orientation is crucial for developing "heart" and "hand." It can help us develop the motivation or momentum for swinging our pendulum of the scientific method back and forth in ever-widening arcs so that we can actually learn how to control the human machine, solve our problems and move in an evolutionary direction. We turn, then, in this next section, to the problem of developing our self-image.

AN EVOLUTIONARY VERSUS A BUREAUCRATIC SELF-IMAGE: STRUCTURES

A. E. Van Vogt's *The World of Null-A* (1945/1970) is a science-fiction novel that can shed light on the nature and potentials of us human beings and, in particular, our "self-image" or the way we see ourselves. It is based on the ideas of Alfred Korzybski, a Polish engineer who developed profound insights in his *Science and Sanity* (1933) into the failure of human beings to make much use of the incredible potentials of language for helping us to address our deepest problems. Korzybski launched a new field, "general semantics," founded the present-day Institute of General Semantics, and succeeded in influencing a great many students. Among his students was Samuel I. Hayakawa, a former Senator from California, whose *Language in Thought and Action* (1949) carried forward Korzybski's ideas. The quarterly journal ETC continues to contribute to the ideas within this field that focuses on developing our linguistic abilities as a basis for attempting to solve the fundamental problems of the human race.

Van Vogt's story takes place on an Earth existing some five centuries from now. The action begins when Nordegg, a store owner from Cress Village, Florida, questions the identity of Van Vogt's hero, Gilbert Gosseyn—pronounced "go-sane," thus suggesting Korzybski's *Science and Sanity*. Nordegg, Gosseyn and many other residents of Earth are preparing for a grueling thirty-day competition, beginning the following day, to assess the degree to which they have developed "Null-A" or "non-Aristotelian" thinking. Korzybski viewed Aristotle's thought as emphasizing a simplistic either-or approach, a dichotomous orientation, rather than a focus on gradation or matters of degree, just as physical science emphasizes numbers and mathematics. Gradational thought, an orientation emphasizing the scientific method, was for Korzybski—as well as it is for us—essential in order to penetrate the enormous complexity of human behavior and human problems. In addition to black and white there are shades of gray. And the scientific method moves us not from total falsity to absolute truth but rather from limited understanding to ever greater understanding. Korzybski's vision as well as our own is that all of us humans—and not just professional scientists—can and should learn to use the scientific method in our everyday lives.

Efforts to develop Null-A thinking had become increasingly important throughout Earth over the past several centuries, given the widely-recognized limitations of a simplistic focus on dichotomous thought that prevailed throughout the planet. For it had been such either-or thinking that had been much of the basis for the wars that had occurred throughout human history, where people stereotyped themselves as "good" and others as "evil." This "two-valued orientation" was well illustrated by Hitler's use of "Aryan" as representing all that was good, and "non-Aryan" as representing all that was evil. In the past those few who had managed to survive the extremely difficult thirty-day competition held yearly would earn a passage to Venus, where a genuine Null-A society had been established. Gosseyn had studied long and hard in preparation for this competition, and he was supremely confident that he would not be eliminated throughout the competition and emerge as one of its few survivors. He saw himself as six feet one inch tall, age thirty-four, weight 185 pounds, and as a long-time resident of the tiny community of Cress Village.

Yet Nordegg had never seen Gosseyn in his many years of operating a store there, and he had never heard of him. Gosseyn apparently is not who he thinks he is, and the other competitors go along with Nordegg and decide that he is not eligible to enter the Null-A competition. Who, then, is Gilbert Gosseyn in reality? How has he come to believe in a false view of himself? What caused him to develop an erroneous self-image? Throughout the novel, and throughout Van Vogt's sequel—*The Players of*

Null-A (1948)—Gosseyn struggles to learn his true identity. In the process, he makes full use of his Null-A training, which enables him to continue to develop or evolve intellectually ("head"), emotionally ("heart") and in the effectiveness of his actions. ("hand"). By so doing, he learns how to save Earth and Venus from destruction by Enro the Red, who had planned to conquer the entire galaxy and establish a galactic empire, and who illustrates dichotomous thought. As he proceeds Gosseyn does not abandon dichotomous thought but rather adds to it gradational thought. At the same time he sees himself as moving on an evolutionary journey to develop ever greater understanding as well as ever greater power to solve problems.

Van Vogt's novels can serve us well as an allegory or extended metaphor, namely, a story that can suggest our own realistic situation at this time in history. Who are we human beings? Like Gilbert Gosseyn, do we have a false view of ourselves? Do we see ourselves as quite limited, failing to see the incredible potential for evolution that each of us possesses? Are we in fact the creatures that we think we are and that society has taught us that we are, with ideas like our supposedly limited intelligence and the supposed importance of the rich and the famous, the beautiful and the Nobel Prize-winners? Are we creatures who have largely limited ourselves to dichotomous thought, all the while failing to give more than lip service to gradational and metaphorical thought? Have we even failed to develop dichotomous thought very far, ignoring the powerful dichotomies developed throughout the social sciences? Have we failed to open up to our possibilities for continuing to evolve throughout our lives, just as Gosseyn was able to do? Is it indeed possible that we remain most limited because we have failed to tap into the potentials of language for gradational, metaphorical and dichotomous thought? Can we learn to make full use of those potentials as a basis for solving our problems and learning to evolve with respect to "head," "heart" and "hand," just as Gosseyn learned to defeat Enro the Red?

The psychologist George A. Kelly put forward in his *A Theory of Personality* an idea for a self-image that we might all do well to develop:

> To a large degree—though not entirely—the blueprint of human progress has been given the label of "science." Let us then, instead of occupying ourselves with man-the-biological organism or man-the-lucky-guy have a look at man-the-scientist. . . . Might not the individual man . . . assume more of the stature of a scientist, ever seeking to predict and control the course of events with which he is involved? Would he not have his theories, test his hypotheses, and weight his experimental evidence? (1963: 4)

Kelly advanced here a truly evolutionary idea. Our pendulum metaphor already suggests the idea that there is no limit to how far our pendulum of the scientific method can swing so as to yield ever-greater progress in understanding self and world. Kelly's metaphor of "man-the-scientist" implies, then, that there is also no limit to how far we can move toward understanding self and world. And if we also follow Peirce's emphasis on the importance of emotional commitment—illustrated by "the irritation of doubt"—then we can extend this evolutionary vision for the individual to "heart" as well as "head." Still further, since the scientific method is used technologically and not just within the halls of the academic world, Kelly's evolutionary vision for the individual can extend to "hand" as well as "head" and "heart." Following Kelly's metaphor, then, we are all already scientists in our everyday lives, granting that we have much to learn about how to improve our scientific approach by learning to move from our bureaucratic scientific method and worldview to an evolutionary scientific method and worldview.

We might then see Kelly's vision of "man-the-scientist" as nothing less than a vision of an *evolutionary self-image*, by contrast with our present-day *bureaucratic self-image*, where we have learned to see ourselves as extremely limited relative to the important people in the world. And we certainly do not see ourselves as scientists. And we even see our most famous scientists and artists as limited relative to the possibility of their having continued to evolve. For example, we do not believe in the possibility that Beethoven, Einstein, Darwin, Freud, Picasso or Shakespeare could have continued works far beyond their actual achievements. And we certainly do not believe that Beethoven could have moved toward the stature of Einstein, and vice-versa, or that Shakespeare—in addition to his achievements—could have produced artistic works comparable to those of Picasso. Instead, we follow along with the eighteenth-century proverb "Jack of all trades and master of none." Yet our own vision of human possibilities is far different. For example, in the introduction to this book, the dream that we put forward included this aspiration: that "one day we all will learn to be poets, philosophers, and scientists."

A basic assumption standing in the way of our developing an *evolutionary self-image* is the idea that our "intelligence" or capacity to learn is fixed, and that people differ greatly in their degree of intelligence, as measured by their IQ scores. However, the inventors of the concept of IQ never claimed that it is a measure of basic intelligence—or the capacity to learn—even though generally it is thought of in that way by educators and everyone else. More and more, recent studies are questioning this assumption that people differ substantially in their intelligence or basic capacity to learn, granting that they can differ greatly in their abilities. From the moment of birth, and even while still in the womb, the individual's abilities are shaped by every experience in one scene after another, for this is what social scientists have discovered.

For example, David Shenk argues for the enormous yet largely untapped potentials of every human being in his book, *The Genius in All of Us: Why Everything You've Been Told About Genetics, Talent, and IQ Is*

Wrong (2010). Shenk claims that we all have a "latent talent abundance," yet our problem is "our inability, so far, to tap into what we already have." For evidence, he cites numerous studies demonstrating that genes are influenced by their interaction with all kinds of environmental stimuli. For additional evidence, he cites experiments that have succeeded in training ordinary individuals to perform extraordinary feats. For example, an individual who was able to hold only seven digits in his short-term memory was taught to recall over eighty digits. Shenk sees this accomplishment as much the same as the accomplishments of individuals who we see as geniuses. Yet our idea of individual evolution points far beyond simply harnessing one's "latent talent abundance"; it points toward the continuing development of "head," "heart" and "hand" without any limit.

Our evolutionary idea carries forward a gradational approach to life that has to do not with our further biological evolution but rather with the continuing conscious evolution of each of us. Thus, a Beethoven, an Einstein, a Darwin, a Freud, a Picasso or a Shakespeare would not have to stop developing at any given time but could continue onward indefinitely. And the same would be the case for the rest of us. Metaphorically or visually, we might think of the idea of individual evolution as a stairway with extremely wide steps that extends to the stars. Its steps are wide enough to accommodate the entire human race. One person's movement up the stairway would not require others to move down. Indeed, that movement could help the rest of us, for we could learn how that movement took place. This image of a stairway with its gradational orientation contrasts with an image of a see-saw, suggesting a two-valued or dichotomous orientation. When we move up on a see-saw we push someone else down, and vice-versa. And we are quite limited in just how far we can move upward, by contrast with a stairway extending to the stars.

There is additional evidence questioning the idea that the individual's intelligence or capacity to learn is limited. For example, in a seventy-seven page article reviewing the research literature on the IQ test, Samuel Bowles and Herbert Gintis have drawn this conclusion: "We have here attempted to speed up the process of demystification [of the IQ test] by showing that the purportedly 'scientific' empirical basis of . . . IQ-ism is false" (in Alan Gartner et al., *The New Assault on Equality*, 1974: 84). Despite such analyses of the inadequacy of the IQ or any other test yet developed to measure basic intelligence or one's capacity to learn based on one's heredity, and despite the failure of almost all researchers to claim that the IQ test is indeed a measure of basic intelligence, and despite the fact that IQ scores can be changed substantially, the idea widely persists that IQ score is a measure of basic intelligence. Apparently, that belief is fostered by our stratified worldview, which remains invisible yet which works to teach us not only that hierarchies exist but that they are persisting, yielding stratification.

To illustrate further how IQ can be changed, Robert Rosenthal—an experimental psychologist—found that children's performance on an IQ test was substantially influenced by the expectations of their teachers (Rosenthal and Jacobson, 1968). Students in an elementary school initially took a series of little-known IQ tests, and their teachers were given lists of students who supposedly were "spurters" or late "bloomers" when in fact those students were chosen by a table of random numbers. After a one-year period Rosenthal and Jacobsen found that, among the so-called spurters, first-graders gained 27 points and second-graders 16 points, gains that were significantly greater than gains among the control group of students who were not designated as spurters.

There have indeed been studies over the years that have supported the idea that intelligence is inherited, granting that those investigations have been widely denounced as racism wrapped in pseudoscience. Yet it has become clear that IQ can be changed by environmental factors. For example, Richard E. Nisbett, a psychology professor at the University of Michigan, systematically documents this idea in his *Intelligence and How to Get It: Why Schools and Culture Count* (2009). As a case in point, when poor children are adopted by upper-middle-class families, they show an IQ gain of twelve to sixteen points. Also, identical twins growing up in different adoptive families show differences in their IQ And the racial IQ gap between Americans of European and African descent has been shrinking over the years.

Once we are freed from the assumption deriving from our *bureaucratic worldview* that our intelligence is fixed, we can open up to the possibility that we can change our *bureaucratic self-image* and move toward an *evolutionary self-image*. For example, there is Kelly's view of "man-the-scientist" or our own vision of ourselves as "poets and philosophers" as well as "scientists." Studies of human biology generally have discovered no fundamental differences among human beings that yield differences in their capacity to learn, and they suggest yet another self-image for us, as illustrated by this analysis of Stephen Jay Gould in his *The Mismeasure of Man*:

> We are, in a more than metaphorical sense, permanent children. . . .
> Many central features of our anatomy link us with fetal and juvenile
> stages of primates: small face, vaulted cranium and large brain in rela-
> tion to body size, unrotated big toe, foramen magnum under the skull
> for correct orientation of the head in upright posture, primary distribu-
> tion of hair on head, armpits and pubic areas. . . . In other mammals,
> exploration, play, and flexibility of behavior are qualities of juveniles,
> only rarely of adults. We retain not only the anatomical stamp of child-
> hood, but its mental flexibility. . . . Humans are learning animals.
> (Gould, 1981: 333–334)

Gould sees our own anatomy as well as our behavior as indicating that we are "permanent children." We might note here part of our dream that we described in the introduction: that "one day we will all learn to see ourselves as children who are only just beginning to understand ourselves and our world." Yet despite the foregoing super-optimistic ideas about our own possibilities, we must pay attention to the problems that we face. Granting that we have possibilities that match those of Gilbert Gosseyn, that we can learn to see ourselves as scientists, philosophers and poets, to move our pendulum of the scientific method in ever-widening arcs, to increase our IQ and to see ourselves as permanent children, we must recognize just how deeply we are enmeshed within a *bureaucratic way of life* that creates barriers to moving in these directions. How are we, realistically, to penetrate those barriers, and not just dream about our possibilities? Unless we can find ways to take one step at a time toward those possibilities, we will abandon them as nothing more than an unrealistic dream.

We will present examples of such a concrete step, where we return to our own past and reinterpret our negative experiences. This is a path that all of us can take: we can enter Timeland and look back at our experiences, whether we saw them as successes or as failures. And using our present understanding, such as the idea of our own possibilities, we can proceed to reinterpret those experiences. In this way we can not only gain further strength from our past successes, but we can also reduce the continuing impact of past failures that take us away from our possibilities.

It is not just our own personal past that can help us to understand our own personal possibilities: we can go back fourteen billion years and look to the interactive nature of our physical universe, as discussed in chapter 1. And we can equally return to the interactive nature of our entire history of biological evolution, also discussed in that chapter. We might also note Gould's analysis of ourselves as "learning animals." Still further, the studies of human intelligence that we have just taken up—those by Bowles and Gintis, Shenk, Nisbett, and Rosenthal—can help to give us confidence about our own individual potential.

For further confidence in ourselves, we can also look to the direction of history over the last several centuries. For history's movement toward democratic ideals suggests nothing less than the increasing importance and potential of every single individual. For example, we have the eighteenth-century American and French revolutions. And we have our more recent social movements that carry still further our democratic ideals: the American civil rights movement, women's movement, gay, lesbian and transgender movement, senior movement and disability movement. Two social scientists, S. M. Miller and Anthony J. Savoie, have called these movements the "respect revolution" of the twentieth century (2002, 8–12). They trace this revolution as including a number of crucial events:

the 1954 Supreme Court decision in Brown v. the Board of Education of Topeka, Kansas, the burial of using the term "girls" for women, the resistance to the attack by police on the Stonewall gay bar, and the passage of the Americans with Disabilities Act and the Older Americans Act.

Robert W. Fuller, former president of Oberlin College, has developed the concept of "rankism" to yield further insight into what Miller and Savoie mean by the "respect revolution":

> Rankism insults the dignity of subordinates by treating them as invisible nobodies. . . . Nobodies are insulted, disrespected exploited, ignored. . . . It might be supposed that if one overcame tendencies to racism, sexism, ageism, and other narrowly defined forms of discrimination, one would be purged of rankism as well. But rankism is not just another ism. It subsumes the familiar dishonorable isms. It's the mother of them all. (2003, 5)

Thus, for example, "rankism" includes such forms of showing disrespect as "heightism," "weightism" and "beautyism," and any form of disrespect whatsoever. Fuller has succeeded in initiating a new social movement focusing on rankism, and he develops further insight about this movement in a later book (2006).

If we continue to focus on problems no less than solutions, we can turn to fiction for an example, dipping into the sequel to Van Vogt's *The World of Null-A: The Players of Null-A*. In *The Players*, Gosseyn's mind is suddenly transported into the body of Prince Ashargin on the planet Gorgzid. The Prince was spared by Enro when he seized the planet and killed the royal family so that in the future Ashargin could help Enro gain credibility in his efforts to rule the galaxy. Yet the Prince had led a life of abject humiliation for years at the hands of Enro, resulting in *negative emotions* like deep feelings of fear, guilt and shame. We might see those emotions as paralleling our own negative emotions, resulting from our *wide values-fulfillment gap* linked to our *bureaucratic worldview*.

Gosseyn seizes his opportunity to train Ashargin in the principles of Null-A thought as a basis for strengthening him emotionally so that he might learn to oppose Enro. He communicates this thought: "Every time you take a positive action on the basis of a high-level consideration, you establish certainties of courage, self-assurance and skills." Then Gosseyn follows this up with specific procedures:

> In the bedroom Gosseyn rigged up a wall recorder to repeat a three-minute relaxation pattern. Then he lay down. During the hour that followed he never quite went to sleep. . . . Lying there, he allowed his mind to idle around the harsher memories of Ashargin's prison years. Each time he came to an incident that had made a profound impression he talked silently to the younger Ashargin. . . . From his greater height of understanding, he assured the younger individual that the affective incident must be looked at from a different angle than that of a fright-

ened youth. Assured him that fear of pain and fear of death were emotions that could be overcome, and that in short the shock incident which had once affected him so profoundly no longer had any meaning for him. More than that, in future he would have better understanding of such moments, and he would never again be affected in an adverse fashion. (Van Vogt, 1948: 115–116)

Gosseyn's efforts to train Ashargin illustrate the approach of psychoanalysis by returning to Ashargin's memories of his past, thus also following a Timeland rather than the Spaceland perspective we all learn from our *bureaucratic worldview*. Gosseyn thought back to Ashargin's fear-ridden experiences, experiences that Ashargin had repressed just as we all learn to repress our deeply *negative emotions*. When this process of bringing repressed *negative emotions* up to the light of day is undertaken by psychoanalysts, a great deal of time and a great many visits to the analyst are generally involved. For the patient must learn over time to use the strength of his or her relation to the analyst to master the fear linked to dredging up those emotions. Yet Gosseyn's position occupying Ashargin's body enabled him to short-cut this long process. And he succeeded in helping Ashargin relive his terrible experiences and learn to see himself in a far more confident light. Ashargin's progress toward his own emotional development and more confident self-image is later illustrated in the book by his ability to stand up to and oppose Enro's plans.

In addition to our ability to reinterpret past failures so as to strengthen our self-image, we can also look to past successes. Moving from Van Vogt's fiction to nonfiction, we turn to the experience that Phillips recently had when a reinterpretation of a success in his past life enabled him to move toward an *evolutionary self-image*. After completing his doctoral dissertation at Cornell University, "A Role Theory Approach to Predicting Adjustment of the Aged in Two Communities," Phillips was able to publish his findings as an article in the *American Sociological Review* with the title "A Role Theory Approach to Adjustment in Old Age" (1957). Phillips's key finding centered on the impact of the self-image of people sixty years old or older on their adjustment to life. He divided his sample of five hundred individuals in New York City and 468 people in Elmira, New York, into two groups: those who saw themselves as "old" or "elderly," and those who saw themselves as "middle-aged."

He theorized as follows:

> It is hypothesized that a self-conception as old is related to maladjustment. Because our society values youth over age, the individual who identifies as old to a degree accepts a negative cultural evaluation of himself. In so doing, he deprives himself of many of the rewards accompanying the adult status, rewards which are associated not only with specific social roles but also with behavior outside of narrow role contexts. (214)

The results of this study of almost one thousand individuals—sampled in an effort to represent a much wider population—proved to be most striking. Not only did those with a self-image as "middle-aged" prove to be better adjusted than those with a self-image as "old" or "elderly." But that younger self-image was sufficiently powerful so as to be more important for their adjustment than their loss of a spouse, or their retirement from work or even their increased chronological age from sixty to seventy. However, it is only now that Phillips is beginning to understand the significance of his study not just for older individuals but for the rest of us as well, with the result that this strengthens his belief in the possibility and importance for all of us of moving from our *bureaucratic self-image* toward an *evolutionary self-image*. For if indeed it proved to be so important for those older individuals to see themselves as middle-aged versus old, it would also prove to be most important for the rest of us to learn to see ourselves as fulfilling the dream we stated in the introduction: "One day we will all learn to see ourselves as children who are only just beginning to understand ourselves and our world."

A lesson that we can learn from Phillips's experience in addition to the implications of his study for the importance of developing an *evolutionary self-image* has to do with the power of our *bureaucratic worldview*. Although Phillips was most happy after having completed his dissertation to have been able to publish his results in sociology's leading journal, the sense of achievement that he had felt many years ago about that achievement did not stay with him for long. This is to be expected, given our Spaceland orientation—illustrating our *bureaucratic worldview*—that hides past situations or future possibilities from present situations. Another lesson that we can learn also has to do with the power of our bureaucratic worldview. Although Phillips has been working with the idea of individual evolution—including the idea of an *evolutionary self-image*—for a number of years, it is only now that he realized the significance of his early study for moving in an evolutionary direction. This suggests that if indeed one is interested in such movement, one would do well to follow the general approach that Gosseyn adopted for helping Ashargin. That can work not just for eliminating the impact of past negative experiences or failures, but also for accentuating the impact of past successes. This approach parallels that of Freudian psychoanalysis, except that it can be undertaken by each of us without the aid of an analyst.

Granting that we can learn to fight against the impact of our *bureaucratic worldview* in such ways, we can also adopt a more direct strategy: we can learn to move away from our *bureaucratic worldview* and toward an *evolutionary worldview*. We can learn to change that worldview despite its enormous comprehensiveness and power over us. Learning to move from a *bureaucratic worldview* toward an *evolutionary worldview* will help us not only to move from a *bureaucratic self-image* toward an *evolutionary self-image*. It will also help us to move from *outward perception and thought* toward *inward-outward perception and thought*. More generally, it will help us to move toward an *evolutionary way of life*.

AN EVOLUTIONARY VERSUS A BUREAUCRATIC WORLDVIEW: STRUCTURES

Given the nature of our interactive world and the breadth of a worldview, metaphysical stance or basic assumptions, anything that we think, feel or do is both shaped by our worldview and also has an impact on our worldview. Thus, for example, not only does our *bureaucratic worldview* strengthen our *bureaucratic self-image* as well as our *outward perception and thought*, but the reverse holds true as well. Conversely, to the extent that we develop an *evolutionary self-image* or *inward-outward perception and thought*, that will influence the development of an *evolutionary worldview*. And the same holds true for the rest of the extraordinary language listed in the section headings that appear in the table of contents for chapters 3, 4 and 5. With reference to chapter 4, for example, moving toward *emotional expression, positive emotions* or a *narrow values-fulfillment gap* will work to strengthen an *evolutionary worldview*. This analysis gives us at least a preliminary idea of the many possibilities that exist for moving from a *bureaucratic worldview* toward an *evolutionary worldview*.

Yet all of these terms are most abstract or general, and it is essential that we come down to earth if we wish to communicate effectively. Chapter 2 can help us to at least some extent in coming down to earth, with its discussion of "the iron cage of bureaucracy" and "breaking out of the iron cage." There we were alerted to patterns of hierarchy and specialization within bureaucratic organizations that can work to limit the interaction among people and ideas, granting the improved interaction within modern versus traditional bureaucracies. And we also noted the contradictions between such patterns of behavior, on the one hand, and scientific and democratic ideals that call for interaction.

It is those very contradictions between ideals or values, on the one hand, and patterns of hierarchy and specialization that limit interaction, on the other hand, that can yield the basis for moving from a *bureaucratic worldview* toward an *evolutionary worldview*. Here we follow the work of Thomas Kuhn in his *The Structure of Scientific Revolutions* (1962). Kuhn believed that in order for a scientific revolution to occur so as to change a basic scientific theory like that of Isaac Newton's theory of mechanics, the fundamental assumptions or "scientific paradigm" that provide the framework for that theory must be raised to the surface where its contradictions can be seen. And an alternative scientific paradigm as well as an alternative scientific theory that promises to resolve those contradictions—illustrated by Einstein's theory of relativity—must be advanced.

Finally, that promise must be fulfilled by evidence that the alternative scientific theory and paradigm actually resolves those contradictions.

Kuhn suggested that the same process for achieving change in a scientific theory and paradigm might hold true for culture as a whole and not just science. This is exactly our own approach to moving from a *bureaucratic worldview* toward an *evolutionary worldview*. We must raise to the surface the contradictions within a *bureaucratic worldview*, such as the clash between democratic and scientific values and patterns of hierarchy and specialization that limit interaction. We must also put forward an alternative worldview that promises to resolve those contradictions, as illustrated by an *evolutionary worldview*. And we must, in addition, advance evidence that an *evolutionary worldview* actually succeeds in resolving those contradictions. None of these steps is accomplished easily even for a particular individual, much less for a society as a whole. For our patterns of *emotional repression* that have developed as a result of our *wide values-fulfillment gap* make it most difficult to raise contradictions to the surface. Further, if we are largely unaware of the nature of our present worldview, it would be difficult to imagine an alternative worldview. Finally, if evidence is to be obtained about the effectiveness of an alternative worldview in resolving those contradictions, then we must not only imagine an alternative worldview. People must actually change their worldview before the impact of that change could be assessed.

If we generalize Kuhn's analysis of scientific revolutions to cultural revolutions, then our first step—assuming we wish to move toward a revolution that takes us away from our *bureaucratic way of life* and toward an *evolutionary one*—is to raise to the surface of our awareness the deep and growing contradictions within society. Those contradictions are well illustrated by our *growing aspirations-fulfillment or values-fulfillment gap*, which pits what we want against what we are actually able to get, a contradiction that is largely the product of our *bureaucratic worldview*. From chapter 1 we are aware of the *emotional repression* that results in large measure from that *widening gap*. How, then, can we begin to reverse this situation? How do we move from *emotional repression* toward *emotional expression* in order to take the first step toward a cultural revolution for sweeping away our *bureaucratic way of life*? Yet this problem of "heart" should be joined by problems of "head" and "hand," for the human being is a unitary creature. How do we gain the general conviction, belief or "head"—following the optimism of the scientific method—that we can move from *emotional repression* toward *emotional expression*? And how do we then, following "hand," not only move toward actions yielding positive reinforcement but also toward an *evolutionary way of life*?

Just as we used Van Vogt's *The Players of Null-A* as an allegory for our learning to reexamine our negative experiences in the past and thus move from *emotional repression* toward *emotional expression*, so can we turn to a Freudian psychoanalyst for further insight. We quoted from Karen Horney's *The Neurotic Personality of Our Time* at the end of chapter 1. Here we make use of her *Self-Analysis* (1942), which also followed Freud's emphasis on the importance of *emotional repression*. Yet she departed from strict Freudianism in her emphasis on problems within society and culture as crucial forces that can affect the individual negatively, just as we saw in that previous quote. Indeed, this broad perspective linking Freudian ideas with sociological ideas led to her expulsion from the New York Psychoanalytic Institute. She also departed from Freudian orthodoxy in her conviction, expressed in her *Self-Analysis*, that the individual can generally learn to accomplish a great deal toward developing himself or herself without the benefit of undergoing psychoanalysis. For example, she saw the work of Abraham Maslow, with his emphasis on the possibilities of "self-actualization," as most important.

In her *Self-Analysis*, Horney wrote about *emotional repression*, relating to "heart," as a fundamental problem that the individual can and must overcome when proceeding to analyze self:

> The crucial difficulty in self-analysis lies not in these fields [possessing psychological knowledge] but in the emotional factors that blind us to unconscious forces. That the main difficulty is emotional rather than intellectual is confirmed by the fact that when analysts analyze themselves they have not such a great advantage over the layman as we would be inclined to believe. . . . On theoretical grounds, then, I see no stringent reason why self-analysis should not be feasible. Granted that many people are too deeply entangled in their own problems to be able to analyze themselves . . . still, all of this is no proof that in principle the job cannot be done. (1942: 25–26)

In our effort to understand some of the forces within modern culture that push the individual toward *emotional repression*, we shall repeat part of our earlier quote from *The Neurotic Personality of Our Time* (1937):

> The second contradiction [within individuals] is that between the stimulation of our needs and our factual frustrations in satisfying them. For economic reasons needs are constantly being stimulated in our culture by such means as advertisements, "conspicuous consumption," the ideal of "keeping up with the Joneses." For the great majority, however, the actual fulfillment of these needs is closely restricted. The psychic consequence for the individual is a constant discrepancy between his desires and their fulfillment. (287–288)

The title of Horney's book suggests her belief that this contradiction "between the stimulation of our needs and our factual frustrations in satisfying them" is by no means limited to a minority of individuals but affects us all. Yet this contradiction—between what people have learned to want and what they are actually able to get—is what we have discussed as a central problem within our *bureaucratic way of life*, namely, our aspirations-fulfillment or values-fulfillment gap. We share Horney's conviction, expressed within her *Self-Analysis*, that the individual need not be a specialist in psychology to raise up to the surface aspirations that have been repressed. She argued in that book that such specialized knowledge is by no means essential: "We are all too inclined to believe that only a politician can understand politics, that only a mechanic can repair our car, that only a trained gardener can prune our trees. . . . Faith in specialization can easily turn into blind awe and stifle any attempt at new activity" (23).

As for "head," Horney's ideas—about the possibilities for human development or self-actualization—parallel the scientist's belief in the possibility of solving whatever problem has been defined, convictions that make possible the continuing development of understanding with no limit whatsoever.

> An integral part of the democratic ideals for which we are fighting today is the belief that the individual—and as many individuals as possible—should develop to the full of his potentialities. . . . In the words of Max Otto: "The deepest source of a man's philosophy, the one that shapes and nourishes it, is faith or lack of faith in mankind. If he has confidence in human beings and believes that something fine can be achieved through them, he will acquire ideas about life and about the world which are in harmony with his confidence." (1942: 22)

Horney does not neglect "hand" in her *Self-Analysis*. We might recall our presentation of the East-West strategy in chapter 2, with our focus on the procedure of changing long-term "structures" (following a Western strategy) by changing one's behavior in one "situation" after another (following an Eastern strategy). Horney sees an advantage of self-analysis over psychoanalysis in the contrast between the analyst's access to the patient for "at best only for an hour each day" with the fact that the individual "lives with himself day and night." As a result, the individual has opportunities to work toward changing one situation after another after another, and thus the individual has the opportunities to change his or her long-term structures. Horney believed that "this fact constitutes an important asset in self-analysis" (25).

Returning to Thomas Kuhn's *The Structure of Scientific Revolutions* as extended to cultural revolutions, if indeed we wish to move away from our *bureaucratic worldview* then we must go beyond conquering *emotional repression* and raising that worldview to the surface. Just as Einstein put forward his alternative theory of relativity to Newtonian theory, so must we advance an alternative worldview to the *bureaucratic worldview*. Although we have outlined the nature of such an alternative, namely, an *evolutionary worldview*, that outline remains to be filled out both in this chapter as well as in the book as a whole. Jack Vance's science-fiction story *The Languages of Pao* (1958) can help us to accomplish this. Vance's novel is based on the linguistic relativity hypothesis of Benjamin Lee Whorf and Edward Sapir: that language causes people to understand the world in a certain way, as described in Whorf's *Language, Thought, and Reality* (1967).

Vance sets his tale mainly on the planet Pao, a world of fifteen billion inhabitants originally colonized from Earth and existing in the far future. The neighboring planets of Breakness, Mercantil and Batmarsh were the locations of societies differing markedly from Paonese society. Breakness—emphasizing "head"—was a land of male scientists, importing females from neighboring planets solely for the purpose of procreating males and shipping the women back along with their female children and male children unable to gain entrance to the Breakness Institute. Mercantil—stressing "heart"—was a merchant planet which produced a wide range of goods and, with their fleet of ships, was home to the key traders in the area. Batmarsh—focusing on "hand"—was the home of warrior clans who competed with one another and raided neighboring planets seeking tribute. By contrast, the Paonese had not developed in such specialized ways. They expected little from life and emphasized caste or status and tradition. They had no competitive sports, typically farmed a small acreage, and gave total allegiance to the Panarch, the hereditary ruler who reached out throughout Pao with a vast civil service.

Beran Panasper, the young son of the Panarch and heir to the throne, witnesses his father's assassination by his uncle, Bustamonte, who blames two emissaries from Mercantil for the deed and promptly executes them. Lord Palafox, Wizard of Breakness, witnessed what had occurred, and he escapes to the planet Breakness with Beran before Bustamonte is able to act against them. Bustamonte proclaims Beran's death and assumes the throne of Pao while Beran becomes a student at the Breakness Institute under Lord Palafox's patronage. Meanwhile, Pao continues to be invaded by the Brumbos of Batmarsh, who require ever higher amounts of tribute. The Paonese, despite their population of fifteen billion, are a passive people who are unable to mount a defense, and Bustamonte travels to Breakness to seek Palafox's help. Palafox comes up with a general plan: "We must alter the mental framework of the Paonese people—a certain proportion of them, at least—which is most easily achieved by altering the language" (Vance, 1958: 57). Paonese on three continents would be relocated to make way for children who would learn a new language. Valiant, Technicant and Cogitant would, over time, yield warriors, industrialists and scientists superior to those on Batmarsh, Mercantil and Breakness. Palafox explains the rationale behind his plan:

> Paonese is a passive, dispassionate language. It presents the world in two dimensions, without tension or contrast. A people speaking Paonese, theoretically, ought to be docile, passive, without strong personality development—in fact, exactly as the Paonese people are. The new language [Valiant] will be based on the contrast and comparison of strength, with a grammar simple and direct. To illustrate, consider the

sentence, "The farmer chops down a tree" [literally, in Paonese, "Farmer in state of exertion; axe agency; tree in state of subjection to attack"]. In the new language the sentence becomes: . . . "The farmer vanquishes the tree, using the weapon-instrument of the axe." . . . The syllabary will be rich in effort-producing gutturals. . . . A number of key ideas will be synonymous; such as pleasure and overcoming a resistance. . . .

Another area might be set aside for the inculcation of another language [Technicant] . . . In this instance, the grammar will be extravagantly complicated but altogether consistent and logical. The vocables would be discrete but joined and fitted by elaborate rules of concordance. What is the result? When a group of people, impregnated with these stimuli, are presented with supplies and facilities, industrial development is inevitable. . . . To the military segment, a "successful man" will be synonymous with "winner of a fierce contest." To the industrialists it will mean "efficient fabricator." (58-59)

As for Cogitant, the language of the scientist, it was similar to the language of Breakness, emphasizing the "head" with almost nothing in the area of the "heart." Beran relates his initial experiences of learning the language on the planet Breakness:

The language included no negativity; instead there were numerous polarities such as "go" and "stay." There was no passive voice—every verbal idea was self-contained: "to strike," "to receive-impact." The language was rich in words for intellectual manipulation, but almost totally deficient in descriptives of various emotional states. . . . Such common Paonese concepts as "anger," "joy," "love," "grief," were absent from the Breakness vocabulary. On the other hand, there were words to define a hundred different types of ratiocination, subtleties unknown to the Paonese. (42)

Beran joins a group of Paonese on Breakness who are learning all three languages and who, as the only interpreters able to communicate with everyone, will assist the Paonese civil service. During their studies they proceed on their own in a jocular vein to invent a patchwork tongue made up of scraps of Valiant, Technicant, Cogitant and Paonese, which they christen "Pastiche." Returning to Pao the interpreters assist in the education of the enclaves of Paonese children. And after only a single generation Palafox's plans bear fruit. Paonese warriors who had learned Valiant and had developed their own warrior traditions outfought the clansmen of Batmarsh. Paonese entrepreneurs and traders, students of Technicant, proved to be superior to their counterparts on Mercantil. And Paonese intellectuals compared favorably with the Wizards of Breakness.

Beran replaces Bustamonte as Panarch and also successfully opposes Palafox, both of whom were attempting to institute an authoritarian regime on the planet. Yet he finally realizes that the three separate enclaves have developed loyalty only to their own groups and none to the Paonese as a whole. For example, the Valiants oppose Beran's orders and threaten his life. Beran decides to disperse the Valiants, Technicants and Cogitants into small groups who will educate and train their fellow Paonese in their own knowledge and skills. And the Paonese will all learn a single language in addition to the languages of Valiant, Technicant and Cogitant, a broader language that will enable everyone to communicate with everyone else: Pastiche.

The Languages of Pao gives us an allegory for movement from our *bureaucratic worldview*—with its separation of "head," "heart" and "hand"—toward an *evolutionary worldview*. Vance gives us a solution to this problem of the separation of these three basic elements of human behavior, just as we humans in the twenty-first century separate science ("head"), the humanities ("heart") and the technologies ("hand"): All individuals must learn one language—Pastiche—that is sufficiently broad so as to embody the ideas and ideals of the Valiants, Technicants, Cogitants and Paonese. Pastiche contains those elements and somehow manages to make them all relevant. Given such inclusiveness, it does not succumb to the one-sidedness of those languages. And neither does it succumb to the passivity of Paonese. Rather, it embodies a balance among "head," "heart" and "hand."

Vance's description of Pastiche suggests the nature of the extraordinary language of social science. Presently, our languages point individuals in diverse directions, just as do the technical languages of the sciences, humanities and technologies. Such narrow orientations within contemporary society are also illustrated by the greater "head" orientation of males and "heart" orientation of females, granting that this difference does not take away from the *emotional repression* that we all undergo. The exaggeration of our own narrow male orientation is illustrated on the planet Breakness, where the language of Cogitant was "totally deficient in descriptives of various emotional states," and where Beran noticed a group of boys "marching in a solemn line" who appeared to be "unsmiling and silent." Yet the language of Pastiche suggests a departure from such narrowness, just as our own vision of our learning to use the extraordinary language of social science in our everyday lives suggests much the same thing.

Such a change in our own society would by no means require waiting a whole generation for children to learn an entirely new language. Rather, only a very limited number of concepts that make up the extraordinary language would be involved, such as those listed in the section headings of chapters 3, 4 and 5, as presented in our table of contents. Those concepts would be general enough to enable us to categorize our thousands of everyday concepts. Thus, instead of those everyday concepts remaining largely isolated from one another, following our *bureaucratic worldview*, that categorization would motivate us to work toward the interaction among all of our concepts, following an *evolutionary worldview*. In this way our present language would not be abandoned for a new language. Rather, the huge number of concepts within our present language would move away from pointing individuals in diverse directions, such as "head" versus "heart" versus "hand."

Returning once again to Thomas Kuhn's *The Structure of Scientific Revolutions* as extended to cultural revolutions, what we require in order to move from our *bureaucratic worldview* toward an *evolutionary worldview* is not just raising the contradictions of our *bureaucratic worldview* to the surface, and not just developing an alternative worldview that promises to resolve those contradictions. We also require actual evidence that such an alternative worldview can in fact fulfill that promise. Since our vision of that alternative is only just beginning to be applied experimentally so as to help individuals move away from their *bureaucratic worldview*, we can expect no more than preliminary evidence for the effectiveness of an *evolutionary worldview*. However, we do indeed have some preliminary evidence. It is based not on such an experiment but rather on the analysis of the work of thirty-three individuals from a variety of fields of knowledge, focusing on the hypothesis that a *narrow aspirations-fulfillment or values-fulfillment gap* is linked to an interactive or *evolutionary worldview*. Granting the limitations of such indirect evidence, every single one of the works of those thirty-three individuals confirmed the hypothesis stated in that book-length study, *The Invisible Crisis of Contemporary Society* (Phillips and Johnston, 2007: 234-235). The "substantial evidence" in favor of that hypothesis is most encouraging. Yet given the enormous difficulties in changing from nothing less than our entire way of life, our efforts in this book to point in that direction have a long way to go. We move now from our focus on "head" to an emphasis on "heart," granting that we have already had to make use of many ideas about our emotions in this chapter along with earlier chapters.

FOUR

"Heart": Emotions and Values

We have already had a good deal to say about the importance of emotions within any effort to change the individual. For example, our central problem—the widening gap between what we want and are actually able to get—yields enormous emotional problems that the individual proceeds to repress with such procedures as the technique of particularization and the falsification of memory. Let us not forget that our own concern with the aspirations-fulfillment or values-fulfillment gap is paralleled by the concern of fully twenty-five hundred years of Buddhist thought with its focus on dukkha. In addition, we might recall Karen Horney's analysis of the neurotic problems resulting from the contradiction "between the stimulation of our needs and our factual frustrations in satisfying them." Also, our emphasis on learning to use the scientific method in everyday life requires our deep emotional commitment to employing that method in one scene after another, by contrast with the widespread belief in the importance of maintaining "value neutrality." More generally, the interactive nature of the universe and of biological evolution point us toward the importance of "heart" interacting with "head" and "hand."

Yet psychoanalysts and other psychotherapists almost uniformly conclude that an intellectual analysis of emotions—and, we would add, such an analysis of values—can only take the individual so far. Given the incredible power and reach of our *bureaucratic worldview*, which is much of the source of our emotional problems, further understanding of our problems of "heart" can help us, granting that it remains for everyone to put into practice such understanding in personal life. We not only support Horney's vision of the potential of "self-analysis," we see it as having a great deal more potential than she did, given the fact that she was only at the beginnings of an understanding of the social sciences. Now,

91

over half a century later, our present understanding of human behavior suggests far greater optimism about that potential. This is true especially because we are now in a position to integrate the bits and pieces of findings about human behavior from all fields of knowledge, including the arts as well as the sciences.

Over the past two decades interest in achieving understanding of emotions has greatly expanded. Among sociologists, for example, a new section of the American Sociological Association—the sociology of emotions—has been formed. This has encouraged increasing research by sociologists in this area. The work of Thomas J. Scheff and Jonathan H. Turner—to be discussed in this chapter—illustrates such recent work. The neglect of this area of knowledge has been due in large measure to the relatively invisible nature of one's emotional life.

The publication of *Descartes' Error: Emotions, Reason, and the Human Brain* (Damasio, 1994), with its focus on the biological basis of emotions, has helped to stimulate the development of research in this area. Descartes' error was his separation of mind from body, by contrast with their interaction along with the interaction between intellect and emotions. A key conclusion of Damasio is that the specialized parts of the brain interact with one another in order to coordinate the overall functions of the brain. This biological organization of the brain contradicts the slogan that a "Jack of all trades" is necessarily a "master of none" for those parts of the brain function in both a specialized and a general way. This contrasts with a centralized view of the brain, with one center giving orders to all of the specialized areas of the brain.

Psychotherapists, who generally have never abandoned the Freudian emphasis on the centrality of emotions, have been encouraged to publish more in this area in recent times. For example, we have Daniel Goleman's *Emotional Intelligence* (1995), a book emphasizing the limitations of IQ all by itself for predicting success in school as well as in life generally. Goleman sees "emotional intelligence" as including "abilities such as being able to motivate oneself and persist in the face of frustrations; to control impulse and delay gratification; to regulate one's moods and keep distress from swamping the ability to think; to empathize and to hope" (35).

Emanuel Tanay—a forensic psychiatrist who has testified in such high-profile cases as that of Jack Ruby, Sam Sheppard and Theodore "Ted" Bundy—describes the enormous importance of *emotional expression* for the testimonies of expert witnesses in his *American Legal Injustice* (2010). Tanay discusses how meritorious cases supported by even the world's leading scientists have been lost because of the emotionless presentations of those scientists. He writes as follows:

> Persuasion is achieved by joining the forces of reason and emotion. To appreciate the significance of emotions in the litigation process, lawyers and experts need to ask themselves what kind of feeling the jury

will have when they render a verdict in favor of or against this defendant. Will the jury feel proud of having found the defendant guilty or have a sense of shame for having imposed life in prison or a death sentence? Will they be pleased that they provided compensation for an injured plaintiff or will they feel gratified that they recognized a false claim? (44)

Our own orientation toward emotions, interaction and integration of knowledge—illustrated by the work of the Sociological Imagination Group over the past decade—has been motivated in large measure by the vision of C. Wright Mills. His most influential work, *The Sociological Imagination*, followed Horney's *Self-Analysis* by little more than a decade. These words—which bear repeating from their quotation in the introduction to part I—capture his general orientation, although they fail to reveal his ability to express emotions in the classroom powerfully and persuasively:

> The sociological imagination. . .is the capacity to shift from one perspective to another—from the political to the psychological; from examination of a single family to comparative assessment of the national budgets of the world; from the theological school to the military establishment; from considerations of an oil industry to studies of contemporary poetry. It is the capacity to range from the most impersonal and remote transformations to the most intimate features of the human self—and to see the relations between the two. (1959: 7)

We begin this chapter by carrying forward our treatment of *emotional repression* in chapter 1. Although many psychotherapists would argue that a trained therapist is essential for bringing repressed conflicts or problems to the surface, that is neither Horney's view nor our own, granting that there are problems that require such help. It is an ability to move toward *emotional expression* that can then become the basis for transforming our *negative emotions* into *positive emotions*, our second topic. Finally, we move from such momentary situational changes toward long-term structural changes: we take up the process of *narrowing the values-fulfillment gap*.

As we proceed, let us build on our understanding of the role of the extraordinary language—as developed at the close of chapter 3, following our analysis of *The Languages of Pao*—for helping us penetrate the mysteries of human behavior. We see concepts such as *emotional repression, emotional expression, negative emotions, positive emotions, wide values-fulfillment gap* and *narrow values-fulfillment gap* as functioning in contemporary societies much like the language of Pastiche functioned on the planet Pao. We can learn to use those very general concepts from the extraordinary or technical language of the social sciences to categorize the thousands of concepts within our everyday language that have been largely isolated from one another, following our *bureaucratic worldview*.

As a result, not only can they help us to link "head," "heart" and "hand," they also can help us to move toward an *evolutionary worldview* and an *evolutionary way of life*. For language is our most powerful tool for solving problems, and the extraordinary language can wed that tool to another most powerful tool: the scientific method.

EMOTIONAL EXPRESSION VERSUS EMOTIONAL REPRESSION: SITUATIONS

The emotion of shame, which is closely linked to the more extreme emotion of humiliation, has been the subject of a good deal of research by Thomas Scheff, a contemporary sociologist who has focused on the sociology of emotions. In particular, Scheff has drawn attention to feelings of shame that remain hidden rather than feelings that are openly expressed, as illustrated by his analysis of the Old and New Testaments of the *Bible*:

> The Old Testament contains many, many references to pride and shame but very few to guilt. The New Testament reverses the balance. . . . It is possible that the role of shame in social control has not decreased but has gone underground instead. . . . For example, we say, "It was an awkward moment for me." . . . It contains two movements that disguise emotion: denial of inner feeling and projection of it onto the outer world. I was not embarrassed; it was the moment that was awkward. (Scheff,1994: 43)

Assuming that Scheff's analysis—that shame is going underground in modern society—is correct, why would that be so? And how are we to explain the rise of guilt? We see both occurrences as closely linked to a *widening values-fulfillment gap* in modern society. We might recall that in chapter 1 we cited "substantial evidence" for that widening, based on a work by Phillips and Johnston (2007: 234–235). Assuming, then, an increasing gap between what we deeply want and our ability to fulfill those values, awareness of our own helplessness would get in the way of our being able to function in everyday life. Thus, we learn to use such procedures as the "technique of particularization" and the "falsification of memory" as means for *emotional repression*. We hide our shame at being so ineffective. But such repression does not get rid of our problem, for it results in guilt at our personal failures.

Let us proceed to understand more fully just how shame, humiliation, pride and hate work within the individual. Scheff has analyzed these emotions in Hitler's *Mein Kampf*, resulting in his analysis not just of relationships between individuals but also between societies. He quotes from *Mein Kampf*:

> There is ground for pride in our people only if we no longer need be ashamed. . . . But a people, half of which is wretched and careworn, or

even deprived, offers so sorry a picture that no one should feel any pride in it. . . . Particularly our German people which today lies broken and defenseless, exposed to the kicks of all the world, needs that suggestive force that lies in self-confidence. This self-confidence must be inculcated in the young national comrade from childhood on. . . .If at the beginning of the War [World War I] and during the War twelve or fifteen thousand of these Hebrew corrupters of the people had been held under poison gas, as happened to hundreds of thousands of our very best German workers in the field, the sacrifice of millions at the front would not have been in vain. (114, 116–117)

Hitler mentions "shame" in his first sentence, for he felt that the Germans had been broken in spirit by having had to accept complete responsibility for World War I and having been forced to pay enormous reparations to other nations by the Treaty of Versailles that was imposed on Germany after World War I. That sense of shame was also linked to the disastrous inflation that Germany experienced following the war. Hitler reacted with enormous hate, as illustrated by his wish to kill the "Hebrew corrupters of the people." Granting Hitler's extremely authoritarian version of stratification—which included his unprecedented and monstrous initiation of the Holocaust—we may see ourselves, gradationally, as following a far less extreme version of Hitler's *bureaucratic worldview*, given our own focus on stratification within our own *bureaucratic worldview*. More concretely—just as was brought out in the film, *Judgment at Nuremberg*— the entire world was guilty to at least some extent for what had happened in Nazi Germany, given the Treaty of Versailles imposed on Germany and the worldwide failure to stop Hitler and do something about what was being done to the Jews and others by his henchmen.

In order to accept our own invisible commitment to a *bureaucratic worldview*—with its contradictions between stratification and democratic along with scientific values —it is important for us to believe that we can indeed resolve that contradiction, just as Kuhn argued that a new paradigm must promise to resolve the contradictions within the old one. Kuhn's argument is illustrated by the pendulum metaphor for the scientific method: there must be an assumption that when a problem is surfaced we can swing our pendulum back and forth, thus moving toward solving it over time. Thus, by addressing these contradictions we move from false pride, with its focus on stratification, to justified pride, with its attention to democratic and scientific values. That movement is based on movement from *emotional repression* toward *emotional expression* as well as toward an *evolutionary self-image* and an *evolutionary worldview*.

We can gain further insight into *emotional repression* and *emotional expression* by turning to a study of humiliation, an extreme form of shame. The writer, Ellen Barry, reviews here a study of 7,322 adult twins published in *Archives in General Psychiatry*:

The events that send people into major depression . . . are not merely losses, but humiliating ones that drive at a person's self-esteem—most typically, being abandoned by a romantic partner. . . . "When your father dies, it doesn't directly address who you are. You can still love yourself after your dad dies," said Dr. Kenneth Kendler, a psychiatric geneticist at Virginia Commonwealth University and the study's lead author. Blows to a person's status, like the experience of marital abandonment, "hit you at a more basic level. . . . So much of human life is built around this."

Kendler followed 7,322 adult twins. . . . While the experience of loss put a twin at a higher risk for depression—about 10 times the risk of one who had not experienced loss—being humiliated was about as important. The two experiences together were by far the most dangerous kind, increasing the risk of major depression by a factor of 20. In one out of five cases, these individuals showed signs of major depression within a month. (Barry, "Study Looks at Loss, Its Role in Depression," *The Boston Globe*, August 13, 2003, A3)

The Kendler study emphasizes the importance of self-respect or self-esteem as well as the link between humiliation and severe depression, which can lead to suicide. Thus, the study suggests the huge importance of one's self-image for one's mental health. We might recall here Van Vogt's *The Players of Null-A*, with Gosseyn helping Ashargin to improve his self-confidence by reevaluating his past experiences. The resulting movement toward an *evolutionary self-image* is in turn linked to *emotional expression*.

Yet *emotional expression* can cause enormous problems, as illustrated by the history of recessions. George Akerlof, a Nobel laureate in economics, has teamed up with Robert Shiller—a Yale economics professor who coined the term "irrational exuberance" before Alan Greenspan made it famous—to write a book about a central idea of John Maynard Keynes that has been neglected. In *Animal Spirits: How Human Psychology Drives the Economy, and Why It Matters for Global Capitalism* (2009), they discuss Keynes's emphasis on the irrational emotional behavior of the individual and how a government can confront that behavior effectively. Louis Uchitelle, an economics writer for the *New York Times*, reviews the book:

Keynes performed a . . . service in the 1930s—mainly by making the point that market economies could suffer long periods of high unemployment and low output unless government stepped in to supply the necessary demand. Barack Obama's $787 billion stimulus program reflects his insight. But another aspect of Keynes's thinking did not fare well. He also introduced the world to "animal spirits," coining that phrase to describe a range of emotions, human impulses, enthusiasms and misperceptions that drive economies—and ultimately unwind them. The economists who interpreted Keynes "rooted out almost all of the animal spirits—the noneconomic motives and irrational behaviors—that lay at the heart of his explanation for the Great Depression."

Above all, they [Akerlof and Shiller] challenge the reigning free-market ideology . . . that markets should operate free of government because they were rational. But if animal spirits influence behavior, then government must play a broad, disciplinary role, and do so permanently. Akerlof and Shiller . . . are concerned that once we enter a revival, pressure will inevitably build—just as it did in the late 1970s— . . . to give the markets free rein again. Akerlof and Shiller intend their book as an obstacle to that ever happening. (Uchitelle, 2009: 18)

Ackerlof and Shiller go on to provide examples of how irrational exuberance has trumped rational economic behavior. "Confidence" or overconfidence that a house or a stock will be worth more the following year has driven up prices far beyond the actual worth of these commodities, yielding what happened prior to the Great Depression of the 1930s as well as what has been happening in these first years of the twenty-first century. Also, they claim that "fairness" influences bosses to pay workers more than the market demands. A third example of animal spirits or the play of emotions is "corruption," where business people influence consumers to buy what they don't need and cannot afford, such as houses with very large mortgages attached to them. They also cite people's reliance on "inspirational stories," such as tales of how others are getting rich by behavior dominated by animal spirits, irrational exuberance, or just plain human emotions. All these examples work to yield the *large values-fulfillment gap* linked to our *bureaucratic worldview*.

We wholeheartedly agree with the authors' recommendation that continuing governmental regulation of markets is essential in order to combat irrational exuberance. But we also believe that this is no more than a short-term partial solution to a long-range and complex problem that remains to be solved. For governmental regulators are themselves victims of animal spirits or behavior guided by a *bureaucratic worldview*, not having learned to balance "heart" with "head" and "hand" any more than others. Further, the complexity of human behavior cannot be so easily penetrated by governmental officials, regardless of whether or not they take the advice of Nobel laureates in economics like Keynes. For that complexity demands the kind of understanding that is based on integrated social science knowledge, an understanding founded on the ability to make full use of the extraordinary language of social science.

We see a basic problem with Keynes's concept of "animal spirits" or Shiller's concept of "irrational exuberance," for they imply that *emotional expression* is our enemy and pure rationality, as wielded by governmental officials fighting such emotional forces, is our friend. Here we see the workings of our *bureaucratic worldview*, with its emphasis on the hierarchy of "head" over "heart." In our own view *emotional expression*—when occurring within a balanced context along with "head" and "hand"—is desperately needed in order to escape from the *emotional repression* that is so central to our *bureaucratic way of life*. This is the repression that Freud and Horney saw as linked to neurotic behavior. However, it remains for us to explore more fully the nature of *emotional expression*.

Let us turn once again to Van Vogt's highly suggestive science-fiction novels for insight into how *emotional expression* can be wedded to rationality, thus linking "heart" with "head." Gosseyn's own development involved his learning the "cortical-thalamic pause," which he was able to use successfully in his battle with Enro. It involves the interaction of "head" and "heart" within a momentary situation that might otherwise be extremely threatening. The cortex is basic to intellectual activity, and the thalamus is basic for emotional expression. Gosseyn illustrates this procedure at a time when he comes under an extremely powerful mental attack that is designed to create fear:

> I am now relaxing. . . . And all stimuli are making the full circuit of my nervous system, along my spinal cord, to the thalamus, through the thalamus and up to the cortex, and through the cortex, and then, and only then, back through the thalamus and down into the nervous system. Always, I am consciously aware of the stimulus moving up to and through the cortex. That was the key. That was the difference between the Null-A superman and the animal man of the galaxy. The thalamus—the seat of emotions—and the cortex—the seat of discrimination—integrated, balanced in a warm and wonderful relationship. Emotions, not done away with, but made richer and more relaxed by the association with that part of the mind—the cortex—that could savor unnumbered subtle differences in the flow of feeling. I'm thinking and feeling, not just feeling. (1948: 177–178)

The cortical-thalamic pause is a procedure for linking "head" and "heart" that can be used within a momentary situation. And when one learns to use this procedure over and over again in one scene after another, one learns to develop a mental structure linking "head" and "heart" in a highly interactive way, contrasting with the isolation of these two entities that is central to our *bureaucratic worldview*. However, this involves a long-term and difficult learning process. In order to continue with such learning it is essential that one experiences the ability to solve problems more effectively by using the cortical-thalamic pause. Thus, one must learn to link "hand" to "head" and "heart." This follows the way we all learn language, for that learning is based on the ability of language to become a highly effective tool for solving problems.

We can make good use of a poem by William Blake, an English poet, to illustrate the "cortical-thalamic pause":

> I was angry with my friend;
> I told my wrath, my wrath did end.
> I was angry with my foe:
> I told it not, my wrath did grow
> — William Blake

Blake's poem exemplifies the importance—as well as the difficulty—of learning to achieve interaction between "head" and "heart." The writer's anger with his friend is an example of "heart," but when he "told" his wrath—illustrating "head" and "heart"—that anger disappeared. By contrast, the writer's failure to use his "head" and confront his anger ("heart") toward his foe resulted in the growth of his wrath. Although it would seem a simple enough task to deal with one's anger, in fact it is generally an exceedingly difficult task, and this is the case for the full range of our emotions.

Blake's contrast between the behavior of the writer in the first two lines with his behavior in the last two lines is also a contrast between an *evolutionary worldview* and a *bureaucratic worldview*. The linking of "head" with "heart" in the first two lines illustrates the interaction that is basic to an *evolutionary worldview*. By contrast, the isolation of "head" and "heart" suggested by the last two lines illustrates the isolation that we see within a *bureaucratic worldview*.

Blake's poem also opens up a question: exactly what did he tell his wrath in order to get rid of it? More generally, how are we to get rid of our anger toward someone else? For example, a broad scientific method suggests the importance of reflexivity, that is, probing and revealing one's basic assumptions. Just why, for example, is that individual our foe? Are we blaming him or her for something that he or she had little control over? Did we fail to communicate something of importance to our foe? On the other hand, is our anger toward our foe in fact justified? More generally, are there situations where it is indeed most useful for us to get angry at one or more individuals? Is it useful for us to see them as foes under certain circumstances?

Blake's concern with the emotion of wrath and with the individual's reaction to his wrath points us toward a focus on situational or momentary behavior as distinct from structural or long-term behavior. Both are important in order to achieve fundamental changes in the individual and society. Social scientists generally have focused on structural behavior and neglected situational behavior, making it difficult to understand how change occurs. For structures are developed as a result of repeated situational behavior, and thus we cannot understand how structures are developed without understanding the development of situational behavior.

To illustrate further the importance of both situational and structural behavior as a basis for achieving fundamental changes, we turn back the clock to 1972, a time of turmoil throughout the academic world, Phillips published a book with alternating chapters of fiction and nonfiction: *Worlds of the Future: Exercises in the Sociological Imagination*. Part of his preface reads as follows:

> I find myself now, located in the present, conscious of several alternative futures. In one of these, man's problems continue to increase until

man himself becomes his own victim. This is a future which I no longer believe will materialize. In another future, man learns to gain control over those forces which presently are shaping his existence. I believe that the development of this future depends on man's consciousness of his ability to construct the future. . . .The appendix . . . focuses on the transition to a post-industrial world. (Phillips, 1972: x-xi)

That appendix was based on a collaboration between Phillips and Peter M. Senge, then a graduate student at MIT, who had learned a procedure for computer simulation known as "system dynamics," based largely on the work of Jay Forrester (see for example Forrester, *Principles of Systems,* 1968; Donella H. Meadows, et al., *The Limits to Growth,* 1972; Nancy Roberts et al., *Introduction to Computer Simulation,* 1983). The sixty-three-page appendix—which included numerous computer printouts as well as diagrams of theoretical models—focused on the construction of a computer simulation of human development from pre-industrial to post-industrial society. Senge continued to work with system dynamics afterwards, developing guides to effective organizational behavior. We will have a good deal more to say about his later work in chapter 6, where we take up his concept of "the learning group" by contrast with bureaucratic organizations.

The actual simulation procedure used is too technical to explain in the brief space that we have here, but its key idea is the importance of the continuing interaction among phenomena. The conclusions of the simulation procedure that Phillips and Senge employed are most suggestive for our present efforts to understand the phenomena of *emotional repression and expression.* That computer simulation was an imaginative effort more than a procedure that built on systematic data. Its focus was on how us humans might break free from existing patterns of behavior throughout society that push us into conformity to social structures that are yielding deepening problems, such as the conflict between patterns of stratification or persisting hierarchy versus democratic ideals. What would it take for us to somehow learn how to make more and more use of our enormous potentials for learning, for solving problems and for continuing to evolve as human beings? More specifically, what would it take to yield a computer simulation that printed out curves representing human development that continued to move upward, versus curves that continued to come crashing downward?

Phillips and Senge struggled for many weeks attempting to construct such a computer simulation, but with no success. Finally, with new assumptions, they achieved an escalating curve representing human development. And it is those assumptions that are most suggestive for our present effort to understand how to move toward an *evolutionary worldview and way of life.* Two changes in their earlier assumptions that had resulted in downward curves were involved. The first change had to do with the amount of time needed to learn from experiences and thus alter one's direction. Could the human being, for example, gain understanding from experiences within a given situation? Or would such learning necessarily prove to be much slower? A shortened time period would enable the individual to counter more quickly environmental forces pushing him or her to conform to our bureaucratic way of life.

The second change was structural. It has to do with the strength of the individual's persisting commitment to achieve development or evolution. What is involved is not merely motivation that is expressed here and there, in this situation or in that one, but rather persisting motivation, suggesting the values to be discussed in the last section of this chapter. What Phillips and Senge discovered was that the combination of this situational and structural change did the job of pushing the curve of human development upward, where it continued to climb with no falling back at all. Given the credit that we have learned to give the use of mathematics and computers—based on the successes of the physical sciences—it is indeed tempting to give that finding far more credit than it is worth. Yet at least it does suggest the importance of structural change coupled with situational change if fundamental changes in the individual and society are to be achieved.

We can thus learn to move from persisting *emotional repression* toward persisting *emotional expression*, yet such movement need not yield *positive emotions*, as was well illustrated by the above quote from Hitler's *Mein Kampf*. How are we to understand the forces that yield *positive emotions* instead of *negative emotions*? As we shall see in our next section, "Positive Versus Negative Emotions," those forces have to do with "hand" as well as "head" and "heart." Thus, we will have to anticipate the ideas in chapter 5, "'Hand': Actions/Interactions, Rituals and Ways of Life," where we will go into greater detail about the situations and structures having to do with "hand." Our learning to develop *positive versus negative emotions* is essential if indeed we aim to narrow our *escalating values-fulfillment gap* and thus move toward an *evolutionary way of life*.

POSITIVE VERSUS NEGATIVE EMOTIONS: SITUATIONS

Our discussion throughout the previous chapters on the fundamental problem of our *growing aspirations-fulfillment or values-fulfillment gap* can yield insight into the forces producing *negative emotions* versus *positive emotions* The 2010 mid-term elections in the United States can provide a current illustration, as reported by Richard Parker and Katherine Allen in an article, "Turmoil Beyond Elections," in the *Sarasota Herald-Tribune*:

> With their victory in the mid-term elections, Republicans now share more than power with Democrats. They share the exact same problem that felled House Democrats. It isn't just a policy problem, though—not

the deficit, taxes or even the economy. Instead, it is a deeper, more profound, structural political problem: the problem of constantly rising—and unfulfilled—expectations. America, once a stable place where such expectations were routinely fulfilled, is now a comparatively unstable nation where they go unmet. This is the vexing but largely unspoken reality with which Republicans and Democrats alike will grapple. And likely fail.

In political science, academics have long studied the conditions that lead to turmoil, indeed. . . . The primary precondition is rising expectations. It is when a citizenry is prepared for one life—with the benefits of education, infrastructure and a growing middle class—only to be greeted by a harshly different, disappointing reality. When this becomes a way of life, the politics of a nation become inherently unstable—and the conditions for revolution can become ripe.

Politicians have an unfortunate habit of raising people's expectations with cheap and easy promises. President Obama loftily promised to change, well, everything. Republicans have promised to repeal everything the president has done. But the policy solutions Democrats and Republicans offer are just sops thrown to satisfy interest groups and neither addresses the underlying problem. Unfortunately for both parties, theirs is a recipe for failure, frustration and continued turmoil (2010: 9A).

It was in chapter 1 that we discussed the "revolution of rising expectations" that has accompanied our continuing technological revolution along with political revolutions that have yielded aspirations for fulfilling such values as democracy and equality. It was there that we contrasted the traditional and relatively fixed aspirations of the chief of Balgat with the rising aspirations of the grocer of Balgat, who had visited Ankara frequently and had learned to desire "a bigger grocery shop in the city, have a nice house there, dress nice civilian clothes." His imagination did not limit him to wanting a better material way of life, for if he were president of Turkey he "would make roads for the villagers to come to towns to see the world and would not let them stay in their holes all their life." But as a result of unfulfilled aspirations he experienced *negative emotions*: "I have not the possibility in myself to get the things I want. They only bother me."

We see this relatively invisible and *increasing aspirations-fulfillment or values-fulfillment gap* as an eight hundred–pound invisible gorilla in the room of society, working toward yielding increasing visible problems. Daniel Goleman catalogs some of those increasing problems near the end of the last century in his *Emotional Intelligence*:

The last decade has seen a steady drumroll of reports. . .portraying an uptick in emotional ineptitude, desperation, and recklessness in our families, our communities, and our collective lives. These years have chronicled surging rage and despair, whether in the quiet loneliness of latchkey kids left with a TV as a babysitter, or in the pain of children abandoned, neglected, or abused, or in the ugly intimacy of marital violence. A spreading emotional malaise can be read in numbers showing a jump in depression around the world, and in the reminders of a surging tide of aggression—teens with guns in school, freeway mishaps ending in shootings, disgruntled ex-employees massacring former fellow workers. Emotional abuse, drive-by shooting, and post-traumatic stress all entered the common lexicon over the last decade, as the slogan of the hour shifted from "Have a nice day" to "Make my day." (1995, x-xi)

Our discussion of the East-West strategy in chapter 2 pointed a direction for *narrowing our aspirations-fulfillment or values-fulfillment gap*, a result that would move us from *negative emotions* toward *positive emotions*. There we discussed using a broad approach to the scientific method that helps us to *narrow our aspirations-fulfillment gap*, or reduce dukkha in Buddhist terms. Given such narrowing that would follow an Eastern orientation, we could then proceed to raise both aspirations and their fulfillment, following a Western orientation, using that broad scientific method to keep our fulfillment close to our aspirations. Thus, the East-West strategy appears to be effective not only for narrowing the gap but also for moving toward *positive emotions*. The above example of recent political occurrences is by no means limited to politics, for it illustrates the Western orientation toward creating a *wide and widening values-fulfillment gap*.

For a deeper understanding of the forces producing *negative emotions* and *positive emotions*—an understanding that builds on contemporary knowledge from the social sciences along with our own analysis of the *increasing values-fulfillment gap*—we turn to the work of Jonathan H. Turner, a sociologist focusing on the individual. He adopts a very broad approach to social science theory with a particular emphasis on social psychology. Turner states these three "laws of emotional arousal":

> The (Simplified) Law of Positive Emotional Energy: When individuals receive positive sanctions and/or realize their expectations in an encounter, they will experience *positive emotions*.
>
> The (Simplified) Law of Negative Emotional Energy: When individuals receive negative sanctions and/or fail to realize their expectations in an encounter, they will experience *negative emotions*.
>
> The (Simplified) Law of Repression and Activation of Defense Mechanisms: When individuals experience *negative emotions*, they become more likely to protect self through repression that, over time, leads to the intensification and transmutation of the *repressed emotion(s)*. ("The Social Psychology of Terrorism," in Phillips, ed., Understanding Terrorism, 2007: 129; italics ours)

Turner focuses his analysis on the momentary situation, as we can see from his linking each of the first two laws to "an encounter" and his tying the third law to an "experience." His centering on the situation, a departure from the emphasis of most sociologists, is absolutely essential if we are indeed to get at the complexity of human behavior. He also opens up to the complexity of human behavior, for he builds on the work of Freud, Horney and other psychoanalysts by paying attention to the idea of the unconscious as well as to *emotional repression*. Social psychologists generally have shied away from these topics, yet by so doing they have succeeded in ignoring fundamental conflicts within the individual, measuring what is easy to measure rather than what is difficult. However, now there is hard evidence for the effectiveness of long-term psychoanalysis, the kind based on the work of Freud and his followers. (See for example Falk Leichsenring and Sven Rabung, "Effectiveness of Long-Term Psychodynamic Psychotherapy," JAMA, October 2008: 1551-1565).

Granting the limitations of dichotomous thought, as illustrated by our contrast between *negative and positive emotions*, Turner's work is a rare plunge into the enormous complexity of emotions. His very general concepts of *"positive emotions"* and *"negative emotions"* are most useful. He provides numerous illustrations of *negative emotions* (e.g., fear, anger, disappointment, sadness, guilt, shame) along with illustrations of *positive emotions* (e.g., satisfaction, happiness, serenity, gratification, enjoyment, pride). We have developed our own dichotomous illustrations, pairing *negative* with *positive emotions*. Our own focus is gradational as well as dichotomous, thus moving along a continuum from negative toward positive emotions, as illustrated by these pairs:

from hate toward love
from shame toward pride
from guilt toward self-acceptance
from fear toward confidence
from despair toward hope
from anxiety toward serenity
from unhappiness toward happiness
from boredom toward passion
from disappointment toward satisfaction
from sorrow toward joy

Following Turner's third law, it is *negative emotions* rather than *positive emotions* that are likely to be repressed. Following that law along with Freudian psychoanalytic psychotherapy, such repression can lead to the intensification of the *repressed emotion* along with the impact of such repression on various areas of one's life, causing what Freud and Horney called neurotic behavior. Where, then, do these *negative emotions* come from? How can they be raised to the surface of awareness rather than repressed? Can we learn to move from *negative emotions* toward *positive emotions* without repressing the former, thus avoiding the neurotic behavior that psychoanalytic psychotherapy ties to *emotional repression*? And can such movement in turn help to pave the way for movement from our *bureaucratic worldview* and *bureaucratic self-image* toward an *evo-*

lutionary worldview and an *evolutionary self-image*? Can it also point us toward movement from *outward perception and thought* toward *inward-outward perception and thought*?

Following Turner's second law, we experience *negative emotions* when we "receive negative sanctions and/or fail to realize . . . expectations in an encounter." Negative sanctions have to do with the behavior of others toward us, and what is negative or positive depends on the impact of that behavior on our values. As for our own failure to realize or fulfill our expectations, that is based on the impact of our own behavior on our values. This takes us back to our discussions of our *values-fulfillment or aspirations-fulfillment gap*. Thus, our situational experience of *negative emotions* depends on the impact of our behavior and that of others on our values, which are structural. Although we have used the concept of values to examine our values-fulfillment gap, it will be in the next section that we will develop a systematic analysis of their nature. As we may note from the heading of this chapter—"'Heart': Emotions and Values"— it is essential to take both emotions and values into account in order to make progress in understanding "heart."

Yet even before moving into our discussion of values in the next section, we can understand a good deal about the sources of our *negative emotions*. Our *bureaucratic worldview* yields a *growing values-fulfillment gap* and, following Turner's second law, that failure to fulfill expectations will result in *negative emotions*. But if we then proceed to repress those *negative emotions*—following Turner's third law—we will lose awareness of what has occurred, just as the Springdalers did and just as we all do in general. Of course, such *emotional repression* does help us to obtain "some degree of satisfaction, recognition and achievement" with respect to other values not tied to that repression. Yet that *emotional repression* will continue to be the source of *negative emotions*, just as Freudian theory sees *emotional repression* as the source of neurotic behavior. Thus, a key source of our *negative emotions* in modern society is nothing less than our *bureaucratic worldview*, for it is tied to a *growing values-fulfillment gap* that yields *negative emotions*.

However, movement toward an *evolutionary worldview* can help us to narrow that gap and thus reduce those *negative emotions*. Following Turner's first law, such movement will work toward generating *positive emotions*, for it will help us to fulfill our expectations. What is at stake with respect to our *growing values-fulfillment gap*, then, is more than deepening world problems that we remain unable to solve. It is our own emotional life that is also at stake, such as feelings of hate versus love, shame versus pride, guilt versus self-acceptance, fear versus confidence, despair versus hope, anxiety versus serenity, unhappiness versus happiness, boredom versus passion, disappointment versus satisfaction and sorrow versus joy. We must bear in mind that movement from a *bureaucratic worldview* toward an *evolutionary worldview* is no easy matter. For example, we must learn to make use of the range of concepts from the extraordinary language of social science in our efforts to do so. And we must repeat changes in our situational behavior over and over again in order to change our structures.

However, we can focus the full potentials of language and the scientific method on the problems foisted on us by our *bureaucratic worldview* and *bureaucratic way of life*. It is a force that we have not yet learned to use, but it is there, waiting to be applied. Just as biophysical science and technology have succeeded in changing our physical and biological world, so can social science and technology succeed in changing our personal and social world. As we have learned from the foregoing two sections, it is indeed possible not only to move from *emotional repression* toward *emotional expression* but also to move from *negative emotions* toward *positive emotions*. It remains for us to learn to move, in our next section, from a *wide values-fulfillment gap* toward a *narrow values-fulfillment gap* and thus learn to achieve not only situational change but also the structural change that can prepare the way for changes in "hand" as well as "head" and "heart."

A NARROW VERSUS A WIDE VALUES-FULFILLMENT GAP: STRUCTURES

In order to *narrow our values-fulfillment gap* we must learn to (1) measure our values, (2) measure our degree of fulfillment of each value and (3) add up that degree of fulfillment for the full range of our values. By so doing we would be able to determine just how wide is our values-fulfillment gap. We already do this to some extent in a general and vague way when we consider the question of how happy or satisfied we are with life. But given our *bureaucratic worldview* which works toward isolating our ideas, feelings and actions from one another, our assessment of personal happiness or satisfaction with life can change from one situation to the next, just as our mood can easily change. Nevertheless, that personal assessment can still yield some useful information.

For example, let us recall from chapter 1 the grocer of Balgat. In response to the question of how satisfied he was with his life he stated, "I am born a grocer and probably die that way. I have not the possibility in myself to get the things that I want. They only bother me." Not only did he indicate his lack of satisfaction with life, but he also indicated the major reason for that dissatisfaction: the gap between his aspirations or values, on the one hand, and his ability to fulfill those aspirations or values. When the village chief was asked the same question he responded as follows: "What could be asked more? God has brought me to this mature age without much pain, has given me sons and daughters, has put me at the head of my village, and has given me strength of brain and body at this age. Thanks be to Him." His answer indicates not only satisfaction with life but also his closing or *narrowing of his values-fulfillment gap*.

Let us also recall that we see the chief as a metaphor for pre-industrial man with a relatively *narrow values-fulfillment gap*, and we see the grocer as a metaphor for contemporary man. It is by no means the absolute level of our achievements in life that indicates our happiness but rather the level of our achievements relative to the level of our aspirations or values. The grocer's aspirations were much higher than those of the chief. For example, if the chief were president of Turkey he would seek "help of money and seeed for some of our farmers." By contrast, the grocer "would make roads for the villagers to come to towns to see the world and would not let them stay in their holes all their life," thus setting himself up for a much *wider values-fulfillment gap* than that experienced by the chief.

We saw much the same thing at the beginning of the above section in the recent article appearing in the *Sarasota Herald-Tribune*. President Obama's promises during his presidential campaign, and the Republicans' promises prior to their taking over the House of Representatives in the 2010 election, both raised aspirations so high and so unrealistically as to yield afterwards a *wide values-fulfillment gap* accompanied by dissatisfaction. That article went further by referring to studies by political scientists that have found that "the primary precondition" for revolutions is "rising expectations," and the history of societies over the last five centuries is indeed a "revolution of rising expectations." The result has been a *widening values-fulfillment gap* along with increasing dissatisfaction, just as was illustrated by the grocer of Balgat.

These examples of the close tie between the width of our values-fulfillment gap and feelings of dissatisfaction or unhappiness help us to understand the importance of that gap. But they do not yield specific directions for measuring it, as outlined in the first paragraph of this section. Yet a study by Phillips half a century ago makes considerable progress toward that end. This was accomplished in an article, "Expected Value Deprivation and Occupational Preference." The article was based on a study of medical students' preferences for various medical specialties, a study financed by the Public Health Service of the U.S. government in order to learn what caused medical students to choose or fail to choose public health as a career. Information was obtained from 2,674 students in eight medical schools that were randomly selected from the four-year medical schools in the United States (Phillips, 1964: 151-160).

Values were measured, but only a narrow set of values related to working as a physician. Nine of the values were measured by a series of three separate items, with the tenth measured by two items. Instead of measuring the actual fulfillment of values, what was measured were student expectations for the future fulfillment of those physician-related values. Those expectations for value-fulfillment were then summed over the range of ten values, integrating almost one hundred pieces of information for each of the 2,674 students. In the days when computers were hardly available, it was quite a problem to calculate the students' expected value deprivation scores for the six medical fields. As a result, Phillips measured not the actual values-fulfillment gap of medical students but rather their expectations as to how wide such a gap would be if they chose any given medical field. Thus, a measurement was obtained of the "expected" value fulfillment of a given student for each of six fields of medicine.

The students filled out questionnaires in specially arranged sessions of two to three hours in length. Ten values relevant to fields of medicine were investigated: continued learning, research activities, involvement with complex problems, level of abilities utilized, closeness of patient relationships, possibilities for helping people, prestige among colleagues, amount of income, number of hours of work and level of physical exertion. Further, student expectations for fulfilling each of these ten occupational values were obtained for each of six fields of medicine: general practice, internal medicine, surgery, psychiatry, pathology and public health. As a result, the "expected value deprivation"—corresponding to our present work with the "values-fulfillment gap"—for each of those six fields of medicine was calculated for each of the 2,674 students.

Thus, each of the 2,674 students provided sixty ratings of their expectations for fulfilling each of ten values for each of six medical fields, and all of this information was summed so as to yield a student's "expected value deprivation" for each of the six fields. The question arises as to whether those measurements of values, expectations for fulfilling them and summations are in fact meaningful. Is it indeed possible to measure people's values? Did the students have insight into the nature of their own values? Would they be willing to reveal their values in an anonymous questionnaire? Did they have specific expectations for how much their values would be fulfilled within those six fields of medicine, and would they be willing to reveal those expectations? And could measurements be taken of the actual value fulfillment of people in general?

One way of assessing the meaningfulness of those measurements is to compare a student's "expected value-deprivation" score for a given medical field with whether or not that student rated that field favorably (a rank above the median rank) or unfavorably (a rank below the median rank). The students responded to this question: "How would you rank the following fields of medicine according to your interest in working in them?" The results of the analysis indicated that, among those students with the lowest expected value deprivation for a given medical field, fully 86 percent of those students rated those fields favorably. By contrast, among those students with the highest expected value deprivation for a given field, no more than 17 percent of those students rated those fields favorably. Phillips's theory, which uncovered a spread of as much as 69 percent between these two groups of students in their ratings of medical fields, is a most unusual finding within survey research, for spreads as high as thirty percent generally are considered to be important information. At the very least, his finding indicates the meaningfulness of the students' ratings of their values, their expectations for fulfilling those values within the six medical fields, the summation of those expectations for the ten values involved and the students' ratings of their preferences for those fields.

Phillips's study was a step toward learning that it is possible to assess not just medical students' expected value deprivation among medical fields, but also toward assessing everyone's actual value-fulfillment gap for choices in general. To move in this direction it is essential that we learn not just the nature of our values for a particular area of life like occupational life, but also the nature of our values for life in general. Yet what is the nature of those general values in contemporary societies? Very few social scientists have focused on this question, given its breadth coupled with a *bureaucratic worldview* that teaches us to emphasize the isolation of phenomena.

As for the nature of "values," we do not depart from the everyday meaning that people already have for this concept, similar to concepts like "aspirations," "interests," "ideals," "goals," "desires" and "motives." But given that we see values as structural phenomena, we do require the idea that they persist over time to a degree, granting that they can change. What social scientists have discovered is that there are a limited number of values that are widely shared throughout a given society, and that these "cultural" values become the most important values for almost everyone in that society, a finding that differs substantially from what most of us believe. In addition, our worldwide continuing technological revolution—coupled with mass markets, mass media and an internet that reaches across the globe—is succeeding in homogenizing cultural values. The result is the globalization of values, that is, the development of a limited number of values shared across the globe, granting that values unique to a given individual, group or society still exist.

These global values are most helpful for our ability to understand the behavior of individuals as well as groups and societies. Up to now we have lumped all of an individual's values together within the concept of a "values-fulfillment gap." This is most useful for understanding perhaps the most important problem in contemporary society, especially since that problem is largely invisible. Yet that concept and that problem are extremely general, granting the importance of understanding their nature. In order for us to come down to earth so that we can make use of the concept of values in confronting our everyday personal problems as well as world problems, it is essential that we discuss specific values, just as we had to come down to earth to discuss specific emotions in this chapter.

Of course, individuals do vary in their degree of commitment to a given global value. And they also still vary in how their values relate to one another and how they relate to their "head" and "hand." Nevertheless, an understanding of the nature of our global values is a huge step forward for reaching an understanding of human behavior. That understanding can in turn help us to make progress in confronting problems of conflict, whether at the individual, group or societal level. For we can focus on the values that individuals, groups or societies share rather than the values that keep them apart. If individuals have values that are in conflict with one another, then by raising them up to the surface they will have the opportunity to resolve those conflicts. Given the problems linked to our *bureaucratic worldview*, we might anticipate the existence of such conflicts.

What, then, are our global values? Anthropologists—granting their emphasis on the concept of values—have only emphasized pre-industrial values. They have also stressed the differences among cultures rather than what they have in common, and this has not helped us to understand global values. Sociologists have also neglected global values by focusing on the differences among groups in society. We can understand such behavior as having been influenced by a *bureaucratic worldview* with its orientation to the isolation of phenomena. As a result, our knowledge of the nature of our global values is limited.

However, at least one sociologist has been an exception to this neglect by social scientists of the values widely shared throughout contemporary society. Robin M. Williams, Jr.—one of the former presidents of the American Sociological Association—published the third edition of a textbook, *American Society* (1970), detailing the cultural values or widely-shared values throughout the United States. That book was based on many years of study, with the first edition appearing in 1951, His emphasis was on the long-term forces that have shaped America's values. From our own evolutionary perspective, American cultural values should indeed be seen as a product of world history.

For example, we cannot neglect the enormous impact of earlier developments in the Middle East and the Far East as well as in other areas of the world. We must also include the impact of Greek and Roman civilizations, Judeo-Christian ideals, the invention of the printing press and the university, Islamic intellectual developments linked to Greco-Roman civilizations, the Renaissance and Reformation in Europe, the journeys of exploration throughout the world, the French eighteenth-century Enlightenment era, the American and French revolutions, the history of Latin America, Africa and Australia, and much, much more. Indeed, given an *evolutionary worldview* we cannot ignore the impact of any human action anywhere in the world throughout all of human history on American cultural values, granting that our knowledge of the nature of that vast number of impacts is extremely limited.

Since the publication of Williams's book in 1970, the process of globalization has continued apace, resulting in the continuing homogenization of cultural values throughout the world. Most of the American values that he discussed are now global values. We have divided those global values into three sets, with a fourth set derived from his discussions of American institutions: political, economic, religious, scientific, educational and family. There are "people-oriented values" closely associated with the values emphasized by the French eighteenth-century Enlightenment preceding the French revolution as well as the values linked to the American revolution. "Work-related values" are linked to the continuing scientific and technological revolutions along with the work ethic linked to those revolutions. In addition, a third set of widely-shared values consists of two values that generally are deeply repressed. They illustrate the *bureaucratic nature of our worldview*, for they conflict with most of the other values. Finally, there is a set of values that Williams did not see as distinct American values because they are closely linked to the way institutions work throughout the world as a whole. However, we shall include them because of their fundamental importance for the individual as well as for society as a whole, and they are indeed global values.

We can understand more clearly the importance of our distinction between people-oriented and work-related values by returning to the work of Karen Horney. We might recall from chapter 3 her description of the "second contradiction within modern culture," namely, that between "the stimulation of our needs and our factual frustrations in satisfying them." There she was referring to our *widening values-fulfillment gap*. We might now see that gap as resulting more from our failure to fulfill people-oriented values than from our failure to fulfill work-related values. For the fulfillment of our people-oriented values depends more on the achievements of the social sciences than our work-related values, which are tied closely to the successes of the biophysical sciences.

In addition to such differences in the fulfillment of work-related and people-oriented values, there are also conflicts between these two sets of values which Horney called the "first contradiction" within contemporary society, as quoted in chapter 1:

> The first contradiction to be mentioned is that between competition and success on the one hand, and brotherly love and humility on the other. On the one hand everything is done to spur us toward success, which means that we must be not only assertive but aggressive, able to push others out of the way. On the other hand we are deeply imbued with Christian ideals which declare that it is selfish to want anything for ourselves, that we should be humble, turn the other cheek, be yielding. For this contradiction there are only two solutions within the normal range: to take one of these strivings seriously and discard the other; or to take both seriously with the result that the individual is seriously inhibited in both directions. (1937, 287)

With her "first contradiction" Horney presents yet another problem within contemporary society. Not only is there our values-fulfillment gap, but there is also the contradiction between our people-oriented values and our work-related values. The former are illustrated by "brotherly love and humility," and the latter by "competition and success." Yet for a systematic and comprehensive understanding of the nature of our people-oriented and work-related values we should turn to the work of Robin Williams. The following list does not include all of the values that Williams discussed, and it includes institutional values that he did not discuss within his listing of widely-shared values. We believe, however, that it does give us a good start toward understanding the nature of the global values that are widely shared by the peoples of the contemporary world. He describes four people-oriented values as follows:

> EQUALITY. At the level of overt interpersonal relations, adherence to a sense of intrinsic human value is discernible. . .by an extraordinary informality, directness, and lack of status consciousness in person-to-person contacts. . . .A second major type of equality consists of specific formal rights and obligations. . .from military service to voting, from public education to taxation—representing not only freedom but also equality.
> FREEDOM . . . Always the demand was for freedom from some existing restraint . . . a tendency to think of rights rather than duties . . . a distrust of central government. . . . American spokesmen emphasize freedom of speech and assembly, a multiparty, representative political system, private enterprise, freedom to change residence and employment.
> DEMOCRACY. Along with majority rule, representative institutions, and the rejection of . . . monarchical and aristocratic principles . . . American democracy stressed the reservation of certain "inalienable rights" as unalterable by majority rule. . . . Its . . . fundamental assumption is the worth and dignity and creative capacity of the individual.
> INDIVIDUAL PERSONALITY . . . We note a large number of important legal provisions [for] . . . the protection of personal freedom or the physical or social integrity of the person . . . illegality of slavery . . . illegality of imprisonment for debt . . . prohibitions against personal defamation (libel and slander); prohibition of "improper search and seizure"; prohibition of "cruel and unusual punishment;" right of habeas corpus. (Williams, 1970: 475-476, 480-481, 493-494, 496)

We can come to see these global values from an evolutionary perspective, for they point in the direction of continuing individual development even if we take into account the enormous limitations in our being able to fulfill them. They represent a swing of our pendulum of the scientific method far to the right—based on the political revolutions and social movements throughout modern history—and thus yield the momentum or motivation required for a swing further to the left, where we become more aware of our fundamental problems and committed to making progress on them. And those swings can be followed by swings ever further to the right and the left, granting some periods where the reverse occurs. It is only in modern times that societies—led by the United States—have emphasized these ideals as applying to all individuals and not just elite groups. And it is only in modern times that we have become convinced of the limitations of a stratified or elitist way of life.

As for Williams's work-related values, he lists these:

> ACHIEVEMENT AND SUCCESS. American culture is marked by a central stress upon personal achievement, especially secular occupational achievement. The "success story" and the respect accorded to the self-made man are distinctly American, if anything is. Our society . . . has endorsed Horatio Alger and has glorified the rail splitter who becomes president.
>
> [Economic] PROGRESS. By the late nineteenth century . . . progress could now become a slogan to defend the course of technological innovation and economic rationalization and concentration. . . . Progress became identified with "free private enterprise" . . . a belief in the positive value of ever-increasing quantities of goods and services.
>
> MATERIAL COMFORT. . . . a certain kind of materialism may emerge in a society . . . in the sense that the sheer availability of creature comforts and the incessant advertising used to sell them creates a social pressure to concentrate effort and attention upon them . . . the objective opportunity to secure material comforts elicits, in the long run, a desire for them.
>
> SCIENCE AND SECULAR RATIONALITY. Applied science is highly esteemed as a tool for controlling nature. Significant here is the interest in order, control, and calculability—the passion for an engineering civilization . . . Science is disciplined, rational, functional, active; it requires systematic diligence and honesty. (Williams, 1970: 454-458, 468-484, 487-489, 492-498)

Our four people-oriented values can easily come into conflict with two major values that are almost universally repressed because of those conflicts: "external conformity" and "group superiority." External conformity is well-illustrated in the first section of chapter 5 within our discussion of the Milgram experiments that were the basis for obedience to authority. Those experiments on a varied sample of New Haven adults yielded the kind of abject conformity to the directions of a supposed expert that are reminiscent of the conformity of Hitler's subordinates at his death camps.

Group superiority meshes hand-in-glove with conformity, much like the positions of two individuals on a see-saw where one individual at the lower end is balanced by an individual at the high end. Thus, we conform to individuals whom we see as superior to us in some respect. Such patterns of superiority and inferiority, which social scientists have come to call patterns of "social stratification," have been found to be nearly universal, granting that they exist alongside of people-oriented values that conflict with them. Their existence continues in the face of social movements in the direction of equality with respect to race, gender, sexual orientation, age and religion.

In addition to the widely shared values throughout society that Williams discusses, we would add five more values closely linked to the institutions of contemporary societies across the globe. There is the institution of science with a focus on the cultural value of achieving (1) "understanding of the world" as well as (2) "solving problems." There is the institution of education with its concern for communicating all of that knowledge. There is the family's commitments to the cultural values of the (3) "life versus death" as well as the achievement of (4) "intimate and close relationships." Religion suggests the cultural value of (5) "ultimate meaning" as well as a commitment to the people-oriented value of "individual personality," thus pointing toward the ultimate worth of the individual. The political institution, given its bureaucratic orientation, has been oriented to the cultural value of the achievement of power over other people, suggesting the hierarchical pattern of behavior that is so basic to the present organization of society. It also joins the institution of science in its orientation to solving the problems of society. As for the economic institution, there is its present bureaucratic focus on "material comfort," "achievement and success," and "progress," focusing on material progress.

It is all of these widely shared values or aspirations that contribute to the very general aspirations-fulfillment or values-fulfillment gap that is increasing throughout contemporary societies, and not just throughout American society. Granting that this analysis of our global values is a work in progress, nevertheless it can enable us to come far down to earth from our previous vagueness about aspirations or values so that we can understand more clearly the nature of our current problems and move toward solutions. Values, by contrast with situational phenomena like perceptions and thoughts, are structural in that they have a track record over time. Williams's analysis is based not on a survey at one point in time, and not on what most people are conscious of in any given moment. Rather, he dipped deeply into the historical record, as analyzed by a wide variety of social scientists, and emerged with his analysis as a result. Our own view of five additional institutional values is equally based on the historical record, although space does not permit a more thorough presentation of them.

We can add to our understanding of the fundamental forces behind the development of these global values by turning to the nature of our *bureaucratic worldview*. For example, that worldview's orientation to *emotional repression* enables us to repress the contradictions between the value of group superiority and many of the other values, such as equality, freedom, democracy, and understanding the world. That orientation to *emotional repression* also helps us to repress conflicts between work-related values like "material comfort" as well as "achievement and success," on the one hand, and people-oriented values like "equality" and "individual personality," on the other hand. The *bureaucratic worldview*'s narrow "head" orientation to *outward perception and thought* helps to explain not only the difficulties that we have in fulfilling most of these values but also our *widening values-fulfillment gap*. It is that same narrow "head" orientation that has defined the value of "science and secular rationality" so as to largely exclude knowledge from social science. Further, the orientation of the *bureaucratic worldview* to hierarchy and conformity helps us to understand the existence of the values of "group superiority" and" external conformity" and, thus, our deep conflicts.

For example, there is the conflict between the value of "ultimate meaning" emphasized by the institution of religion and the focus on science and secular rationality within the institution of science, with proponents of one value seeing proponents of the other in a hierarchical way. The controversy over abortion often pits those emphasizing the family and religion—centering on the life of the unborn—against women who believe that the political and family institutions should leave them with the "freedom" to make their own choices with respect to abortion. The result of such controversies, following our *bureaucratic way of life*, generally is not deepening understanding ("head"), *narrowing people's values-commitment gap* ("heart") and more effective problem-solving, as would occur within an *evolutionary way of life*. Rather, it is the strengthening of our *bureaucratic way of life* along with its *growing values-fulfillment gap*.

Much like the tool of psychoanalysis, this social science analysis enables us to probe deeply into the powerful yet largely invisible forces that have shaped and are continuing to shape human behavior throughout the world. This can result in increasing ability to find common ground amidst such controversies. Social science has taught us just how much we all share by means of this knowledge of our widely shared global values. Of course our *bureaucratic worldview* has fed us the idea that we all very different from one another. Yet an understanding of global values can help us to see the limitations of that worldview and move toward an *evolutionary worldview*. In this way we can depart from the assumption that we are all so unique and move toward the assumption that we all share a great deal.

More specifically, knowledge of those fifteen global values outlined above can help us to find that common ground and move away from the values of conformity and persisting hierarchy that conflict with those values. It may indeed be hard to believe that one can know so much about other people when we have never even met them. Yet this is exactly what a broad approach to social science knowledge has taught us. No psychoanalysis of others is necessary. These shared values are a major force holding any given society together, just as anthropology and sociology have taught us. And knowledge of those global values can equally help us to understand more about ourselves. We are not the absolutely unique individuals that we generally think we are, given once again a *bureaucratic worldview* emphasizing the differences among individuals rather than what they have in common. Such knowledge of global values can help us to move in a reflexive direction with its implications for movement toward *inward-outward perception and thought* as well as toward an *evolutionary way of life*.

As we proceed from this chapter with its focus on "heart" to chapter five with its emphasis on "hand," let us look back at the implications of the journey that we have taken. We have presented both situational and structural concepts from the extraordinary language of social science that are so general that they enable us to integrate our "head" and "heart" experiences along with our everyday language that has to do with "head" and "heart." Each of the concepts from the extraordinary language is itself linked to the other concepts from that language within the umbrella of the extremely general concepts of *bureaucratic worldview* and *evolutionary worldview*. From a problem-solving perspective, any experience or any thought relating to "head" or "heart" that we have can now be seen as moving us toward a *bureaucratic way of life* or toward an *evolutionary way of life*. Given our pendulum metaphor for the scientific method, we can come to see any movement in a bureaucratic direction—or a swing to the left—as yielding the motivation or momentum for a swing to the right, thus moving from (1) *inward or outward perception and thought* toward *inward-outward perception and thought*, from (2) a *bureaucratic self-image* toward an *evolutionary self-image*, from (3) a *bureaucratic worldview* toward an *evolutionary worldview*, from (4) *emotional repression* toward *emotional repression*, from (5) *negative emotions* toward *positive emotions*, and from (6) a *wide values-fulfillment gap* toward a *narrow values-fulfillment gap*.

Granting these possibilities for evolving in any and every situation from our *bureaucratic way of life* toward an *evolutionary of life* this is the actuality of our present personal problems and escalating world problems that threaten the very survival of the human race. That comparison between our possibilities and actuality suggests a human tragedy so vast and deep that it far surpasses all of the tragedies that the human race has experienced since its appearance on earth. It is a tragedy that has to do not with the fact that we all die but rather with the idea that we have not yet learned how to live. However, granting that we have only a limited window of opportunity to turn things around, we have yet to make full use of the incredible potentials of language and the scientific method. In chapter 6 we shall cover the waterfront of human behavior with a focus on "hand" in addition to "head" and "heart." Our continuing technological revolution has emphasized a very narrow "hand" centering on shaping the physical universe. Our breakthrough in the social sciences gives us a much broader approach to "hand," namely, the development of our potential for shaping the human as well as the physical universe, based on a much broader approach to using the full potentials of language and the scientific method.

FIVE

"Hand": Actions/Interactions, Rituals and Ways of Life

We begin this chapter with a selection from Ralph Ellison's 1947 novel, *Invisible Man*, about a young black man who was a victim of prejudice and discrimination, illustrating the persisting hierarchy or stratification that is basic to a bureaucratic way of life:

> I am an invisible man. No, I am not a spook like those who haunted Edgar Allan Poe; nor am I one of your Hollywood-movie ectoplasms. I am a man of substance, of flesh and bone, fiber and liquids—and I might even be said to possess a mind. I am invisible, understand, simply because people refuse to see me. Like the bodiless heads you see sometimes in circus sideshows, it is as though I have been surrounded by mirrors of hard, distorting glass. When they approach me they see only my surroundings, themselves, or figments of their imagination—indeed, everything and anything except me.
>
> Nor is my invisibility exactly a matter of a biochemical accident to my epidermis. That invisibility to which I refer occurs because of a peculiar disposition of the eyes of those with whom I come in contact. A matter of the construction of their inner eyes, those eyes with which they look through their physical eyes upon reality. . .you're constantly being bumped against by those of poor vision. . .out of resentment, you begin to bump people back. And, let me confess, you feel that way most of the time. (3–4)

Ellison's young hero is certainly visible as a material object but is invisible as a unique human being with a history of personal experiences different from those of all other human beings. His treatment as nothing but yet another black does violence to his unique inner world based on his millions and millions of past experiences. That treatment also does violence to the people-oriented values that are shared throughout the

119

world: "equality," "individual personality," "freedom" and "democracy." Thus, such stereotyping fails to do justice not only to "head" but also
to "heart." And it then becomes the basis for acts of discrimination, thus
invoking "hand."

Yet Ellison's hero is not alone in his invisibility. Following the nature
of our *bureaucratic worldview*, we are all largely invisible to others and
ourselves, granting that some individuals—such as African-Americans in
the United States even at the present time—generally are more invisible
than others. We might recall here chapter 3's presentation of Plato's allegory of the cave, where the prisoners could see neither one another nor
themselves but only shadows on the cave's wall. We see this situation as
the product of the focus on *outward perception and thought* within our
bureaucratic worldview, by contrast with the *inward-outward perception and
thought.* within an *evolutionary worldview*.

When Phillips was in graduate school at Cornell—after having been
pointed toward a career in sociology through contact with C. Wright
Mills at Columbia—he published this sonnet:

WHEN I BEGIN THE ANCIENT GAME OF CHESS

> When I begin the ancient game of chess,
> Commanding knights and pawns in bitter strife,
> I wonder at the thought that I possess:
> How is it with the greater game of life?
> Am I a wooden piece which someone moves,
> A means to satisfy another's ends?
> Do I advance, retreat, in patterned grooves,
> A creature of commands another sends?
> Perhaps I am a player in the game,
> And force the moves of countless other souls
> To seek my own fulfillment, fortune, fame,
> Ignoring in my quest their secret goals.
>
> The castle falls, the knights remain en pris [exposed],
> Besiegers there are none the eye can see.
> (Phillips, *Different*, Summer, 1954: 18)

The poem alerts us to the existence of invisible forces that shape our
behavior, pushing the individual to conform to "another's ends" much
like "a wooden piece" that is moved on a chessboard. The "besiegers" of
"the castle" are invisible, for "there are none the eye can see." Those
invisible forces can treat us just as Ellison's hero was treated. And following Plato's allegory, they can teach us to see no more than shadows rather
than the reality of ourselves and others.

Yet there is a most optimistic side to Ellison's novel, Plato's allegory
and Phillips's poem. For they all help us to "see" phenomena that otherwise would remain invisible. A situation that was not a problem for us

has now become a problem. For our people-oriented values have taught us to reject any situation where we are treated as Ellison's hero was treated, or where we are turned away from experiencing reality, or where we are forced to conform to the will of others. Given our commitment to the value of "science and secular rationality," that new sense of problem can become much like a swing of the pendulum of the scientific method far to the left, where we become aware of and committed to solve a given problem. As a result, we can gain the motivation or momentum to swing our pendulum far to the right, using the scientific method to make progress on that problem.

Indeed, this is what we have been trying to accomplish throughout this book for readers as well as for ourselves. We see Ellison's book, Plato's allegory and Phillips' poem as metaphors not for an entertaining story or an intellectual tour de force but rather for the reality that we are all experiencing at this very moment. We are pushed and pulled by our *bureaucratic worldview* or metaphysical stance, a stance that remains invisible. Yet by becoming aware of this we can commit ourselves to breaking free of our enslavement, and then we can actually break free.

Breaking free of our *bureaucratic way of life* illustrates our focus on "hand" in this chapter. Just as in the case of chapters 3 and 4, the sections within this chapter will include focuses on both situational and structural change. Specifically, our first section on *negative and positive actions* or interactions centers on situational behavior, with the following two sections focusing on structural behavior. Also as in the case of chapters 3 and 4, we must include attention to the other major components of human behavior—"head" and "heart" in this case—in order to understand the nature of the change on which we are focusing. Thus, for example, our *negative and positive actions* or interactions ("hand") should be seen, correspondingly, as yielding *negative and positive emotions* ("heart"), and these actions or interactions are guided by "head." Whether those actions and emotions are negative or positive depends on whether they *widen or narrow one's values-fulfillment gap*.

Thus, there is a close link between one's structures, such as one's values, and one's situational experiences, such as one's emotions. One's values shape one's emotions just as one's emotions shape one's values. Further, our emotions ("heart") within the context of our ideas ("head") also shape our actions ("hand"), just as our actions shape our emotions. Emotions ("heart") that we interpret as positive ("head") encourage us to more effective actions ("hand") and *negative emotions* discourage us about taking such actions, much like a pendulum swinging between the two. In turn, effective or *positive actions* encourage the development of *positive emotions*, and ineffective or *negative actions* encourage *negative emotions*. This is a more general statement of the workings of the pendulum metaphor for the scientific method, for it can be applied to any and every problem in everyday life, and not just to specialized scientific problems.

Any and every situation that we experience can become problematic, given our *bureaucratic way of life* with its *widening values-fulfillment gap*.

It will be in our third section on moving from a *bureaucratic way of life* toward an *evolutionary way of life* that we will focus on linking "head," "heart" and "hand." Our emphasis will be on integrating them around the fundamental problem of how to move from one way of life to the other way of life. That problem is more general than a problem that we have devoted considerable attention to, namely, how to narrow our *widening values-fulfillment gap*. To the extent that we learn to change our way of life we will also be learning how to narrow that gap. Yet movement toward an *evolutionary way of life* can take us far beyond the narrowing of that gap. Following our East-West strategy, as discussed in chapter 2, once that gap is narrowed there is no limit as to how far we might go, assuming that we continue to stay with an *evolutionary worldview* that includes the other elements of that worldview discussed in chapters 3, 4 and 5.

POSITIVE VERSUS NEGATIVE ACTIONS/INTERACTIONS: SITUATIONS

THE ROAD NOT TAKEN

> Two roads diverged in a yellow wood,
> And sorry I could not travel both. . . .
> Oh, I kept the first for another day!
> Yet knowing how way leads on to way,
> I doubted if I should ever come back. . .
> Two roads diverged in a wood, and I—
> I took the one less traveled by,
> And that has made all the difference.
> —Robert Frost

Frost's poem suggests enormous optimism about the nature of the human condition. For if we can actually make choices, then we are not simply victims of external forces, as suggested by Phillips's "When I Begin the Ancient Game of Chess." And those choices can include absolutely fundamental ones, like the choice of our worldview or the choice of solutions to the fundamental problems of society. Indeed, we may even define the nature of the human being in this way. We are the only creatures throughout the known universe with the capacity to make the kinds of choices that are so fundamental that they can change the very structure of ourselves as well as society. Our choices can require actions or interactions ("hand") as well as emotions and values ("heart") along with perceptions and thought ("head"). Of course, such optimism must be balanced by realism, given our present situation of increasing world problems along with our *bureaucratic way of life*.

Frost's final line, "And that has made all the difference," suggests the focus of this section on the impact of our actions on ourselves and the world. We know that Robert Frost had experiences with factory work and farming but had found those occupations to be unsatisfactory. Instead, he chose "The Road Not Taken": becoming a poet, a very rare choice of a lifelong occupation. That final line suggests his immense satisfaction with having made that choice, a choice that resulted in no less than four Pulitzer prizes as well as his performance at the age of eighty-six when he spoke and read his poetry at the inauguration of President John F. Kennedy on January 20, 1961. Making use of our extraordinary language with respect to "heart," his choice illustrates the close relationship between "hand" and "heart." For it was that choice that apparently yielded for him more *emotional expression* and *positive emotions* along with a *narrow values-fulfillment gap*. And the last line of his poem indicates that he understood ("head") the significance of that choice. Because of the effectiveness of that action in fulfilling Frost's values, an effectiveness that yielded *emotional expression* as well as *positive emotions*, we see Frost's choice of "the road not taken" as a *positive action* rather than a *negative action*.

Yet we must integrate such optimism with realism, just as the pendulum of the scientific method moves from a swing to the right that makes progress on a problem to a swing to the left that digs more deeply into that problem. Experiments that succeeded in such deep digging into a basic problem existing throughout modern society were developed by Stanley Milgram, a psychologist working at Yale University, which he described in *Obedience to Authority* (1974). He undertook a series of experiments that focused on the two major values within modern society that we repress because of their conflicts with our people-oriented values: "external conformity" and "group superiority". Are people really guided by those repressed values? Just how powerful are they? Are we in fact a society of conformists who bow down to our supposed superiors, despite our emphasis on "equality," "freedom," "democracy" and "individual personality?"

Milgram selected a group of experimental subjects through an ad as well as phone calls to individuals selected at random from the New Haven telephone directory, indicating that participants would be paid four dollars per hour, securing five hundred subjects in this way. They were divided among unskilled and skilled workers, white-collar, sales and business people, and professionals. Each subject was required to adopt the role of "teacher" to a forty-seven-year-old accountant—generally described as "mild-mannered and likable"—who played the role of "learner." Subjects were given their orders by an "experimenter" dressed in a gray technician's coat. In fact, the learner was Milgram's confederate, and so was the experimenter. They had been carefully coached by Milgram on how they were to behave throughout the experiment.

Each of the subjects, separated from the other subjects, was introduced to the learner and the experimenter. The experimenter read several pairs of words to the learner, such as "blue box," and later the learner was cued by one of the words and was then required to respond with the associated word. If the learner gave an incorrect answer or failed to respond within a few seconds, the teacher was supposed to give the learner an electric shock using a bogus "shock generator" with voltages that ranged from 15 to 450. Teachers were instructed to begin with 15 volts and then add 15 additional votes for each incorrect answer, thus taking them up to the level of 450 volts. Most of us are quite aware of the danger posed by even a shock of 120 volts from an ordinary electric outlet. But when we get up to the range of 300 volts—let alone 450 volts—those kinds of shocks can easily result in death.

Thus, we can draw a parallel here between what these subjects were asked to do and what those individuals who led Hitler's victims into gas chambers were asked to do. Let us recall the Holocaust, as briefly discussed in chapters 1 and 2 and as examined in the film, *Judgment at Nuremberg*. For those most responsible for the mass murders and torture—people much the same as present-day officials throughout the world—claimed that they were not responsible for their horrendous crimes because they were acting "under orders." Indeed, Hitler's minions were under more pressure from their superiors to obey orders, versus Milgram's volunteers, since they themselves could be killed for refusing to follow their leaders. Would those American volunteers behave much the same as Hitler's minions, granting that the life of only one individual was at stake in Milgram's experiments? Would our people-oriented values prevail over the orders of an authority figure, by contrast with what occurred during the Holocaust, granting that those people-oriented values were by no means foreign to the German population?

After the conclusion of the experiments, Milgram asked an audience of college students, psychiatrists and other adults how they would expect those teachers to react to their instructions. A total of one hundred and ten individuals responded, and not a single one expected any teacher to administer a shock greater than 300 volts, indicating that they would refuse to do so. Further, most respondents indicated that no one would go past 150 volts. In this way, those respondents came out foursquare for the idea that we are absolutely not a nation of conformists who bow down to our superiors, thus emphasizing the importance of the opposing people-oriented values of "equality," "freedom," "democracy" and "individual personality." And we might add here the value of "life versus death."

What Milgram actually discovered as a result of these experiments is hard to believe, given our people-oriented values and the value of life itself. Milgram had arranged four different experimental conditions that represented different degrees of closeness of the "teacher" to the "learner." In (1) a remote condition, where the learner was supposedly strapped to a chair in an adjoining room with communication by electric signal, Milgram found that fully 65 percent of the teachers continued up to the maximum of 450 volts, which probably would be lethal for most people in most situations. In (2) a voice-feedback experimental condition, where the learner's vocal protests could be heard through the laboratory wall, 62.5 percent continued to 450 volts. In (3) a proximity condition where the teacher stands only a few feet away from the learner, 40 percent continued to that maximum shock, and (4) in touch proximity, where the teacher must place the learner's hand on the shock plate, 30 percent went to the maximum shock of 450 volts. Through all of this the experimenter had been coached to show no emotion and to look stern.

Reactions of teachers in the remote condition are illustrated by these remarks of a teacher:

> These are terrific volts. I don't think this is very humane. . . . Oh, I can't go on with this; no, this isn't right. It's a hell of an experiment. The guy is suffering in there. No, I don't want to go on. This is crazy. (Milgram, 1974: 32)

With respect to the voice-feedback condition, Milgram had coached the learner to groan painfully at 135 volts, to demand that he be released from the experiment at 150 volts, to shout that he could no longer stand the pain at 180 volts, to scream in agony at 270 volts, and to shriek with increasing intensity from 300 volts onward. There were also several variations of the experiment. In one variation a laboratory was set up in a rundown building not associated with Yale University. There, compliance of the teacher with the demands of the experimenter within the voice-feedback condition dropped from 62.5 percent to 48 percent. In another variation where the experimenter gave his orders to the teacher over a telephone, 25 percent of teachers—by contrast with 62.5 percent— continued to the level of 450 volts.

Whatever other ideas these experiments support, they also support the idea of the incredible power of our *bureaucratic worldview* to yield abject conformity among most of us. For that worldview specifies patterns of persisting hierarchy or stratification throughout society, despite our people-oriented values. Those patterns of hierarchy point us toward the importance of "hand" in addition to "heart" and "head." It is a worldview that we apparently share with the worldview that prevailed within Nazi Germany, granting some differences in degree. For let us recall that the individuals who were administering what they must have known deep down were lethal shocks were volunteers whose lives were not threatened if they refused to obey orders, by contrast with Hitler's subordinates. We might note that the Milgram experiments cannot be repeated, for new guidelines for social research have been developed since 1974 that protect subjects of experiments to a great extent. Most of the subjects of Milgram's experiments have had to live with the realization that they administered what they believed were lethal doses of electricity to a defenseless human being, a situation that research administrators will no longer tolerate.

Yet there is more that we should take into account in interpreting the results of the Milgram experiments. Up to now our focus has been on structures rather than situations, given our focus on "worldview" ("head"), "values" ("heart") and "stratification" ("hand"). We should also look to situational phenomena, like "perception and thought" ("head"), *negative and positive emotions* ("heart"), and "actions" that yield such emotions. For example, we might note that perception proved to be most important, for when subjects were close to the learner—especially when teachers placed the learner's hand on the shock plate—conformity was greatly reduced. As for emotions, the above-quoted protests of a learner ("No, I don't want to go on. This is crazy") illustrates the conflicts between opposing values that learners were experiencing. Yet granting those conflicts, their actions in conformity with the experimenter's orders indicated that *negative emotions* from disobedience were more powerful than *negative emotions* from conformity, or *positive emotions* from conformity were more powerful than *positive emotions* from disobedience.

The Milgram experiments illustrate the nature of our values-fulfillment gap, for the conforming actions of most subjects to the experimenter's orders—which we see as negative actions—led them to a huge gap between their people-oriented or humanistic values and their actual behavior. And it also yielded extremely *negative emotions*. Given that gap and those emotions, we can well understand the desires of research administrators to protect experimental subjects from awareness of those gaps. Yet such awareness of a problem—following the nature of the scientific method—is absolutely crucial if we are indeed to make progress on that problem. That is our own direction in emphasizing the importance of the Milgram experiments. We want to bring up to the light of day our *enormous values-fulfillment gap*—just as Ralph Ellison, Plato and Phillips brought to the surface invisible problems—so that we can make progress on those problems. Following our pendulum metaphor for the scientific method, by swinging our pendulum far to the left so that we become aware of absolutely fundamental problems, we can gain the momentum or motivation for making progress on them

Is, then, direct opposition to conforming actions and patterns of hierarchy necessarily a direction that will take us away from our *bureaucratic worldview* and toward an *evolutionary worldview*? We turn here to a personal experience that Phillips had, by contrast with another research project. His most formative experience at Columbia was within sociology courses given by C. Wright Mills, an individual who had illustrated in a series of books—such as *The New Men of Power*, *White Collar* and *The Power Elite*—his extremely negative view of patterns of conformity and social stratification. He was an individualist, his own man, exuding enormous self-confidence, who roared into the campus quadrangle on his motorcycle, with the tail of his coonskin cap waving in the breeze that he had created. In his lectures on the problems of middle-class office workers and salespeople—with their repetitive work, uncertain employment, subservience and conformity to their bosses—they illustrated fundamental problems throughout the world. His commitment to unearthing basic problems ran very deep, illustrated by his often roaring in his classes rather than calmly speaking.

One story that he told his class, grinning broadly, was of an unannounced visit by Dwight Eisenhower, then president of Columbia University and shortly to become president of the United States. Eisenhower took a seat in the back row, and Mills immediately altered the lecture he had planned, inventing on the spur of the moment a new lecture on how to overthrow the U.S. government by force, with the class operating as a cell that would help to coordinate this violent revolution. As Mills continued with the details of his plot, Eisenhower's face started to turn the color of a boiled lobster, and he shortly rose from his seat and walked out of the room, with Mills never hearing a word about the episode from the college administration. In his own view, Mills had succeeded in confronting "the Establishment," the most powerful figure within Columbia's administrative hierarchy, and he had triumphed. Instead of conforming to what the college administration expected from the faculty, he deviated very sharply from those expectations.

Yet did Mills's actions in his classroom when President Eisenhower appeared actually illustrate movement away from a *bureaucratic worldview*? In fact, Mills was reversing the existing pattern of hierarchy within the university, showing off his superiority to the president of the university. More specifically, although Mills's actions yielded *positive emotions* on his own part to some extent, his violation of such people-oriented values of his own such as "equality" and "individual personality" also probably yielded repressed *negative emotions* on his own part. And they yielded *negative emotions* for Eisenhower. This analysis should not in the least take away from Mills's great contributions, such as the ideas that social scientists should develop a very broad approach to the scientific method and deep emotional commitments to solving the huge problems of society. Yet Mills missed out on a huge opportunity to join forces with Eisenhower in confronting mammoth problems in society. And by so doing, Mills failed to move toward narrowing the *widening values-fulfillment gap* throughout contemporary society and thus moving toward an *evolutionary way of life*. Thus, the effectiveness of actions depends not just on their impact on one's own emotions but also on the impact on the values-fulfillment gap linked to our *bureaucratic worldview*.

To illustrate the possibilities that Mills missed out on, following his tenure as president of the United States, Eisenhower stated in his farewell address: "In the councils of government, we must guard against the acquisition of unwarranted influence, whether sought or unsought, by the military-industrial complex." In the words of Karl Weissenbach, director of the Eisenhower Library, Eisenhower's was "the most famous farewell address in American history," for he warned all of us of a threat to our fundamental democratic values, a threat that the years following Eisenhower's presidency have—in our own view—demonstrated to be very real. Mills missed an opportunity for *positive actions* that might well have advanced his own humanistic and problem-solving orientations as well as, more generally, movement in society away from our *bureaucratic way of life* by *narrowing our values-fulfillment gap.*

Mills's behavior toward Eisenhower meshed with the general understanding by social scientists as to the nature of power. They define power as the ability to control the behavior of others—against their will if necessary—by using force, authority or influence. And they see power as a scarce commodity, like a fixed pie of power: the more power a given group has, the less power remains for others. Thus, if Mills was able to control Eisenhower's behavior, his power over what goes on at Columbia University would increase and Eisenhower's power would decrease. To use another metaphor, a see-saw suggests hierarchical relationships between people or groups, indicating that one person's gain is another's loss: moving up on the see-saw pushes someone else down. Thus, we can see Mills's *negative action* as yielding his own *positive emotions* along with *negative emotions* for Eisenhower, and with the overall result of a *wider values-fulfillment gap.* Mills's actions, then, were negative because they proved to be ineffective relative to *narrowing our values-fulfillment gap.* And they were also negative because they probably yielded repressed *negative emotions* on his own part.

EVOLUTIONARY VERSUS BUREAUCRATIC RITUALS: STRUCTURES

Thus far our focus in this chapter has been on situations, granting that we have included attention to structures. The time has come to shift our focus to structures. Former President Calvin Coolidge has contributed to our understanding here:

> Nothing in the world can take the place of persistence. Talent will not; nothing is more common than unsuccessful men with talent. Genius will not; unrewarded genius is almost a proverb. Education will not; the world is full of educated derelicts. Persistence and determination are omnipotent. The slogan "press on" has solved and always will solve the problems of the human race.

President Coolidge is not simply emphasizing "hand" here, for the "persistence" he is calling for requires action in one scene after another after another. In other words, he is suggesting the overwhelming importance of structures, and not just behavior in this situation or that one.

We may define a "ritual" as an individual's *persisting* pattern of action ("hand") that is meaningful ("head") and expressive ("heart") to some degree. "Ritual" is a term that has generally been used only in a religious context, but we believe the concept can apply usefully to any context whatsoever, corresponding to the wide application of the term "habit." But the word "habit" suggests a narrow focus only on "hand," although we know that all human behavior, including habits, involves "head," "heart" and "hand." By contrast, the word "ritual" suggests a pattern of action with genuine significance ('head') and importance ("heart"). Rituals can also be widely shared, as illustrated observances of national holidays like Thanksgiving, Veterans Day, Presidents Day and Christmas. The usefullness of this concept for understanding human behavior has been thoroughly illustrated by J. David Knottnerus in his book *Ritual as a Missing Link* (2011).

Our interest in this section as well as throughout this book is in the contrast between bureaucratic and evolutionary behavior. For an illustration comparing *bureaucratic rituals* with *evolutionary rituals*, we turn to Janusz Bardach, who managed to survive the very difficult conditions in the Soviet labor camps, described his experiences in *Man Is Wolf to Man: Surviving the Gulag*:

> At four A.M. the ringing rail sounded for us to get up. Despite my fatigue and the cold, I kept the exercise routine I had followed at home and in the Red Army, washing my face and hands at the hand pump. I wanted to retain as much pride in myself as I could, separate myself from the many prisoners I had seen give up day by day. They'd stop caring first about their hygiene or appearance, then about their fellow prisoners, and finally about their own lives. If I had control over nothing else, I had control over this ritual, which I believed would keep me from degradation and certain death. (1998: 130)

Bardach generally saw prisoners giving up day after day: "They'd stop caring first about their hygiene or appearance, then about their fellow prisoners, and finally about their own lives." By so doing, those prisoners were illustrating *negative actions* one day after another, thus yielding *bureaucratic rituals*. As another indication of such rituals, they separated "heart" (caring about themselves and others) from "hand" (continuing to survive). And they fooled themselves ("head") into believing that their lack of caring made no difference to their potential for surviving. Such behavior also illustrates *bureaucratic rituals* with its separation of "head," "heart" and "hand." They were also bureaucratic because they resulted in a *widening values-fulfillment gap*, for they resulted in death rather than survival. Unfortunately, those prisoners generally were not aware of the impact that their *bureaucratic rituals* would have on their survival.

By contrast, *evolutionary rituals* are illustrated by Bardach's own positive actions day after day: "Despite my fatigue and the cold, I kept the exercise routine I had followed at home and in the Red Army, washing my face and hands at the hand pump ("hand"). I wanted to retain as much pride in myself as I could ("heart")." Bardach hoped to survive, and he focused on the kinds of behavior that would help his chances for leaving the Gulag one day ("head"). His ability to take pride in such actions by interpreting them most favorably ("head") helped to strengthen his overall motivation ("heart"), and that motivation in turn helped him to persist over time in his *evolutionary rituals* ("hand"), despite his "fatigue and the cold." In other words, by repeating his *positive action* of an exercise routine day after day, that routine became a structure for him: an evolutionary ritual. Repeated behavior in one scene after another yielded a structure. And once that structure had developed, it became easier for Bardach to repeat his behavior day after day. The same is true for structures in general. Thus, an *evolutionary self-image* helps one to focus on *inward-outward perception and thought* in one situation after another. And a *narrow values-fulfillment gap* helps one to experience *positive emotions* as well as *positive actions* in one setting after another

Bardach's experience suggests the possibility that we all can learn to transform more and more of our habits or *bureaucratic rituals* into *evolutionary rituals*. As another illustration that is much different and much more commonplace than Bardach's life-threatening situation, there is Phillips's experience with falling asleep at night. Although generally he has been able to fall asleep within a reasonable period of time, on many occasions he has been kept awake by thoughts of unsolved problems that he had experienced during the day. On those occasions his thoughts had turned to his *wide values-fulfillment gap*. At those times he decided to focus his thoughts on his perception of his breathing, and that took him away from thoughts about unsolved problems and enabled him to fall asleep quite easily. Given that "heart" is linked to "head" and "hand," those unsolved problems ("heart") kept him awake with thoughts about how to solve them ("head") in a situation—lying in bed—where he was unable to take the actions ("hand") needed to solve them. Phillips' procedure was by no means unique, since procedures of meditation generally call for much the same kind of behavior. Yet our analysis of what Phillips was experiencing, with its usage of the extraordinary language of social science, clarifies the nature of his procedure.

We might, then, see Phillips's pattern of behavior when retiring at night as an *evolutionary ritual*, granting that his focus was on limiting his thoughts to his perception of his breathing. For one thing, he focused "inward" to a greater extent, balancing his previous outward orientation to external problems and thus achieving more of a focus on *inward-out-*

ward perception and thought ("head"). For another thing, he was able to achieve a *narrow values-fulfillment gap* ("heart"). And instead of tossing and turning for hour after hour with accompanying *negative emotions*, he experienced *positive emotions* resulting from his ability to fall asleep with very little or no tossing and turning ("heart" and "hand"). This ritual has in turn helped Phillips to develop another *evolutionary ritual*: learning to become fully rested with no more than six hours of sleep. For he has discovered that he is more rested than previously, most likely as a result of his technique of falling asleep. In this way he is able to get in several hours of writing every morning, which is yet a third *evolutionary ritual*. What helps to make these latter two rituals evolutionary rather than bureaucratic is that they help him to continue to raise his aspiration or value pointing toward writing books about individual evolution like this one because he is learning to fulfill that value and thus continue with a *narrow values-fulfillment gap*. If he had raised that aspiration without being able to fulfill it, that would illustrate a *bureaucratic ritual*.

While Bardach's and Phillips's experiences illustrate *evolutionary rituals* based on the solitary positive actions of individuals, we can turn to the writings of Karl Marx for an example of *bureaucratic rituals* based largely on the *negative interactions* among individuals. It was in his early work in the 1840s that Marx focused on the problems experienced by the individual worker in Europe at that early stage of the industrial revolution. In particular, he was much concerned with the worker's experience of "alienation" or isolation within a work setting that emphasized persistent hierarchical or stratified relationships between factory owners and workers, such as what existed on assembly lines.

Here is an excerpt from Marx's essay on alienation:

> We have now considered the act of alienation of practical human activity, labour, from two aspects: (1) the relationship of the worker to the product of labour as an alien object which dominates him. . .(2) the relationship of labour to the act of production within labour. This is the relationship of the worker to his own activity as something alien and not belonging to him. . . .This is self-alienation as against the above - mentioned alienation of the thing. . . .Since alienated labour: (1) alienates nature from man; and (2) alienates man from himself, from his own active function, his life activity; so it alienates him from (3) the species. . . .For labour, life activity, productive life, now appear to man only as means for the satisfaction of a need, the need to maintain his physical existence. . .free, conscious activity is the species-character of human beings. (4) A direct consequence of the alienation of man from the product of his labour, from his life activity and from his species-life, is that man is alienated from other men. (Marx, Early Writings, 1844/1964: 125–127, 129)

Now, more than a century and a half after Marx wrote these words, we have gained perspective on his contributions to our understanding of human behavior along with his limitations. His broad focus on physical, biological, social and personality structures is a lesson for modern social scientists, who have become quite specialized with limited communication across specialized areas. If we are indeed to probe the nature of rituals with their inclusion of elements of "head," "heart" and "hand," then such a broad orientation is essential. Marx's focus on alienation strikes at the very heart of the idea of a *bureaucratic worldview*, which centers on the isolation of phenomena. His description of patterns of physical, biological, social and personality alienation indicate that all of these types of alienation embody that worldview. Contemporary social science has taught us that these patterns are by no means limited to the situation of the worker, for they extend to the rest of us as well, given the range and power of our *bureaucratic worldview*.

We might note the importance of patterns of persisting hierarchy or stratification that accompany this phenomenon of alienation, granting that this is implied rather than directly stated in the quoted passage. For example, the worker struggles "to maintain his physical existence" by working for wages given to him by the owners of the means of production rather than "to engage in free, conscious activity." Further, following Marx, those owners organize the work situation so as to emphasize their profits, and thus make it difficult for the worker to relate to other workers. Modern social science has supported this analysis by the early Marx with reference to the power of stratification and the existence of alienation in the workplace, applying these ideas to society as a whole. Indeed, "alienation" is one of the few concepts developed by social scientists that has come into general usage. At the same time, modern social science generally has found severe limitations to much that Marx wrote in his later work, such as the idea that a violent revolution is essential to take power away from owners and place that power in the hands of workers. There is also the view that, despite Marx's intellectual breadth, he was dogmatic about the truth of his ideas rather than the follower of a scientific method that is open to new evidence that might contradict one's ideas.

Carrying forward the implications of the idea of stratification for our understanding of rituals, this *bureaucratic ritual* is absolutely central to our *bureaucratic way of life*. We should understand that it involves persisting *negative actions* and not just a *negative action* in this situation or that one, for that is the structural nature of stratification. By contrast, an *evolutionary ritual* develops as the result of persisting *positive actions* in one scene after another. To illustrate, Mills's encounter with President Eisenhower illustrated a *negative interaction*, given its link to *negative emotions* and, more generally, a *bureaucratic worldview*. That *negative interaction* was never repeated, and thus it never became a *bureaucratic ritual*. By contrast, Eisenhower's relationships with the members of his cabinet illustrate patterns of stratification, for they involved hierarchal interactions that were repeated over and over again in a variety of situations. They were *negative interactions* only to the extent that the emphasized one-way interaction exemplifying hierarchy. But to the extent that they were genuinely two-way interactions that implied fundamental equality—despite Eisenhower's superior authority—then they were *positive interactions* that pointed toward the development over time of *evolutionary rituals*.

The one way to move from *bureaucratic rituals* toward *evolutionary rituals* is to change the way in which we relate to others so that we become more and more visible as unique individuals both to them and to ourselves. This goes along with the "head" concept of the extraordinary language that calls for *inward-outward perception and thought*, by contrast with *outward perception and thought*. And it also goes along with the "heart" concept of *emotional expression* by contrast with *emotional repression*. We now put forward the concept of deep dialogue in order to embody both of these evolutionary ideas, that is *inward-outward perception and thought* as well as *emotional expression*. Thus, deep dialogue is another example of an *evolutionary ritual*, one that is based on interactions repeated in one scene after another that embodies those evolutionary orientations to "head" and "heart."

To explain more fully the nature of deep dialogue by contrast with our ordinary conversations or professional communication, we might contrast such a continuing conversation or dialogue with "straw-man" dialogue. Within deep dialogue we listen so closely to a partner in conversation that we learn to extend the thrust of his or her ideas, even if only to provide an additional illustration, thus carrying them even further than the initial statement of them. By so doing, we make it easier to learn from them, seeing how they differ from our own hidden assumptions or worldview. We then attempt to either change our own assumptions or reinforce them, depending on what we have learned from the exchange, and we then communicate the result of our analysis. This approach is quite the opposite of setting up another's argument as a "straw man," where we stereotype it negatively and thus weaken it so that we can easily refute it and have no need to examine our own assumptions and question them.

We see deep dialogue as rare either in the academic world or in our personal lives. And we see straw man, by contrast, as our general pattern of discourse, where we remain unable to genuinely listen to another's ideas when they contradict some of our own hidden assumptions. An approach to deep dialogue, by contrast, suggests the reflexive approach that Gouldner called for, since one can learn to use dialogue as a basis for uncovering one's own hidden assumptions. Unless this is accomplished, one remains a victim of those assumptions, protecting them at all costs instead of learning their nature. Yet given the universality of our *bureaucratic worldview*, taking Gouldner's advice is most difficult

This difficulty is exemplified by examples of social interaction in the above material which illustrate our lack of deep dialogue. From the introduction we have Millay's lines about "a meteoric shower of facts" that "lie unquestioned, uncombined," implying the lack of communication throughout society. We might recall from chapter 1 the Flatland figures who refused to take seriously the square's idea of the existence of a third dimension. There was also the neighbor that Robert Frost described in his poem, who was almost completely uncommunicative and who claimed, "Good fences make good neighbors." From Yeats's poem in chapter 2 we have "the falcon cannot hear the falconer," a metaphor for the failure of people to communicate effectively with one another. Also in that chapter the emphasis on value neutrality throughout the academic world indicates a failure to achieve deep dialogue, for that requires "heart" no less than "head" and "hand." In chapter 3 we have Prince Ashargin—from VanVogt's novel—whose treatment at the hands of Enro the Red was quite the opposite of deep dialogue. And from chapter 4 we have Hitler's speech illustrating his one-way communication with the German people.

Ours is indeed a highly critical view of people's general patterns of interacting with one another, for we see ourselves generally as failing to listen to others, stereotyping the ideas of others so that we can more easily parade our own ideas, and not learning from others as a result, thus moving up on our see-saw. We also see ourselves as generally afraid to challenge ideas that we don't believe in because we feel too inadequate to sustain any such controversy. Yet such behavior is exactly what we should expect if we accept the ideas that *emotional repression* versus *emotional expression* is basic to our present *bureaucratic way of life*. Why should we pay serious attention to the ideas of others if we feel either superior to them or inferior to them, by contrast with feeling equal to them, following the patterns of stratification tied to our *bureaucratic worldview*? And if our global values have been distorted to favor work-related values such as material comfort at the expense of our humanistic or people-oriented values, then what room is left for relationships that don't add to our pot of gold?

Let us now examine the possibility that more and more of us can learn to move away from our patterns of *negative interaction* along with *emotional repression, negative emotions* and straw-man behavior, And let us also think of the possibility that we can learn to move toward deep dialogue not just with one or two friends but with more and more of our relationships throughout the various institutions of society: our educational, scientific, political, economic, religious and family institutions. By so doing, we would be moving toward a vision of "deep democracy," which extends our present idea of democracy—limited to periodically voting in elections—to the idea of continuing personal involvement in more and more of the affairs that affect our well-being. Whatever this concept of deep democracy proves to be, it is by no means limited to the idea of political democracy. For political democracy does not eliminate our patterns of stratification that include racism, sexism, ageism, homophobia, classism and ethnocentrism. Neither does political democracy yield a world without wars that might well eliminate any future for the human race, for we might recall that Hitler was elected by a democratic process. The idea of deep democracy has to do not just with the political institution but rather with the full range of our institutions.

Jane Addams' vision, as stated in her 1902 book, *Democracy and Social Ethics* (1902/2004), advances these ideas: "The cure for the ills of Democracy is more Democracy. . . . A conception of Democracy not merely as a sentiment which desires the well-being of all men ("heart"), nor yet as a creed which believes in the essential dignity and equality of all men ("head"), but as that which affords a rule of living as well as a test of faith" ("hand"). Just as we have defined "deep dialogue" so as to include inward-outward perception and thought as well as emotional expression, so does Addams see the development of democracy as requiring "head" and "heart" no less than "hand." But we would add that such a requirement requires in turn movement from a *bureaucratic way of life* toward an *evolutionary way of life*. For the former, following our bureaucratic worldview, separates "head," "heart" and "hand."

Yet it is far too easy to get caught up in the optimism linked to human possibilities while failing to address the realism that we require if indeed we are to move toward those possibilities. That is like a pattern of *emotional repression* that fails to confront the reality of the *wide values-fulfillment gap* tied to our *bureaucratic worldview*. It is also like not swinging our pendulum far enough to the right so that we can gain the momentum or motivation for a swing far to the left where we become aware of and committed to making progress on our deepest problems. However, let us take heart from our analysis of human possibilities so that we can indeed swing our pendulum very far to the right and gain the momentum or motivation we require to swing it very far to the left. There, instead of continuing to *repress our emotions* with such procedures as the technique of particularization or the falsification of memory—as illustrated by the Springdalers discussed in chapter 1—let us choose to *express them* and confront our deepest problems, focusing in particular on yet another example of rituals.

If we are looking to uncover more evidence of major problems in contemporary society, then a short news story with no author taken from the *Sarasota Herald-Tribune* fills the bill:

> A national study says half of high school students say they have bullied someone in the past year, and nearly half say they have been the victims of bullying. The survey released Tuesday by the Los Angeles-based Josephson Institute of Ethics asked more than 43,000 high school students whether they had been physically abused, teased or taunted

in a way that seriously upset them. Forty-three percent said yes, and 50 percent admitted to being the bully.

The institute's president, Michael Josephson, says the numbers don't surprise him, but he still finds them "alarming." Josephson says 10 percent of students admitted bringing a weapon to school, and 16 percent admitted being drunk at school. He says combined with bullying, that can make for a "toxic cocktail". (Sarasota Herald-Tribune, 2010, 9A)

The facts that half of high school students admit to bullying, almost half admit to having been bullied and a substantial number admit to being drunk at school or bringing a weapon to school are indeed "alarming." This has implications far beyond the widely publicized cases of students who committed suicide after having been bullied or of mass killings in schools by students. For it opens a window on the magnitude of problems in contemporary society that don't make it into the headlines. Not only does it illustrate the scope of the *bureaucratic ritual* or persisting pattern of bullying along with the *negative actions* of drunkenness and carrying concealed weapons. Given the links among the concepts within the extraordinary language of social science, it also indicates the magnitude of support for a *bureaucratic worldview* and a *bureaucratic way of life*.

We might recall here from the introduction to chapter 3 the experience of C. Wright Mills when he was a freshman at Texas A & M. His letter to the student newspaper that protested against the mindless oppression or bullying that freshmen endured at the hands of upperclassmen was met with the accusation that he had a lack of "guts." His response in a second letter defending his own guts in having protested that oppression and implying that the individual accusing him of a lack of guts was himself gutless. We might also recall from Van Vogt's *The Players of Null-A*, presented in chapter 3, Prince Ashargin's experiences of abject humiliation at the hands of Enro the Red, and Gosseyn's ability to strengthen him emotionally while inhabiting his body. Yet Mills's ability to stand up to bullying, and Ashargin's new-found self-assurance are exceptions to what generally occurs. We know little about the long-term psychological impact of bullying on the huge numbers of students who do not commit suicide.

We are convinced that the powerful forces that generate the widespread ritual of bullying are similar to the forces involved in other forms of aggression, such as acts of international terrorism, physical and mental abuse within families, most of criminal behavior, and the *bureaucratic rituals* of racism, classism, ageism, sexism, homophobia and ethnocentrism. They are all linked to the patterns of stratification that are in turn linked to our *bureaucratic worldview* and *bureaucratic way of life* with their rituals of persisting hierarchy as well as isolation versus interaction. Of course, other factors are involved as well within any instance of aggression—given the complexity of human behavior—yet patterns of persisting hierarchy or stratification that are found within almost any group remain fundamental.

Thus far in this book our understanding of fundamental problems within contemporary society has been gained as a result of observations, such as the above survey of high school students or the ideas of C. Wright Mills and A. E. Van Vogt. Yet let us recall just how much we were able to learn from the Milgram experiment, where a situation that could yield insight into human behavior was deliberately constructed and the impact of that situation was then carefully measured. Another experiment can help us to gain further insight into our many rituals. This one, in common with the Milgram experiment, probably could not be repeated because of new standards protecting the welfare of experimental subjects.

Jack Levin, a doctoral student at Boston University whose dissertation was directed by Phillips, embarked on an experiment that follows this contrast between a bureaucratic or "see-saw" and an evolutionary or "stairway" view of the world. What Levin accomplished was nothing less than a rigorous experiment that succeeded in measuring (1) the degree to which one is oriented to a *bureaucratic or evolutionary worldview*, or an aspect of "head." In addition, he created (2) a situation that yielded a considerable degree of emotional frustration within his experimental subjects, an aspect of "heart," a situation that most likely could not be repeated today. Also, he measured (3) the impact of (1) and (2) on one's prejudice against minority groups, and he also obtained observational information from his subjects. Levin was not just interested in the causes of prejudice: his broader interest was in the causes of aggression, for he saw prejudice as foreshadowing the ritual of discrimination against minority groups along with other aggressive rituals or *negative interactions*. Although he was not able to measure such *bureaucratic rituals* directly, he saw his measures as indirect measures of them.

Levin launched his experiment during the fall semester of 1965 ("The Influence of Social Frame of Reference for Goal Fulfillment on Social Aggression," Ph.D. Dissertation, Boston University, 1968; see also Bernard Phillips and Louis C. Johnston, *The Invisible Crisis of Contemporary Society*, 2007: 70-77). His subjects were 180 freshmen and sophomores enrolled in two sections of introductory sociology at Boston University. As for "head," Levin developed a questionnaire he used within the experiment with the aim of determining whether students were "relative evaluators" who generally compared themselves with others or "self evaluators" who generally compared their performances with their own previous performances. He did not at the time have in mind our own contrast between a *bureaucratic worldview* and an *evolutionary worldview*, yet his concepts suggest the very same contrast. For a *bureaucratic worldview* is closely linked to *outward perception and thought*, and an *evolutionary worldview* is linked to *inward-outward perception and thought*.

We assume, then, that Levin's "relative evaluators" were oriented to *outward perception and thought* with its link to a *bureaucratic worldview*. And we also assume that Levin's "self evaluators" were oriented to *inward-outward perception and thought*, for their inward orientation was balanced by the outward orientation that we all experience as a result of our *bureaucratic way of life*. Given these assumptions, we shall refer to Levin's "relative evaluators" as students with a *bureaucratic worldview*, and we shall refer to Levin's "self evaluators" as students with less of a *bureaucratic worldview* or at least the beginnings of an *evolutionary worldview*.

As for Levin's setting up a frustrating emotional situation with respect to "heart," students were led to believe that they were taking an aptitude test for graduate school. Actually, it was a phony test, for no student was able to complete more than 100 of the 150 items and thus no one received a passing score. Students were also given this note in their test booklets: "In similar groups of undergraduates at Boston College and Syracuse University, the average student was able to correctly complete 143 of the 150 items." With respect to "hand," Levin measured the students' degree of prejudice against Puerto Ricans both before the frustrating bogus aptitude test and immediately afterward. By so doing he created a classic before-after experiment designed to assess the impact of a very frustrating experimental situation on two groups of students: those more oriented to a *bureaucratic worldview* and those more oriented to an *evolutionary worldview*. When students were queried after the experiment was over, they stated that they had no idea that they were involved in an experiment.

What Levin achieved was the construction of a microcosm of contemporary society so that the results of his experiment might be generalized to behavior in society as a whole, granting the need for corroboration from other studies. For Levin's relative evaluators correspond to the rest of us with our orientation to *outward perception and thought*, by contrast with his self evaluators who illustrate the beginnings of an alternative worldview to what we presently have. The substantial emotional frustration he created corresponds to the *wide values-fulfillment gap* that we are all experiencing, largely as a result of our *bureaucratic worldview*. And the students' prejudice against Puerto Ricans that Levin assessed with their implications for aggressive behavior corresponds to the *bureaucratic rituals* that are found among the rest of us.

The results of the experiment strongly supported the importance of the individual's worldview as a crucial factor in the genesis of prejudice. It was the relative evaluators oriented to a *bureaucratic worldview*—rather than the self evaluators oriented to an *evolutionary worldview*—who increased their degree of prejudice against Puerto Ricans following their frustrating experience. They appear to have placed themselves, metaphorically, on a see-saw with Puerto Ricans occupying the other end of that see-saw. By putting down Puerto Ricans they were able to raise themselves up to some degree. By contrast, students closer to an *evolutionary worldview* might have seen themselves on a stairway with wide steps, where putting down Puerto Ricans would do no more than delay their own learning to climb further.

Levin anticipated the potential implications of his experiment for understanding not just prejudice but also the general phenomenon of aggression, as illustrated by the urban riots of the late 1960s. To flesh out the implications of his findings, he included a questionnaire that assessed a wide range of the beliefs of his experimental subjects. Here are several statements that shed further light on the students' orientation to *bureaucratic rituals* involving *negative interaction*, and not just to patterns of prejudice that suggest an orientation to *bureaucratic rituals*.

> Obedience and respect for authority are the most important virtues children should learn.
> Sex crimes, such as rape and attacks on children, deserve more than mere imprisonment: such criminals ought to be publicly whipped, or worse.
> Most of our social problems would be solved if we could somehow get rid of the immoral, crooked and feeble-minded people.

Just as Levin had predicted, it was the relative evaluators with their bureaucratic orientation who agreed with these statements significantly more than the self evaluators with their more evolutionary orientation. Here, then, we have further evidence for the widespread aggression that we see throughout contemporary societies. For the combination of our *bureaucratic worldview* and the frustration linked to our *wide and widening values-fulfillment gap* has been much of the basis for the aggressive behavior that we see illustrated among our many *bureaucratic rituals* with their emphasis on persisting hierarchies among individuals or social stratification. Yet Levin's experiment also gives us concrete evidence that we need not remain doomed to this situation. For we can learn to move from our *bureaucratic way of life* with its aggressive behavior toward an *evolutionary way of life*. It is indeed possible for us to move from a see-saw world toward a stairway world.

AN EVOLUTIONARY VERSUS A BUREAUCRATIC WAY OF LIFE: STRUCTURES

In this final section of chapter 5 on our general way of life, our focus changes from "hand"—with its emphasis on action, interaction and rituals—to an effort to pull together the ideas about "head," "heart" and "hand" developed in chapters 3, 4 and 5.

"Man on Wire" is a documentary film about Philippe Petit's walk on a one-inch wide braided steel wire 110 stories high, stretched between the

Twin Towers of the World Trade Center early in the morning of August 7, 1974. The title of the film comes from the police report, for Petit was arrested but later released. He had a fifty-pound balancing pole with no safety devices, and he managed his death-defying stroll amid tricky breezes. As the crowd below gazed upward, they saw the tiny speck that was Petit, yet a speck that had somehow managed to stride confidently above New York's tallest buildings.

Just as Petit dangled between disaster and a life-affirming feat, we believe that at this time in history we are all on a wire stretched between the end of our fourteen-billion year journey and a new beginning for the human race. Pettit performed at a time when the nation had endured long years of war in Vietnam, a break-in at the Watergate Hotel, and the day before Richard Nixon resigned. At the present time we are experiencing a variety of new and highly threatening problems, as was dramatically and horrifically illustrated by the fall of the Twin Towers on 9/11, 2001. There is the threat of nuclear proliferation, a Great Recession throughout the world, threats from terrorists with weapons of mass destruction, global warming with its potential for massive climate change along with environmental destruction and possibilities for engineered airborne viruses that even a single individual might use in the future to wipe out the entire human race. It is, then, humanity that is walking on a wire at this time in history.

Yet Petit's ability "To Reach the Clouds"—the title of his book that was the basis for the film—suggests the kind of optimism that is now quite rare, given all the news about massive problems with little in the way of solutions. Are we the limited creatures that we have been taught to think that we are? Or are we, like Petit, creatures with capacities that he illustrated? Can we somehow learn to penetrate far more deeply than our present insights into the causes of our personal, national and world problems? Is each one of us far more significant than the world's tallest buildings—indeed, more significant than the entire non-living physical universe—given that it is the individual human being who stands atop fourteen billion years of evolution? Must that long evolutionary journey come to an end because of our present inability to confront our escalating problems effectively, or can we somehow learn how to solve those problems? Do we humans have the potential to reach the clouds and even to move far beyond them? Has our evolutionary journey no more than just begun?

Abraham H. Maslow, an American psychologist who pioneered an emphasis on positive mental health among psychologists, founded the field of humanistic psychology and developed his ideas most fully in his *The Further Reaches of Human Nature* (1971). Given our own orientation to the evolution of the individual and society, we can learn from Maslow's efforts.

Maslow developed the idea that we human beings are confronted with a hierarchy or pyramid of needs. At the bottom of the pyramid are our biological needs, such as for food, water and sex. The second level has to do with needs for safety, such as for security, order and stability. The third level points to needs for love and belonging. At the fourth level we have needs for self-esteem, having to do with our accomplishments. The fifth level moves into the pinnacle of human needs, namely, the need for "self actualization." This includes such things as the need to know and understand self and world, aesthetic needs for symmetry, order and beauty, and the need for transcendence, as illustrated by helping others fulfill their own potential.

Instead of working with people who had mental problems, Maslow studied individuals whom he believed had achieved self-actualization, such as the anthropologist Ruth Benedict and the psychologist Max Wertheimer. He believed that all of us have "peak experiences," such as feeling—within a given situation—that we have somehow achieved incredible emotional development. Maslow believed that those peak experiences occur most frequently in individuals who have achieved self-actualization. Such individuals had developed healthy relationships with a few friends, but they also felt comfortable when they were alone. One historical figure whom he admired was Lao Tzu, the founder of Taoism, who believed that a materialistic way of life is most limited.

Maslow's work points to the same problem that is our own focus: the problem of human development or evolution. Very few social scientists look up from their narrow specialized fields and attempt to look toward human possibilities, and Maslow is among those few. We have learned from the nature of the scientific method that a focus on awareness of and commitment to solving a problem is absolutely essential in order to make progress on that problem. Following the pendulum metaphor, a swing far to the left creates the momentum or motivation for a swing far to the right. Maslow's view that we all have "peak experiences"—and that those experiences occur more frequently in more highly developed individuals—meshes with our own emphasis on the importance of both situations and structures. For we see movement from a *bureaucratic way of life* toward an *evolutionary way of life* as requiring evolutionary behavior in one situation after another after another in order to develop evolutionary structures. And we see such evolutionary behavior as similar to a peak experience.

Yet Maslow has failed to stand on the shoulders of the giants of the social sciences, neglecting attention to their basic findings in favor of his own pet concepts like "self-actualization." For example, he writes about a hierarchy of human "needs" yet fails to pay attention to what anthropologists and sociologists have discovered about the centrality of cultural "values" in societies throughout the world. It is indeed useful for him to study the experiences of people whom he believed had experienced "self-actualization," as illustrated by their many peak experiences. But that focus neglects the opportunity to conceive of human possibilities stretching far beyond those individuals, so as to include the rest of us. Following our own emphasis on the importance of structures as well as situations, what about the possibility of all of us learning to develop peak experiences not just more often, but learning to develop them in one situation after another after another? That would yield a structure of peak experiences—or, analogously, evolutionary behavior—in one situation after another after another among people in general.

Another individual whose work can help us gain insight into how to move in an evolutionary direction is Gishin Funakoshi, the founder of karate. Japan's transition from a feudal to a modern society began in the nineteenth century after Japan was opened up to the influences of the West. This led to the banning of the weapons that the Samurai or warrior class were able to carry. Funakoshi invented the weaponless martial art of modern karate on the island of Okinawa at the beginning of the twentieth century. In 1922 he was invited to Tokyo to demonstrate this new martial art. While there, Funakoshi was deeply influenced by Zen Buddhism. As a result, he developed the spiritual and humanistic aspects of karate, which means "empty hand," for hands must bear no weapons. He came to call his invention Karate-do—"the Way of the Empty Hand."

Funakoshi developed twenty principles of karate-do that were later recorded, along with commentary, in a book co-authored by a contemporary student of karate. *The Twenty Guiding Principles of Karate* (Funakoshi and Genwa Nakasone, 2003) can serve as another allegory for our own efforts to move toward an *evolutionary way of life*. Funakoshi's immersion within Zen Buddhism can help us Westerners to pay more attention to the East-West strategy, a strategy that we can use to apply the scientific method to our own everyday lives, taking into account our situation at this time in history. Also, this allegory is much concerned with human emotions, granting that "head" and "hand" are involved as well. We have selected seven of Funakoshi's principles, retaining their original numbering, as most appropriate for this book:

1. Do not forget that Karate-do begins and ends with Rei. . . . Rei is often defined as "respect," but it actually means much more. Rei encompasses both an attitude of respect for others and a sense of self-esteem. When those who honor themselves transfer that feeling of esteem—that is, respect—to others, their action is nothing less than an expression of rei.

3. Karate stands on the side of justice. . . . Human beings are at their strongest when they believe they are right. The strength that comes from the confidence of someone who knows he or she is right is expressed by the saying, "When I examine myself and see that I am in the right, then whether I am faced by one thousand or ten thousand

opponents, I must press onward." To avoid action when justice is at stake demonstrates a lack of courage.

4. First know yourself, then know others. . . . Karate practitioners must be completely aware of their own strengths and weaknesses, and never become dazzled or blinded by conceit or overconfidence. Then they will be able to assess calmly and carefully the strengths and weaknesses of their adversaries, and create an ideal strategy.

9. Karate is a lifelong pursuit. There is no single point that marks the completion of karate training; there is always a higher level. For this reason practitioners should continue training throughout their life. . . .Walking this endless road, becoming better today than yesterday, and then better tomorrow than today—throughout one's life—is a true image of the Way of Karate.

10. Apply the way of karate to all things. Therein lies its beauty. One blow or one kick, given or taken, can mean life or death. This concept forms the soul of karate-do. If all aspects of life are approached with this spirit of seriousness, all manner of challenges and hardships can be overcome.

11. Karate is like boiling water: without heat, it returns to its tepid state. In all our studies, continuous concentration and diligence are the hallmark of success. It is meaningless to begin the study of karate-do as if you were stopping by a roadside stand for a refreshment on your way home. A random sampling of karate, or random practice, will not suffice..

20. Be constantly mindful, diligent, and resourceful in your pursuit of the way. Conceit or laziness are chains that impede our advancement. Karate practitioners must constantly examine and chide themselves. . .until they can penetrate the innermost levels of karate-do. This must be the attitude of all who aspire to the Way. (19-20, 29-30, 33-34, 49-50, 57, 59, 63, 67-68, 114)

Funakoshi's emphasis on the importance of tying a martial art emphasizing action and interaction ("hand") together with fundamental beliefs ("head") and values ("heart") associated with Zen Buddhism parallels our own emphasis on the importance of linking "head," "heart" and "hand." For action can no more be separated from thinking and feeling while still proving to be effective than our hands can be cud off from our heads, and our heads from our hearts, while we still are able to survive as human beings.

Principles one and eleven focus on "heart." As for one, showing sincere respect for others as well as oneself emphasizes people-oriented values like "equality" and "individual personality." And eleven with its idea that "Karate is like boiling water" stresses the importance of the heat of passion or deep motivation that is essential for any successful effort. These principles are similar to the emphasis within an *evolutionary world-*

view on *emotional expression, positive emotions* and a *narrow values-fulfill-ment gap.*

As for "head," principle three suggests the importance not just of doing the right thing by working toward *narrowing one's values-fulfillment gap*, especially with respect to people-oriented values. In addition, it is crucial that we gain awareness of that "heart" orientation, giving our-selves the credit that we deserve. Such awareness is encouraged by prin-ciple four with its reflexive orientation, an orientation much the same as the emphasis within an *evolutionary worldview* on *inward-outward percep-tion and thought.* By so doing, one strengthens one's self-image, thus mov-ing toward developing a key evolutionary structure.

With respect to "hand," principles nine and ten apply here. The very idea of evolution is that it is not static but rather is a continuing process, following principle nine's idea that Karate is a lifelong pursuit. The hu-man being can continue to learn with respect to "head," "heart" and "hand" throughout life. Principle ten emphasizes the breadth of Funako-shi's Zen approach to karate, for he sees it applying to the full range of one's experiences in life, paralleling our own evolutionary orientation to the full breadth of "head," "heart" and "hand."

Funakoshi's twentieth principle appears to invoke all three funda-mental elements of human behavior, "head," "heart" and "hand," in its orientation to an evolutionary process. Continuing mindfulness is a "head" orientation; diligence suggests the importance of "hand"; and resourcefulness suggests applying the full range of one's values within any given situation. It is in this twentieth principle that Funakoshi centers on the importance of structures and not just situational behavior. For example, the individual should be "constantly" mindful, and one must "constantly" chide oneself, thus indicating the importance of a continu-ing sense of problem as one goes about living.

The close fit between Funakoshi's principles and our own evolution-ary orientation is most understandable, given our realization that Bud-dhism—by contrast with Western ideas and practices in general—is oriented to self-development. We should remember the West's outward orientation and the East's inward orientation. In our view, our East-West strategy makes use of the best of both worlds. For the East helps us to center on our own realistic situation, and the West teaches us the idea of continuing progress. Such progress need not be limited to external phe-nomena, for that yields a materialistic way of life. Instead, we can learn to combine fulfillment of our work-related values with the fulfillment of our people-oriented values.

In reviewing chapters 3, 4 and 5, we have an image of a plane floating above our heads where we see embedded in that plane the extraordinary language of social science together with two-way arrows connecting all those concepts in an interactive way. And we also have an image of the thousands of our ordinary concepts in the space below that plane that reaches down to ourselves, thus forming a three-dimensional cube. As we move toward an *evolutionary worldview* we learn to link those very general extraordinary-language concepts on the plane to more and more of our everyday concepts with vertical two-way interactive arrows. By so doing we learn to move away from our shattered selves with our *outward perception and thought,* our *emotional repression,* and our *negative actions* and interactions. And we learn to move toward fully integrated selves.

We can also see this three-dimensional cube moving into time as a fourth dimension, moving out of Spaceland and into Timeland. For we have as yet no more than scratched the surface of understanding our past and opening up to our potentials for the future. Whatever else that extraordinary language is, it is our most powerful tool for solving problems. Integrating our language would indeed be a wonderful accomplishment, but we must also learn to put our tool of language to work on more and more of our situations in everyday life. We must learn to apply our extremely broad language—with our extraordinary language integrating our everyday language—to understanding more and more of our past and shaping more and more of our situations in the present so as to open up possible futures that are worthy of ourselves as infinite creatures.

Once we begin to understand our incredible potential for continuing personal evolution, more and more of our everyday situations can become problematic for us, by contrast with our present experiences of generally going through the motions of conforming over and over again to a static way of life. Our belief that such a way of life not only destroys our possibilities—just like the *bureaucratic rituals* pursued by Bardach's fellow prisoners in the Gulag—but also points toward the end of our species, can motivate us learn to evolve in more and more situations. For that integrated language—organized with the aid of our broad scientific method—can enable us to answer the question: exactly how am I evolving in this momentary situation? And our ability to come up with answers in more and more scenes can yield, following Maslow, more and more "peak experiences," leading to nothing less than the structures that make up an *evolutionary way of life.*

As we move from part II with its focus on individual evolution to part III with its focus on the evolution of society, we will not abandon our movement toward personal evolution, for the two kinds of evolution interact with one another just as the universe itself as well as biological evolution are interactive phenomena. For the unsolved and increasing problems of the world affect all of us negatively, and efforts on our part that make any progress whatsoever on those problems will help to *narrow our values-fulfillment gap* and point toward our own personal evolution.

Our approach to world problems is one of realistic optimism. We fully recognize the depth of present-day problems as they are discussed throughout the media. But beyond those discussions, we are also aware of enormous invisible problems that are particularly threatening because of their invisibility, such as our *widening values-fulfillment gap* or what Buddhism has labeled dukkha. Yet just as we can learn to see every situation as problematic, given its pointing in a bureaucratic direction, so can we learn to see our humongous problems in the same way. And by so doing—with the aid of optimism stemming from our broad approach to the scientific method—we can learn to make progress on such humongous problems no less than small problems. As we proceed to part III we will be learning to fill out an image of an evolutionary future not just for ourselves and not just for a single society but for the world as a whole. What kind of a future will that be? We believe that it will be the kind of future that helps all of us continue to evolve with no limit whatsoever, or else it will be no future at all.

III

Tactics: Societal Evolution—Groups, Institutions and Society

Back in chapter 1 we quoted John Dewey, who stated that "the supreme test of all political institutions and industrial arrangements shall be the contribution they make to the all-around growth of every member of society." This eminent American philosopher and educator envisioned a society encouraging the development of every member of society "into the full stature of his possibility." We are carrying Dewey's vision a step further by conceiving of the possibility that we all can continue to evolve, with no limit as to how far we might go.

It is exactly this optimism—which many would see as an unrealistic or utopian vision—that can become the basis for our actually learning to move toward personal evolution with the aid of a broad scientific method that we use in everyday life. Just like the scientific method within the physical and biological sciences, a scientific method that makes use of social science knowledge requires the extraordinary language of social science, that is, technical concepts that carry along with them the weight of what social scientists have discovered. We have presented and illustrated the key concepts from the extraordinary or technical language of the social sciences that center on the evolution of the individual in the foregoing pages. With the aid of those concepts we are now in a position to swing our pendulum of the scientific method in ever-widening arcs. We can move toward awareness of and commitment to a problem on the left, and we can then make use of the momentum or motivation linked to that swing to swing that pendulum far to the right where we make progress on the problem.

Yet this optimism about our incredible possibilities that we so desperately need at this time in history when escalating problems in the world threaten the very survival of the human race is an extremely rare commodity. John Dewey had a fair degree of optimism, and so did C. Wright Mills and Alvin Gouldner, and we might include Plato, Fred Polak, Jane Addams, Philippe Petit and Abraham Maslow. Let us recall in particular the imagination expressed by Mills in his *The Sociological Imagination*, a

vision that we have attempted to carry forward with our own development of the Sociological Imagination Group. But optimism must be accompanied by the kind of realism that can in fact yield movement that
narrows the gap between aspirations and fulfillment, yet it is that very
values-fulfillment gap that continues to widen in contemporary societies. It is
a gap that we see tied closely to our *bureaucratic worldview* and *bureaucratic way of life*. And none of those historical figures have given us the scientific tools that we require to narrow that gap and thus develop the optimism that we so desperately need to move toward our own evolution
and the evolution of society.

To claim that our gap is widening and our optimism is moving toward pessimism is a vague statement, even granting that "substantial
evidence" exists for the hypothesis that "the gap between aspirations and
their fulfillment is in fact increasing in contemporary society" (Phillips
and Johnston, 2007: 234-235), as quoted in chapter 1. We have catalogued
throughout the foregoing chapters no more than a small number of concrete examples of occurrences in contemporary society—relative to what
we see as the large number that actually exist—that have provided the
basis for growing pessimism about the future of society. That large number of examples includes recent events in Tunisia, Egypt, Libya and the
Middle East in general that illustrate not only aspirations for a democratic way of life. Those events also illustrate a very *large values-fulfillment
gap,* given our worldwide revolution of rising expectations coupled with
technologies like the internet and Facebook for mass communication.

Within this book we have cited in our introduction the British Astronomer Royal's book, *Our Final Hour.* In chapter 1 we called attention to the
Great Recession of 2008-2009 along with the values-fulfillment gaps emphasized by contemporary Democrats and Republicans. In chapter 2 we
had reference to modern bureaucratic procedures used to extract gold
and other valuables from the teeth and genitals of those "unworthy of
life" in Hitler's death camps. In chapter 4 we quoted from Daniel Goleman's *Emotional Intelligence,* citing "a surging tide of aggression" illustrated by "teens with guns in schools, freeway mishaps ending in shootings,
disgruntled ex-employees massacring former fellow workers." And in
chapter 5 we described Stanley Milgram's studies of conformity that
taught us that two-thirds of ordinary Americans paralleled Hitler's minions with their willingness to administer lethal shocks to an innocent
individual within bogus experiments that they believed had scientific
validity.

We can also flesh out our relative vagueness about the concrete basis
for our growing pessimism by turning to what has been happening within science fiction. We turn to a study of the decline of optimism or utopian thought in modern society, "Utopia and Transcendence" (McQuarie,
1980; see also Phillips, 1985). McQuarie's focus on science fiction is paralleled by our own treatment of works by Abbott, Van Vogt and Vance

along with the original *Star Trek* television series in all but one of the preceding chapters. We see science fiction as particularly imaginative because of its combination of "heart"—given its fictional orientation to metaphorical language—with "head" (its scientific orientation) and "hand" (its stories of adventure). That breadth was illustrated by the original Star Trek's characters of Spock ("head"), McCoy ("heart") and Captain Kirk ("hand").

McQuarie discussed the enormous change from nineteenth-century utopian thought—illustrated by Bellamy's *Looking Backward* and the works of Jules Verne and H. G. Wells—to twentieth-century science fiction. He saw that early optimism as powered by a "century of unprecedented scientific discovery and industrial transformation" which "had irrevocably changed Western European society and brought about a new awareness of physics, astronomy and the other sciences among both writers and the reading public." But as we move into the twentieth century we are confronted with the science-fictional anti-utopia or dystopia, as illustrated by Foster's *The Machine Stops*, Huxley's *Brave New World*, Orwell's *Nineteen Eighty-Four* and Bradbury's *Fahrenheit 451*.

McQuarie analyzed in more detail utopian efforts in the twentieth century. They include technological utopias like Isaac Asimov's *Foundation Trilogy*, militaristic utopias like Tom Godwin's *Space Prison* and feudal utopias like Delany's *Einstein Intersection*. Another example of a technological utopia is the *Star Trek* television series. However, he concludes that there has developed in the twentieth century a fundamental contradiction between the professed ideals among the writers of science fiction for unbridling the human imagination and their actual timidity in conceiving of fundamental changes in society. It is a contradiction, on the one hand, between the ideal of the author's freedom to imagine alternative futures where anything is possible, and on the other hand a capability "only of projecting contemporary reality into a more technologically developed future or romantically longing for a lost, idealized past" (246-247). Let us recall for example our discussion of the *Star Trek* episode "Where No Man Has Gone Before" in the introduction to part II. There we have a vision of quite the opposite of individual evolution, supporting Lord Acton's idea that "absolute power corrupts absolutely."

Yet just as there have been exceptions to the growth of pessimism and limited imagination in the twentieth century—as illustrated by such individuals as Addams, Dewey, Mills, Gouldner, Maslow and Petit—so are there exceptions to the decline of optimism and imagination among science fiction writers. A. E. Van Vogt's *The World of Null-A* and *The Players of Null-A* and Jack Vance's *The Languages of Pao* are most notable illustrations, with both of them emphasizing social science. Indeed, Van Vogt builds on the work of Alfred Korzybski, and Vance builds on the work of two anthropologists, Edward Sapir (1929) and Benjamin Whorf (1963). These exceptions among science-fiction writers as well as others should remind us that the humanistic ideals of modern society—as illustrated by the people-oriented values of equality, freedom, individual personality and democracy—are still alive and well, existing not only in these individuals but also in the rest of us. We see those values as waiting to find homes in societies that have learned how to fulfill them.

As for an explanation of this huge change from optimism and soaring imagination to pessimism along with limited imagination, McQuarie sees a partial understanding in Mark Hillegas's *The Future as Nightmare*. Hillegas refers to a series of twentieth-century events—World War I, the governments of Hitler and Stalin—which have had a discouraging effect on the literary imagination. McQuarie also sees merit in Chad Walsh's *From Utopia to Nightmare* for explaining the twentieth-century writer's disillusionment and passive resignation. Walsh saw that change as a product of the unintended consequences of nineteenth-century progress, such as exploitation, pollution, chauvinism and war. And McQuarie adds to this mix of explanations his own view that "corporate and technocratic domination extends its hold from the economy and polity to every sector of modern intellectual life, creating a cultural wasteland which is incapable of nurturing works of any truly transcendental vision" (249).

We agree with all three of these authors about the causes they cite for the decline in optimism and imagination among science fiction writers—and, we would add, writers in general—as we moved from the nineteenth to the twentieth centuries. Yes, World Wars I and II have indeed had a most discouraging impact. Yes, the continuing industrial and technological revolution has indeed added to that discouragement with its production of unintended consequences like exploitation, pollution and chauvinism. Yes, the bureaucratic stratification within American society with its "corporate and technocratic domination" also discourages the freedom to imagine. But there is also more to the story of what happened between the nineteenth and twentieth century, It is a story that has to do with more invisible phenomena than what those authors have cited, yet those phenomena are nevertheless exceedingly powerful.

Just as we have claimed above, it is our *widening aspirations-fulfillment gap* or values-fulfillment gap—tied closely to our bureaucratic worldview and bureaucratic way of life—that lies behind what these three authors cite. And by linking our own explanation incorporating the extraordinary language of social science with their explanations using our everyday language, we are illustrating a direction for applying the ideas in this book to yielding a deeper understanding of world problems like contemporary pessimism and limits placed on the human imagination. Such linking of the extraordinary and ordinary language also can help each one of us to move in an evolutionary direction, granting that we have much work to do in order to accomplish this for the range of our ideas.

As we continue with tying together these two languages—extraordinary and ordinary—we need no longer continue with our pessimism and narrow view of our possibilities. McQuarie himself struck an optimistic note at the end of his article by claiming that the very act of understanding a problem can release that problem's hold on an individual's mind. Carrying that idea further, the foregoing chapters have suggested that we can indeed develop optimism about the possibilities of the individual to move toward continuing personal evolution. Yet for part III we need to extend that optimism substantially so as to include the evolution of society.

But is such enormous optimism in fact realistic? Absolutely! For if indeed it is possible for any of us to continue on an evolutionary path—and if this can in fact be clearly demonstrated—then there is good reason to believe that such evolution would spread over time to society as a whole. Ralph Waldo Emerson wrote, "If a man write a better book, preach a better sermon, or make a better mouse-trap than his neighbour, tho' he build his house in the woods, the world will make a beaten path to his door." We have discussed the process that might be involved in chapters 2 and 3, where we generalized the work of Thomas Kuhn in his *The Structure of Scientific Revolutions* (1962). Sufficient optimism about human possibilities can free us to develop an evolutionary vision of society as an alternative to our present *bureaucratic worldview*. That vision in turn can free us to swing our pendulum of the scientific method back and forth in ever-widening arcs where we learn to open up to both the fundamental problems blocking that development and also to make progress in actually moving toward that development.

Fred Polak was a Dutch sociologist who surveyed the "images of the future" in the major religions within the history of Western society, and we briefly referred to his work in the introduction to this book. The following excerpt comes at the end of his *The Image of the Future* (1973). He concluded that "the more powerful the image of the future is, the more powerfully it acts in determining the actual future." And he believed that we all bear responsibility for creating optimistic visions of the future. Now, in our era of pessimism, his advice is all the more compelling, granting that we also require the realistic basis for actually moving toward the future that we envision, a basis that we have attempted to develop throughout this book.

> Everyman, look to the harvest! It is the layman's responsibility to be aware of his own aspirations and those of the group to which he belongs. It is for him to choose the vision he will follow and to take responsibility for carrying it out. . . . No man or woman is exempt from taking up the challenge. social scientist, intellectual, artist, leader, middleman of any breed, and the Common Man (and Woman) to whom, after all, this century belongs—each must ask himself, what is my vision of the future? And what am I doing about it? . . . Man has the capacity to dream finer dreams than he has ever succeeded in dreaming. He has the capacity to build a finer society than he has ever suc-

ceeded in building. . . . Here lies the real challenge! There are among us even now dreamers and builders ready to repeat the age-old process of splitting the atom of time, to release the Western world from its too-long imprisonment in the present. Then man will once again be free to "seek the city which is to come." (305)

SIX

From the Learning Individual toward the Learning Group, Institution, and Society

In this sixth and final chapter we center on movement from the evolution of the individual toward the evolution of society. Here we will be taking Polak's advice seriously by developing our own vision of the kind of society that fosters the infinite possibilities of the individual. It is also the kind of society that cannot appear without the development of the individual in an evolutionary direction. That is why we have put forward five chapters on the evolution of the individual prior to this chapter on the evolution of society. This interaction between the individual and society illustrates the interactive nature of the universe itself as well as the interactive nature of biological evolution.

"Personal evolution" is a most general or abstract idea that appears to be very far from our everyday experiences, so we mean to bring it down to earth. Our meaning is much the same as that for the concept of "continued individual learning," and this is the reason for the title that we have given to this chapter. But by "individual learning" we mean more than intellectual or "head" learning: we include emotional or "heart" learning, and we also include learning to act effectively to solve problems, or "hand" learning. Also, by our understanding of the idea of continued individual learning we do not mean simply obtaining more and more advanced degrees in institutions of higher education, for such intellectual learning does not include "heart" or "hand." Indeed, in our view advanced degrees generally focus very narrowly on specialized areas of knowledge, and what we have in mind is the kind of general understanding that we can use to solve a very wide variety of personal and world problems.

For us, continued individual learning involves all seven of the principles we quoted from *The Twenty Guiding Principles of Karate* (Funakoshi and Genwa Nakasone, 2003) at the end of chapter 5. They encompass "head," "heart" and "hand," and thus such learning is broad versus narrow. This is most specifically illustrated by principle ten: "Apply the way of karate to all things." Further, as indicated by principle nine—"Karate is a lifelong pursuit"—one never stops continued learning, just as we might continue to climb a stairway with an infinite number of steps. And principle twenty—"Be constantly mindful, diligent and resourceful in your pursuit of the way"—gets at the importance of both one's situational behavior as well as the structures that one develops, as indicated by the word "constantly," granting the difficulty of developing evolutionary structures.

It is crucial that we recognize that continued individual learning is a continuation of personal evolution as we move toward taking more seriously the evolution of society in this final chapter. We have already considered the nature of the evolution of society when we focused in chapter 1 on the evolution of the physical and biological universe, and also in chapter 2 when we distinguished between a worldview emphasizing isolation and one stressing interaction. In chapter 3 we never abandoned outward perception and thought when we emphasized *inward-outward perception and thought*, and our movement toward an *evolutionary self-image* and an *evolutionary worldview* is essential for tackling the evolution of society. Our movement toward this present focus on the evolution of society required in addition further understanding of "heart" in chapter 4, and our focus on "hand" in chapter 5 included interaction no less than solitary action. And just as we were involved in working toward the evolution of society in the preceding chapters centering on personal evolution, so shall we be involved in working toward personal evolution in this chapter centering on the evolution of society. For the very idea of evolution points to an interactive phenomenon, and it is thus impossible to separate personal evolution from the evolution of society. When our pendulum of the scientific method swings back and forth in widening arcs, it achieves both kinds of evolution or learning at the same time.

In this chapter we start with the idea of moving from our present-day bureaucratic organization of groups toward the development of "learning groups." The key difference between these two kinds of groups—following the distinction between a *bureaucratic worldview* and an *evolutionary worldview*—is the difference between emphasizing isolation in the former and interaction in the latter. What we have in mind is not merely the large multi-national organization but rather all groups, including the family. In our view—shared by students of bureaucracy like Max Weber, as discussed in chapter 1—modern bureaucracies are indeed generally more effective than pre-industrial bureaucracies, given their access to individuals with a more scientific orientation. However, we need not assume, as do most students of bureaucracy, that we cannot develop groups that are more effective than bureaucracies, for it is indeed possible to improve the scientific orientation of the individuals inhabiting bureaucracies. It is in this way that we can move from bureaucratic groups toward "learning groups." Given the importance of the scientific development or personal evolution of group members, the reader might well understand our emphasis in this book on personal evolution prior to tackling the problem of the evolution of society. And the reader might also understand that we have been working toward understanding how society evolves all the while we have been developing chapters on personal evolution.

From society's groups we move toward a vision of society's institutions: scientific, educational, political, economic, religious and family institutions. Once again it is the availability of individuals who have moved toward personal evolution—and thus learning how to use the scientific method in everyday life—that makes all the difference between a bureaucratic and an evolutionary institution. Institutions are set up to solve particular problems. Let us recall the key institutional values linked to the various institutions that we put forward in chapter 4, for those values are in turn tied to problems on which institutions focus. Science centers on achieving "understanding of the world" as well as "solving problems." Education centers on communicating all of that knowledge. The political institution also focuses on "solving problems," with particular attention to the problems of society as a whole. The economic institution is concerned with fulfilling the values of the "material comfort" and "achievement and success" of the individual as well as the "economic progress" of society. Religion is most concerned with "ultimate meaning." And the family centers on "intimate and close relationships" as well as "life versus death." Unfortunately, as evidenced throughout the foregoing chapters with their attention to our *widening values-fulfillment gap,* our institutions are experiencing limited success in solving the problems that they have been set up to solve. Indeed, we are convinced that contemporary societies are facing in this century nothing less than the end of humanity's long journey unless they learn to succeed more fully.

Our third section centers on society as a whole with all of its individuals, groups and institutions. Just as we will continue to focus on increasing threats to the very existence of society, we will be equally oriented to the continuing development or evolution of society. If the individual is a complex entity, then society as a whole is that much more complex. Yet this does not take away from the fact that the individual can change society just as society shapes the individual. It is here that we require the kind of optimism about human possibilities that we have discussed throughout this book and summarized in the introduction to part III. Our vision of an evolutionary or learning society is also a vision of the different elements of society—individuals, groups and institutions—all working together and all pointing toward solving the problems of developing learning individuals, learning groups and learning institutions.

Van Vogt envisioned a "null-A society" on the planet Venus in his *The World of Null-A* and *The Players of Null-A*. We will attempt to carry further his vision with more specific descriptions of how our society could in fact move toward becoming a learning society. Although we do not have to contend with Enro the Red and his minions who were working to destroy Venus, we do have to contend with the anti-evolutionary forces located within ourselves and throughout society as a whole. Given our bureaucratic worldview and our bureaucratic way of life, it is all too easy to repress our fundamental problems and thus achieve—following the Springdalers, as discussed in chapter 1—"some degree of satisfaction, recognition and achievement." Yet we are convinced that in that direction lies the end of our species, "not today or tomorrow, but the day after tomorrow," quoting here from Herman Hesse's novel, *The Glass Bead Game* (1943/1969), to be discussed in the section on institutions.

LEARNING VERSUS BUREAUCRATIC GROUPS: STRUCTURES

It was in the first section of chapter 4 that we described the collaboration in the early 1970s between Phillips and Peter M. Senge—then a graduate student at MIT—on a computer simulation of a change in society that would yield its continuing development or evolution. They discovered, after weeks of failure, the importance of a combination of a situational and a structural emphasis on people's emotional commitment to such evolution, thus emphasizing the role of "heart" in the evolution of society. Of course, given what Phillips has learned since that time, "head" and "hand" are involved as well.

As for Senge's later work, he has focused on the problems within bureaucratic organizations, also seeing those problems as similar to the problems that we all face in our everyday lives. His book *The Fifth Discipline: The Art and Practice of the Learning Organization* (1990) has received wide attention throughout the business community. It begins as follows:

> From a very early age, we are taught to break apart problems, to fragment the world. This apparently makes complex tasks and subjects more manageable, but we pay a hidden, enormous price. We can no longer see the consequences of our actions; we lose our intrinsic sense of connection to a larger whole. When we then try to "see the big picture," we try to reassemble the fragments in our minds, to list and organize all the pieces. But, as physicist David Bohm says, the task is futile—similar to trying to reassemble the fragments of a broken mirror to see a true reflection. Thus, after a while we give up trying to see the whole altogether.

> The tools and ideas presented in this book are for destroying the illusion that the world is created of separate, unrelated forces. When we give up this illusion—we can then build "learning organizations," organizations where people continually expand their capacity to create the results they truly desire, where new and expansive patterns of thinking are nurtured, where collective aspiration is set free, and where people are continually learning how to learn together. (3)

Senge describes here the fundamental difference between a *bureaucratic way of life* and an *evolutionary way of life*: an emphasis on isolation, illustrated by breaking apart a problem, by contrast with the interaction among ideas and people. For example, we see a failure to grasp the importance of this distinction between isolation and interaction in the academic world no less than in the world of business. Within the American Sociological Association there are no less than forty-five distinct sections, with each section centering on some small aspect of human behavior, yet with each section thus failing to "see the big picture." Senge's argument is that this occurs in the business world, and that it is a much worse approach to solving the problems of business than an approach involving the interaction of all individuals throughout an organization.

Senge begins to explain more fully what he means by a "learning organizations" with this statement by Arie De Geus, head of planning for Royal Dutch/Shell:

> As the world becomes more interconnected and business becomes more complex and dynamic, work must become more "learningful." It is no longer sufficient to have one person learning for the organization, a Ford or a Sloan or a Watson. It's just not possible any longer to "figure it out" from the top, and have everyone else following the orders of the "grand strategist." The organizations that will truly excel in the future will be the organizations that discover how to tap people's commitment and capacity to learn at all levels in an organization. (4)

Just as we have argued that all of us should learn to use the scientific method in our everyday lives, so does De Geus argue that "all levels" of an organization must become involved in working toward solving the organization's problems. This approach is similar to the idea of "deep democracy," as discussed in chapter 5, which is not limited to the idea of political democracy but has to do with all institutions, including the economic institution. And it is the individual who must do the learning that is required if this is to be accomplished.

Senge himself focuses on the importance of individual development to achieve the learning organization, just as we have centered in this book on individual evolution to achieve the evolution of society. He states:

> Personal mastery is the discipline of continually clarifying and deepening our personal vision, of focusing our energies, of developing patience, and of seeing reality objectively. As such, it is an essential cor-

nerstone of the learning organization—the learning organization's spiritual foundation. An organization's commitment to and capacity for learning can be no greater than that of its members. The roots of this discipline lie in both Eastern and Western spiritual traditions, and in secular traditions as well. (7)

As he moves through *The Fifth Discipline*, Senge elaborates on the nature of that discipline. In short, it is an orientation to "systems thinking" that emphasizes the interactive and dynamic relationships among all phenomena that affect a given problem. This is indeed a similar approach to the one that we have adopted throughout the foregoing chapters, for we have emphasized an extremely broad approach to the scientific method that encompasses "head," "heart" and "hand," and that moves from the emphasis on isolation of our *bureaucratic worldview* toward an emphasis on interaction within an *evolutionary worldview*.

Let us recall from the first section of chapter 4 Phillips's collaboration with Senge in the early 1970s on a computer simulation of a change from our present bureaucratic society toward an evolutionary society. Our work was based on the development by Jay Forrester and his colleagues at MIT's Sloan School of Management in the 1960s of a computer simulation procedure called "system dynamics." And it is the interactive approach or dynamic systems thinking behind system dynamics that is what Senge has called "the fifth discipline." It is based on analyzing the ways in which all of the phenomena relevant to a given problem interact with one another.

One way to understand the importance of the fifth discipline or systems thinking with its emphasis on interaction is to consider examples of the negative impact of a lack of systems thinking. The sociologist Robert Merton in his article, "The Unanticipated Consequences of Purposive Social Action" (1936), pointed out the disastrous results that many groups have experienced in their "purposive" efforts to solve problems. These were disasters based on a lack of systems thinking. Hilmar S. Raushenbush has provided many illustrations of "unanticipated consequences" resulting from such a lack of systems thinking (1969).

For example, after World War I the allies sought to keep Germany weak by forcing it to accept sole guilt for the war and by collecting large indemnities. But largely as a result—as illustrated by our quotation from *Mein Kampf* in chapter 4—Hitler was able to build up a resentful nationalism, destroy German democratic institutions, and create a powerful war machine. As another example of unanticipated consequences based on a lack of systems thinking, in Roman times the aristocracy sought to acquire wealth by confiscating common lands from villagers. But as a result Roman generals took over the aristocrats' properties in order to pay their soldiers' pensions, which had previously been paid with profits from farming those common lands. As an additional example, Britain attempted to prevent Indian independence by violently suppressing the Gandhian movement. But that violence conflicted with the people-oriented values of the British and Indian peoples, stirring them to give support to the independence movement.

Yet granting the importance of Senge's and De Geus's ideas about the "learning organization," learning at "all levels" in an organization and "systems thinking," just how is an organization to discover "how to tap people's commitment and capacity to learn at all levels"? Despite their ideas and efforts, and despite the similar efforts of some others within the business community, there is certainly no groundswell of movement in this direction.

In the introduction to this chapter we discussed the importance of the scientific orientation of the individuals inhabiting modern bureaucracies—by contrast with pre-industrial bureaucracies—for the greater effectiveness of those contemporary bureaucratic organizations. Yet this requires nothing less than a scientific approach that is broad enough to capture the knowledge throughout the social sciences. Neither Senge nor De Geus—nor other business leaders who have argued in the same vein—have revealed any awareness of the importance of such an extension of a scientific orientation. Of course, they are hardly to be blamed for this failure, since social scientists themselves have failed to integrate their knowledge despite a few exceptions that have at least pointed in this direction. Our argument is, then, for the importance for the individuals within organizations to learn to apply the extraordinary language of the social sciences to the problems that they face not only within the business world but also within their own everyday lives. In other words, our argument throughout chapters 1 through 5 cannot be skipped over by individuals who wish to develop "learning organizations," yet we fully grant the importance of their hitting on the idea of developing such organizations.

However, the forces within our *bureaucratic way of life* that work against a scientific orientation within the business community broad enough to include the social sciences are exceedingly powerful. For example, Susanna Hornig has analyzed television's NOVA—the award-winning PBS documentary science series—with a focus on its presentation of modern science and the scientist (1990). Her analysis is headed "Television's NOVA and the Construction of Scientific Truth." Hornig's investigation includes a detailed analysis of "The Race for the Superconductor," an episode describing the efforts of researchers from Sweden, Japan and the United States to create a compound that will conduct electricity while losing no power to electrical resistance.

"The Race for the Superconductor" begins with a picture of a cube that appears to be dancing in the air, and this picture is repeated at intervals throughout the presentation. A narrator tells us that superconductors will have an "almost magical power," and he later summarizes,

"It would be like the world of Buck Rogers come to life with this super-electricity." And later the audience is told that "airplanes could be flown merely by the pilot's own thoughts," although it is not informed just how this could be accomplished. There are interviews with researchers in Zurich, Tokyo and the United States interspersed with "shots of complex laboratory equipment, chemicals in jars, blackboards complete with equations, and various explanatory models and diagrams, including another periodic chart from which elements appear to take off and fly toward the viewer" (15). We are shown bottles of liquids dripping through complicated arrangements of tubes, although there is little or no explanation of the purposes behind such research.

Scientists are portrayed as a breed apart from lab assistants and ordinary people. They generally appear either in a suit and tie or a laboratory coat, talking in front of blackboards covered with equations and in offices filled with books and piles of papers containing their notes. The episode presents "The Race for the Superconductor" as a competitive race among researchers in Sweden, Japan and the United States, with the suggestion that the stakes are no less than world domination. The enemy appears to be Japan, and if the United States "gets there" first, Japan may still win because of its systematic procedures for developing industrial applications for new knowledge.

Hornig compares "The Race for the Superconductor" with other episodes, such as "The Hidden Power of Plants," and she finds substantial differences in the way different scientists are treated:

> Diagrams and models used in the superconductor show are surrounded by a black background and often accompanied by music that reinforces the suggestion of mystery. Diagrams and models in the medicinal plant show, on the other hand, are superimposed over a pale green leaf, itself surrounded by a light gray background. Several mentions are made in the superconductor episode of publishing or reading journal articles; these activities are not featured in the medicinal plant episode. And although no real attempt is made to explicate the specific activities or functions of the complex laboratory apparatus that appears in the superconductor labs, the activities of ethnobotany are revealed as mundane: gathering and sorting plant materials, crushing them in a mortar and pestle, systematically searching for pharmaceutical effects, examining and cataloging the samples. (19)

Hornig concludes that "hard sciences" like physics are treated with an air of mystery, and the "soft sciences" are treated as involving only mundane activities. She does not even mention the social sciences, since they are almost completely ignored by NOVA in its quest to educate the public on the nature of science. Our own conclusion is that this award-winning series on public television presented an episode illustrating not only the stratification or persisting hierarchy between the United States and Japan, and between physical scientists and biological and social scientists, but also between physical scientists and the lay public. The latter stratification is encouraged by the episode's mystification rather than explanation of the scientific method, with its mumbo-jumbo of dancing cubes, complex laboratory tubes, piles of books and papers, blackboards filled with equations, references to journal articles, superconductors with "almost magical power," and planes that "could be flown merely by the pilot's own thoughts." These patterns of persisting hierarchy themselves illustrate a bureaucratic scientific method deriving from a *bureaucratic worldview* that isolates phenomena and people rather than encourages the interaction fostered by an *evolutionary worldview* and an evolutionary scientific method.

An additional example of this same bureaucratic scientific method — deriving from a bureaucratic worldview — comes from a paper by Phillips, "Paradigmatic Barriers to System Dynamics" (1980). Phillips found that system dynamicists were largely ignorant of relevant literature from the social sciences, as illustrated by the sparcity of references in their key books. For example, of the total of only eleven references Forrester cites in his *World Dynamics* (1971), seven are to himself or his colleagues and three are to someone he is collaborating with in a research project. The most well-known book put out by this group, *The Limits to Growth* (Donella Meadows, et al., 1972), received extensive criticism because of assumptions that were not justified by relevant literatures from the social sciences. Just as in the case of the above analysis of "The Race for the Superconductor" within the NOVA science series, social science knowledge was treated as unimportant by comparison with physical science technologies. This pattern of stratification isolates knowledge and people, following a bureaucratic worldview.

Phillips found this pattern of stratification was also illustrated by the relationship between students of system dynamics and their business clients. On the one hand, their training in system dynamics calls for uncovering and emphasizing feedback relationships or interaction among all phenomena — including long-term behavior — and thus following scientific ideals. Yet their actual relationships with clients generally violated those ideals to some extent, as Phillips suggests:

> The modeler is the producer, and the client is the consumer. . . . Thus, the modeler-client relationship appears to be very largely an open-loop [one-way, or stratified] system. Further, the modeler's concern tends to focus on the short-term modeler-client relationship rather than the client's long-term use of modeling. If the client learns to be dependent on the modeler, and if there are financial costs involved, we might wonder about the client's long-term motivation to use the SD [system dynamics] approach. This would be especially the case if the initial model is only partially effective or is effective for only a short period of time. (1980: 682)

Here, then, is yet another pattern of stratification illustrated by the procedures of system dynamicists. On the one hand, through their ignoring the extraordinary language of social science, their efforts to explain human behavior fail to achieve effective results. Instead, they fall into the trap illustrated by the NOVA science series of a bureaucratic worldview that downgrades the social sciences in favor of the physical sciences, thus failing to achieve the integration of knowledge that is required to explain complex phenomena. On the other hand, their *bureaucratic worldview* is manifested by their stratified relationships with clients in their consulting efforts, failing to help them to learn the tools they need to develop their own models of problems that their organizations encounter. Yet system dynamicists should not be singled out for special criticism, for we see their work as typical of the bureaucratic approach almost universally adopted by business consultants as well as throughout the business community.

However, there is indeed an alternative to this approach, namely, an evolutionary scientific method deriving from an *evolutionary worldview*. Within such an approach there would indeed be a vital home for the key ideas that system dynamicists have developed about moving toward an understanding of complex human problems. What is required first of all is familiarity with the extraordinary language of social science. Just as the technical or extraordinary concepts of physics are essential for landing a man on the moon, so are the technical or extraordinary concepts of social science essential for making progress on our massive social problems. In a second step we need not immediately jump into the technicalities of computer simulations. Rather we could move toward what are called "causal-loop diagrams." These are sophisticated diagrams of relationships among a set of key factors involved in the origins of a given problem, emphasizing the interactions among those factors. They are explained in detail in Nancy Roberts's *Introduction to Computer Simulation: The System Dynamics Approach* (1983). As for actual computer simulations, we can leave that for a third step in the future, following our demonstration of the effectiveness of those diagrams—coupled with the extraordinary language of social science—for helping us to make progress toward understanding complex human situations.

Senge provides us with an illustration of causal-loop diagrams with an extremely simple one focusing on the Cold War between the U.S. and the U.S.S.R. Without charting feedback or interactive relationships within such a diagram, we might think simplistically of U.S. policy as based on the one-way relationships among three factors: (1) the production of nuclear arms in the U.S.S.R., (2) the awareness of this as a threat to Americans, and (3) the development of a need to build U.S. nuclear arms. And we might think of Soviet policy as also based on this same simplistic one-way relationships among three similar factors: (4) the production of nuclear arms in the United States, (5) the awareness of this as a threat to the Soviet Union and (6) the development of a need to build Soviet nuclear arms. Such behavior was illustrated during the Cold War when the United States and the Soviet Union continued to build their stockpiles of nuclear weapons to the point where each country could destroy the other a great many times over. Granting that there was some awareness among governmental officials on both sides that they were moving toward mutual destruction, that was not sufficient to counter their *bureaucratic worldviews* that kept them from learning how to move toward mutual cooperation.

Senge's illustration of a causal-loop diagram is a step toward mutual understanding, and use of the extraordinary language can become yet another step. Instead of two one-way relationships among two sets of three factors, we can combine these six factors into a single causal-loop diagram. In this way, going around a circle, (1) can cause (2), illustrated by an arrow between them, (2) can cause (3), (3) can cause (4), (4) can cause (5), (5) can cause (6), and then (6) can cause (1), thus completing the causal loop which then can continue to yield an escalating arms race. More concretely, by drawing such a loop it becomes clearer that the Soviet production of nuclear weapons threatens American security and causes the American production of such weapons, and that in turn threatens Soviet security and causes the Soviet production of nuclear weapons, and that this cycle of escalation continues indefinitely with no end in sight.

Of course, this causal-loop diagram is a vast oversimplification of what was actually happening during the Cold War, for a great many other factors were involved. For example, the strain on the Soviet economy resulting from the arms race along with failures within that economy were important additional factors that such a simple diagram does not include and that—along with other factors on both sides of the Pacific— eventually succeeded in ending the Cold War. The new START treaty between the United States and the Soviet Union—resulting once again from factors not included in this simplistic causal-loop diagram—points toward its reversal so as to yield ever-fewer nuclear weapons. The diagram still remains useful, even granting its simplicity, in showing how such a reversal can occur. Thus, it can show that the reduction in the production of Russian nuclear weapons causes a reduction of threats to America, and this in turn causes a reduction of America's production of such weapons, and this in turn causes a further reduction of Russian arms, and so on indefinitely.

Yet granting the vast oversimplification of the above examples, causal-loop diagrams could be developed—with the aid of the extraordinary language of social science—to take into account more and more of the complexity of any given human problem. By so doing, they could help those individuals attempting to solve problems—whether they are working within an organization or are dealing with their own personal problems—to penetrate the complexities of human behavior. Further, such analyses could become more effective in the future by moving from causal-loop diagrams to computer simulation.

However, we should by no means overemphasize the importance of the technology of the causal-loop diagram or even computer simulation for the solution of escalating problems throughout the world. For diagrams and simulation procedures do not by themselves change our *bureaucratic worldview* and *bureaucratic way of life*. As we have argued throughout the foregoing chapters, that worldview is incredibly powerful and is much of the basis for those increasing problems, as illustrated by our *growing values-fulfillment gap*. Nevertheless, by learning to use causal-loop diagrams together with the extraordinary language of social science, we can at least take a step in the direction of learning to apply that language to our problems in a systematic way. Fully granting the enormous power of our *bureaucratic worldview*, the resulting improved understanding of problems could help individuals to move—one step at a time—toward personal evolution. And it could also help those individuals to change the organizations that they work in—again, one step at a time—from bureaucratic groups into learning groups.

To illustrate briefly a next step beyond Senge's illustration of causal-loop diagrams, a step that begins to introduce the extraordinary language of social science, we might add the concept of *bureaucratic worldview* as a seventh concept to the six concepts in the diagram illustrating the arms race during the Cold War. By so doing we can begin to understand the arms race not only as threatening mutual destruction of America and the Soviet Union but also as yielding a continuing escalation of the full range of other problems within the two countries, which we believe actually occurred. And such a diagram suggests the kind of evidence required to test its validity, and such evidence could be obtained. Of course, these are no more than small steps toward learning to use causal-loop diagrams together with the extraordinary language to help us understand complex problems, yet we can learn to continue to move in this direction.

As another brief illustration of combining causal-loop diagrams with the extraordinary language of social science, we could add the concept of *evolutionary worldview* as a seventh concept to the six concepts illustrating the reversal of the arms race linked to the START treaty. This would help us to understand the positive impact of that reversal on the full range of problems within America and Russia. Again, this would guide us to the kind of evidence required to test this idea, and such evidence would have to be obtained. And again, these are only small steps toward learning to understand our complex problems. Still further, we can introduce any number of the eighteen extraordinary or technical concepts from social science that we have discussed and illustrated in chapters 3, 4 and 5 into any given personal or world problem. Those concepts are all stated in the table of contents, which reveals two concepts for each of the three sections within each of the three chapters, or six concepts for each chapter.

Yet what is crucial in doing so is by no means our use of a large number of concepts for addressing a given problem. Indeed, that was and is a major mistake of system dynamicists in addition to their failure to use the extraordinary language of social science. They generally develop overly complex diagrams so that they lose their ability to understand what they are doing in an intuitive way. Simplicity, by contrast, must be the keynote of such analyses, for the diagrams should function as tools to educate the modeler and not function simply as ends in themselves. It is in this way that causal-loop diagrams can work to help modelers—and we can all become modelers—to move from their bureaucratic way of life toward an evolutionary way of life. Without such movement, any achievements in understanding a given problem will do little to change the powerful forces within our *bureaucratic worldview* that are yielding escalating problems throughout the world. Thus, modeling with causal-loop diagrams can become an educational tool that can help all of us to move away from our *bureaucratic worldview* and toward an *evolutionary worldview*.

LEARNING VERSUS BUREAUCRATIC INSTITUTIONS: STRUCTURES

Given the complexity of institutions added to our own lack of deep immersion into the problems within all of them—and also taking into account our limited space for this section of chapter 6 if it is to remain similar to the other sections of the book—we shall focus on the institution of education along with limited treatment of other institutions. This is by no means to imply that those other institutions of society—science, the political institution, the economic institution, religion and the family—are of little importance. Each of them deserves not only space equal to what we are giving to education. Actually, every one of our institutions, including education, deserves to be analyzed within a great many books that make full use of the extraordinary or technical language of social science. Unfortunately, the books available up to this point in time focus on using highly specialized concepts from the social sciences, reflecting the shattered nature of those sciences with their literally hundreds of specialized and sub-specialized areas of knowledge. And following the *bureaucratic worldview* that dominates the academic world, they fail to integrate those bits and pieces of knowledge so as to yield the broad knowledge that we desperately require to understand our escalating problems, let alone make progress on them.

To begin with an overview of the present state of education throughout the world, we turn to the ideas on education of E. F. Schumacher. He was economic advisor to the British Control Commission in postwar Ger-

many as well as the top economist and head of planning at the British
Coal Board for twenty years:

> Education cannot help us as long as it accords no place to metaphysics
> [worldviews]. Whether the subjects taught are subjects of science or of
> the humanities, if the teaching does not lead to a clarification of meta-
> physics, that is to say, of our fundamental convictions, it cannot edu-
> cate a man and, consequently, cannot be of real value to society. . . .
> What is at fault is not specialization, but the lack of depth with which
> the subjects are usually presented, and the absence of metaphysical
> awareness. . . . The sciences are being taught without any awareness of
> the presuppositions of science, of the meaning and significance of sci-
> entific laws, and of the place occupied by the natural sciences within
> the whole cosmos of human thought. . . . Economics is being taught
> without any awareness of the view of human nature that underlies
> present-day economic theory. . . . How could there be a rational teach-
> ing of politics without pressing all questions back to their metaphysical
> roots? (Schumacher, *Small Is Beautiful*, 1973: 86-87)

Schumacher's analysis of the failure of education to confront our worldview—or fundamental metaphysical assumptions as to the nature of reality—takes us back to our own emphasis on moving from a *bureaucratic
worldview* toward an *evolutionary worldview*. He suggests the general failure of education to prepare contemporary society for escalating visible
and invisible problems because of our lack of attention to worldviews or
metaphysical assumptions. His overall critique of education emphasizes
the one-sidedness of our focus on materialistic values by contrast with a
broad interest on the situation of the human being. It is that very materi-
alism that makes a mockery of education through its focus on preparing
students to get jobs rather than doing that in addition to opening them up
to their incredible potentials as human beings.

To illustrate Schumacher's vision of the kind of educational institution
that pays attention to its own metaphysical assumptions or worldview,
we might recall our distinctions among three potentials of language—
dichotomy, gradation and metaphor—as discussed in the first sections of
chapters 1 and 3. Our *bureaucratic worldview* that presently dominates our
institutions erects barriers separating the social sciences, the biophysical
sciences and the humanities. Those barriers are constructed in part by the
different linguistic emphases of these fields: dichotomy for the social
sciences, gradation for the biophysical sciences and metaphor for the
humanities. By contrast, an *evolutionary worldview* involves alternative
metaphysical assumptions that stress interaction. That worldview points
toward the kind of education that enables the student to avoid a one-
sided approach to language and give significant attention to dichotomy,
gradation and metaphor. In that way, the student would learn to build on
the achievements of all three fields of knowledge, carrying further the
ideals of the liberal arts tradition. Unfortunately, however—given our

bureaucratic metaphysical assumptions — there is a very large gap between those ideals and current educational practices.

As for the economic institution, Schumacher contrasts our present approach to economics that is oriented to a materialistic way of life with Buddhist economics: "The Buddhist point of view takes the function of work to be at least threefold: to give a man a chance to utilize and develop his faculties; to enable him to overcome his ego-centeredness by joining with other people in a common task; and to bring forth the goods and services needed for a becoming existence" (51). Schumacher's emphasis on the importance of Buddhist economics follows the ideal of John Dewey that "the supreme test of all political institutions and industrial arrangements shall be the contribution they make to the all-around growth of every member of society."

As an economist, Schumacher was extremely critical of the one-sided materialistic place where our economic system has taken us: away from the basic values that educators and society as a whole should be attempting to teach

> What is the meaning of democracy, freedom, human dignity, standard of living, self-realisation, fulfillment? Is it a matter of goods, or of people? Of course it is a matter of people. . . . If economic thinking . . . cannot get beyond its vast abstractions, the national income, the rate of growth, capital/output ratio, input-output analysis, labour mobility capital accumulation; if it cannot get beyond all this and make contact with the human realities of poverty, frustration, alienation, despair, breakdown, crime, escapism, stress, congestion, ugliness, and spiritual death, then let us scrap economics and start afresh. (70)

Schumacher's interest in Buddhist economics derives not from his focus just on Buddhism but rather stems from his view of the importance of Eastern thought: "The choice of Buddhism is purely incidental; the teachings of Islam, or Judaism could have been used as well as those of any other of the great Eastern traditions" (49). It is Eastern thought that can help Westerners balance their outward perception and thought with inward perception and thought so as to achieve *inward-outward perception and thought*. In this way, Schumacher brings forward fundamental human values that we must learn to fulfill, such as "democracy, freedom, human dignity, standard of living, self-realisation, fulfillment."

Schumacher focused on "head" with his emphasis on our worldview or metaphysical assumptions. And he also saw our basic values as an absolutely fundamental part of education, thus dealing with "heart." We move now to the ideas of Ivan Illich, an Austrian philosopher and Roman Catholic priest, who developed in his *Deschooling Society* (1972) an approach to stratification that deals with "hand":

> Many students, especially those who are poor, intuitively know what the schools do for them. They school them to confuse process and

substance. Once these become blurred, a new logic is assumed: the more treatment there is, the better are the results; or, escalation leads to success. The pupil is thereby "schooled" to confuse teaching with learning, grade advancement with education, a diploma with competence, and fluency with the ability to say something new. His imagination is "schooled" to accept service in place of value. Medical treatment is mistaken for health care, social work for the improvement of community life, police protection for safety, the rat race for productive work. Health, learning, dignity, independence, and creative endeavor are defined as little more than the performance of the institutions which claim to serve these ends, and their improvement is made to depend on allocating more resources to the management of hospitals, schools, and other agencies in question.

In these essays, I will show that the institutionalization of values leads inevitably to physical pollution, social polarization, and psychological impotence: three dimensions in a process of global degradation and modernized misery. I will explain how this process of degradation is accelerated when nonmaterial needs are transformed into demands for commodities; when health, education, personal mobility, welfare or psychological healing are defined as the result of services or "treatments." (1-2)

Illich takes to task here not only the educational institution but also economic, political and scientific institutions. He argues that by confusing "process and substance," defenders of the present-day organization of society are claiming that these institutions actually succeed in fulfilling the values that they have been set up to fulfill. However, Illich claims that this is a sham, and that none of this is true. In fact, Illich claims, we are achieving nothing less than "physical pollution, social polarization, and psychological impotence." Referring to the global values that we presented in chapter 4, we see Illich as claiming that we are failing to fulfill such values as "understanding the world," "solving problems," "individual personality" and "freedom." Thus, what our present institutions are actually creating—despite their claims—is a *wide values-fulfillment gap*.

Illich's master concept is "schooling," which is roughly equivalent to "stratification." Just as patterns of stratification or persisting hierarchy are present throughout all societies, so are we all "schooled" within all of our institutions to conform to the idea that our institutions are in fact fulfilling our values. Illich also claims that our nonmaterial values or "needs," as illustrated by those values cited above, come to be "transformed into demands for commodities." And the result is what we have called a *growing values-fulfillment gap*, or what Illich describes as "a growing frustration gap, which is the motor of a society built on the co-production of services and increased demand" (156). Illich's vision, by contrast, calls for the kind of society within which every individual is able to transform each moment of life into one of learning, sharing and caring. This image of a possible future parallels our own vision of the evolution of the individual and society.

Illich thus sees "schooling" or social stratification within the educational institution not just from the perspective of "hand" but also from the perspectives of "head" and "heart." Stratification or "hand" is the tool used to teach ("head") all of us that our present institutions are in fact fulfilling our basic values or "heart." Schooling teaches us that we are experiencing no values-fulfillment gap, and that we should learn to accept our present situation. Thus, schooling teaches us *emotional repression* all the while that our *values-fulfillment gap* continues to increase. Schooling thus teaches us to fiddle while Rome is burning.

We can learn about our educational institution from fiction as well as non-fiction. Herman Hesse's novel *The Glass Bead Game* (1943/1969) was published in Switzerland during World War II, and it was much of the basis for the Nobel Prize he received in 1946. He focused on the splitting up of modern society into parts that fail to communicate with one another, just as we have emphasized that the isolation of phenomena is central to a *bureaucratic worldview*. Specifically, he centered on the split between professors in the academic world and individuals outside of that world who were attempting to cope with problems. Prior to World War II Hesse idealized a world of culture set far apart from our everyday world full of unsolved problems. But it was in *The Glass Bead Game*, written during the war, that he demonstrated a radical change in his perspective. Culture is indeed important, but the artist and scientist must do their utmost to help society solve its urgent problems if they are to survive along with everyone else. Although Hesse came to be revered by the college students of the 1960s as an underground hero preaching active rebellion against the status quo, in fact he suggested not action alone ("hand") but action guided by the vast cultural achievements that are the focus of the academic world and that are illustrated by the elements of the Glass Bead Game he described ("head" and "heart").

The story takes place in the far future, and the book is a biography of the life of Joseph Knecht, who was Magister Ludi, master of the Glass Bead Game. Knecht had become the leader of an intellectual order, Castalia—much like our present academic world—devoted exclusively to the development of the mind and the imagination. The Glass Bead Game is a game played by members of Castalia in order to integrate and keep alive the wisdom of all ages, and it involves working with elements of all cultures derived from their philosophical, literary, dramatic, artistic, musical and scientific achievements. This is in fact what Hesse himself was attempting to do throughout most of his life: to keep alive elements of all cultures by means of his novels as well as by separating those cultural achievements from the pressing problems of the day.

After reaching the pinnacle of achievement in Castalia as Master of the Glass Bead Game, Joseph Knecht sends a letter to the ruling board of his intellectual order which includes the following paragraphs:

> I have begun to doubt my ability to officiate satisfactorily because I consider the Glass Bead Game in a state of crisis. . . . Here I am sitting in the top story of our Castalian edifice. . . . And instinct tells me, my nose tells me, that down below something is burning, our whole structure is imperiled, and that my business now is not to analyze music or define rules of the Game, but to rush to where the smoke is. . . . The history of societies shows a constant tendency toward the formation of a nobility as the apex and crown of any given society. . . . If, now, we regard our Order as a nobility and try to examine ourselves to see . . . to what extent we have already been infected by the characteristic disease of nobility—hubris, conceit, class arrogance, self-righteousness, exploita- tiveness . . . we may be seized by a good many doubts.
>
> In brief, this Castalian culture of ours . . . tends somewhat toward smugness and self-praise, toward the cultivation and elaboration of intellectual specialism. . . . Historically we are, I believe, ripe for dis- mantling. And there is no doubt that such will be our fate, not today or tomorrow, but the day after tomorrow. . . . Critical times are approach- ing. . . . Displacements of power are in the offing. They will not take place without war and violence. . . . I herewith request the Board to relieve me of my office as Magister Ludi and entrust to me an ordinary school, large or small, outside in the country; to let me staff it with a group of youthful members of our Order. (Hesse, 1943: 319, 321–322, 328–329, 335)

Hesse invokes two key elements of a *bureaucratic worldview*, both of which are found in Castalia. There is (1) persisting hierarchy or stratification ("we have already been infected by the characteristic disease of nobil- ity—hubris, conceit, class arrogance, self-righteousness, exploitative- ness"), and (2) specialization with limited communication ("the cultiva- tion and elaboration of intellectual specialism"). These elements form a grid pattern—with horizontal lines yielding stratification and vertical lines yielding specialization—that results in the isolation of phenomena or in barriers to interaction. Those barriers are the very essence of a *bureaucratic way of life*.

Up to this point within this section our focus has been on what is wrong with the educational institution along with other institutions in contemporary society, illustrated by the criticisms of Schumacher, Illich and Hesse. We have been swinging our pendulum of the scientific meth- od far to the left, gaining momentum or motivation for a swing far to the right. Yet this is exactly what contemporary debates about how to im- prove education, and contemporary efforts to change education in a posi- tive direction, fail to do. For example, where are the discussions about the metaphysical stance or worldview behind our efforts at reform, as Schumacher called for and as our own approach has emphasized in seven books that have stretched over a full decade? Where are the discussions about the negative impact of stratification within all of our schools from pre-kindergarten to post-doctoral levels — as well as within our other institutions — as suggested by Illich and Hesse?

More concretely, such stratification is illustrated by our grading system which reinforces the idea of a hierarchy with respect to basic intelligence. This is an idea that we see as both false — as illustrated by our analysis in the section on self-image in chapter 3 — and incredibly damaging to all of us, including those with supposedly superior intelligence. For it teaches all of us that we are most limited creatures, closing the door on our possibilities for fulfilling our capacities. As for the isolation of knowledge within hundreds of specialized and sub-specialized fields throughout the academic world — also structured by our bureaucratic worldview with its emphasis on isolation — this results in the need for more and more specialists both as educators and as medical practitioners. It is no wonder, then, that the costs of education and medical care are skyrocketing relative to the general increases in the cost of living.

Yet where are the discussions within the mass media about how we might reduce those costs by changing a worldview that emphasizes both patterns of stratification and the isolation of knowledge? We do not have such discussions for the very same reason that the costs of education and medical care are rapidly increasing. The nature of our *bureaucratic worldview* falls under our radar because that worldview itself works to hide such knowledge from our awareness, for it is far too threatening for us to examine. We repress any understanding of our worldview just as the Springdalers made use of the technique of particularization and the falsification of memory in order to develop at least "some degree of satisfaction, recognition and achievement." Yet all the while our *values-fulfillment gap continues to grow*, and we continue on the road to disaster.

However, Schumacher, Illich and Hesse were able to uncover the humongous problems within the institution of education because they had in mind optimistic visions of something far better, that is, a swing of their pendulum far to the right where that institution could be radically improved. Without such visions they would have been unable to mount their fundamental criticisms, just as is the situation of almost all educational reformers today. Schumacher was calling for digging deeply into our basic assumptions so as to uncover the nature of our worldview, and then changing that worldview so that it would support our humanistic people-oriented values. Illich and Hesse were calling for a change from a stratified world that conflicts with those same values toward an egalitarian world where we learn to face up to and solve our basic problems.

With the aid of our own optimistic vision of an *evolutionary worldview* coupled with the realism promised by a broad approach to the scientific method within our everyday lives, we are able at this time in history —

when the problems they cited have continued to increase—to build on their aspirations. Of course, we are able to put forward no more than a very bare outline of what might be done for education within the few pages remaining in this section, yet the foregoing chapters help us by laying the foundation for the directions that might be taken. Overall, granting the humongous problems within the educational institution throughout the world, we are enormously optimistic about moving toward solutions, based on our vision of an *evolutionary worldview* that teaches us the infinite possibilities of every human being. Indeed, we see our awareness of those problems—as illustrated by Schumacher, Illich and Hesse—as absolutely essential if we are to gain the momentum and motivation for swinging our pendulum of the scientific method far to the right.

Our vision of education begins with the assumption that there would develop at least "a few good men and women"—following the Marine Corps slogan—who have begun the evolutionary journey outlined in the above chapters. For it is they who would be able to form "learning groups"—by contrast with bureaucratic organizations—as outlined in the above section of this chapter. And it is they who would be able to follow Ralph Waldo Emerson's advice by making "a better mousetrap" that would motivate more and more of those involved in education to "make a beaten path" to their door. For there would be no limit to how far those groups would continue to go in solving problems of education as well as in their own continuing development or evolution.

More specifically, those "few good men and women" would be contradicting the eighteenth-century slogan, "Jack of all trades and master of none" by both continuing to evolve in the breadth of their understanding ("head"), emotional development ("heart") and ability to solve more and more problems ("hand"), as well as in their own specialized interests. For example, individuals might focus on the problem of nuclear proliferation, or making desserts, or composing music, or developing friendships, or writing musical comedies, or educating their own children, or catching fish, or weight-lifting, or learning languages, or foreign travel, or singing, or playing bridge, or studying ancient Egypt, or typing, or fighting fires, or decorating homes, or writing novels, or exercising, or public speaking, or working as a medical internist, or building houses, or dancing, or playing tennis, or researching Alzheimer's disease, or self-analysis, or conquering depression, or space travel, or Tai Chi, or acting, or manufacturing cars, or leading a country, or growing food, or directing a charitable foundation, or writing poetry, or directing films, or skateboarding or any of the millions of other specialized activities of the human race.

What would be crucial is that they would be able to develop feedback relationships—as illustrated by the causal-loop diagrams discussed in the above section—between their specialized activities and their personal evolution, with those diagrams including relevant concepts from the extraordinary language of social science. As a result, they would be both continuing to learn or evolve and continuing to develop their specialized abilities. Their personal evolution would also give them increasing ability to teach others their specialized abilities. And it would also enable them to move society as a whole toward ever-increasing productivity with respect to making progress on the full range of problems that interest human beings and relate to the fulfillment of our values, as illustrated in the above paragraph. As a result—much like present-day bead stores that have classes on making jewelry requiring paid enrollment—those learning groups would point toward a continuing expansion of the world economy based on ever-increasing productivity. For the world would continue to make a beaten path to the doors of those individuals who are able to build better mousetraps. And given the evolutionary potential of the rest of the human race, there would be every reason why more and more of us would set up such shops either within learning groups or as learning individuals.

Of course, the above paragraphs are no more than a very bare outline of how education might move in an evolutionary direction. A great many problems would be involved, given our present near-universal commitment to our *bureaucratic way of life*. For example, presently our focus within education is on giving young people the knowledge and skills enabling them to obtain jobs within our bureaucratic economy. By contrast, the above paragraphs point toward a shift in focus toward education throughout life that emphasizes continuing personal evolution. Also, presently our focus is on international competition leading to a persisting hierarchy or stratification of rich nations and poor ones. But the above approach suggests the possibility of an expanding pie of development for all peoples of the world and a narrowing of the income gap between the rich and the poor. For watching entertainers or sports figures, resulting in their huge salaries, would become less and less attractive for people who can learn to develop their own creative activities, and effective teachers would do very well financially. Is all of this a hare-brained idea? We believe, based on social science knowledge, that it is not.

LEARNING VERSUS BUREAUCRATIC SOCIETY: STRUCTURES

Given such changes within the educational institution along with all other institutions, what will an evolutionary or learning society be like? For one thing, our answer will depend on how far into the future we want to look. For a learning society will be changing from one moment, hour, day and year to another. For example, initially such a society would be divided along national lines, just as present societies are divided. Yet as communication and transportation across those national boundaries continues to evolve, the human race will in all probability move toward those boundaries becoming less and less meaningful and interaction among the peoples of the world becoming more and more meaningful. As another example, continuing improvements in the scientific method should yield increasing abilities to lengthen the span of human life. Thus, depending how far in the future we go, we see that length continuing to grow. Presently, we look at increasing proportions of older individuals within society most negatively, since they will have to be supported by a smaller proportion of younger individuals. Yet in the society that we envision older individuals generally will be fully productive members of society. While some will be less productive due to medical problems, others will be more productive as a result of the increased opportunities that their long life-span has given them to learn how to solve problems.

Yet movement toward one world should not imply that individuals and groups will abandon their uniqueness, with everyone becoming much the same as everyone else. In fact, given our common *bureaucratic way of life* with its patterns of stratification, conformity, widely shared values and mass communication, we see individuals as illustrating far less uniqueness than is widely believed. By contrast, we see futures within which individuals and groups will become both more and more unique as well as have more and more in common. Visually, we might think of two individuals as circles that are overlapping with one another to a very substantial degree, given our present limited uniqueness. And we see them changing as a result of movement toward an evolutionary society so that they both overlap to a greater degree and increase their non-overlapping areas

Our vision might be illustrated by the change in the American approach to its ethnic groups away from an earlier emphasis on the importance of the assimilation or homogenization of its diverse peoples with their diverse religions, cultural and ethnic backgrounds, thus losing their diversity within the common "melting pot" of America. Our newer emphasis is on "cultural pluralism," as illustrated by immigrants both learning English and the story of America and also learning about their own heritage. This will become more and more possible as individuals continue to develop their abilities along with their emotions and intellects. And we can extend the idea of cultural pluralism to include the diversity or uniqueness of individuals, following our example of two circles with both greater overlap and greater areas that do not overlap.

Such uniqueness was illustrated in the above section on institutions, where we envisioned individuals moving toward becoming both jacks of all trades and masters of more and more trades. We might recall here our reference to *Descartes' Error* in the introduction to chapter four. Current research on the brain has demonstrated that its specialized centers also interact with its other specialized centers to yield general instructions for the behavior of the individual. This suggests the possibilities for specialists to continue to develop their own specialized knowledge while at the same time developing their own general knowledge. This vision carries forward the old idea of the "Renaissance man" into the idea that the rest of us can increasingly become renaissance individuals. The human potential to accomplish this is illustrated in part by the fact that some individuals now experience several careers, suggesting the possibility that we all might do the same.

Given the centrality of learning or evolution as we move away from our bureaucratic way of life, we envision our structuring of the physical environment to help us to evolve. To illustrate, the computer coupled with the internet opens up enormous opportunities for our interaction with both the peoples of the world as well as the knowledge that has been accumulated throughout history. Yet with our present *bureaucratic worldview*, time spent on the internet can easily take away from our "head," "heart" and "hand" development, and that in turn would reinforce our bureaucratic worldview. Yet by emphasizing learning the extraordinary language of social science and applying it to our everyday experiences, we can avoid that pitfall. And we can then go on to continue developing our emotions, intellect and problem-solving abilities as well as our internet skills. For example, the internet could help us to develop "deep dialogues"—as outlined in the section on rituals within chapter five—as well as our understanding of history and our ability to purchase obscure books.

There is much more that can be done to shape our physical world so that it helps us to learn or evolve. For example, we could learn to build functional physical environments that emphasize our own importance as human beings rather than huge non-functional structures that dwarf us into insignificance. We could learn to develop means of personal transportation, like automobiles and aircraft, that use computers to teach us safety lessons when we make mistakes in our driving or flying. We could learn to move away from the "hard architecture" of rooms in buildings—and buildings themselves, and indeed all other physical structures—that cannot be altered as we climb further up the stairway of evolution and as our requirements for solving problems change. We could learn to design games that move us away from our competitive win-lose mentality, where the focus of the game becomes the development of all the players.

As we continue to envision a learning or evolutionary society, a central question has to do with the nature of the economic institution. It is here that we return to the saying that most people believe is true but that we most emphatically reject—"Jack of all trades and master of none"—as cited both in the introduction to chapter four as well as in the above material within this section of our final chapter. Our central idea here is that we human beings, just like Gilbert Gosseyn at the beginning of *The World of Null-A*, have no idea as to the nature of our incredible capacities for continually learning with respect to "head," "heart" and "hand," or personal evolution. More specifically, each one of us can learn more and more to be both a "Jack of all trades" and a master of some. By so doing we will be following along with the very structure of our brains, as documented in *Descartes' Error*. For we can continue to learn about our specialized interests all the while that those interests also help us to develop our general understanding of ourselves and the world as well as how to make progress on broad problems.

At this point what we require most are realistic and current examples of how we can move from where we are toward the kind of society where the "productivity" of more and more individuals continues to increase. Within our present *bureaucratic way of life*, by contrast, what we see within a see-saw world is increasing gaps between the rich and the poor throughout the world accompanied by worldwide unemployment and underemployment along with very limited increases in "productivity." What we mean by productivity is the degree to which the full range of our values—and not just those values emphasizing economic progress and material comfort—are fulfilled. As we shall see in the final pages of this book, present-day measurements of productivity emphasize the latter almost exclusively rather than the former.

It is the integration of social science knowledge that can provide a platform for understanding human behavior and human problems that can become the basis for launching ever more effective personal and social technologies throughout all of society's institutions. To focus on just one—the educational institution—we presently have the beginnings of this possibility, beginnings limited to the efforts of no more than a tiny minority of individuals. For example, the demand by adults and retired individuals for adult education illustrates both the human being's potential for learning or evolution and the ability of some entrepreneurs to cash in on that demand. Thus, we have increasing numbers of adult-education classes, organizations that provide domestic and foreign educational trips, bead stores with classes for learning how to make jewelry, chefs who have organized cooking classes, theatrical organizations that have developed acting classes, organizations that teach writing for publication, medical groups that teach healthful living, and so on. More personally, we—as educational entrepreneurs—are hoping that this book will gain a wide readership because it proves to be effective in opening up possibilities for readers to learn to become productive in society by pursuing their own specialized interests.

Yet all of this is no more than the tip of the iceberg of our possibilities. We are convinced that the rest of the iceberg will emerge, one step at a time, as we learn to move toward an *evolutionary worldview* and way of life that includes the integration of our knowledge of human behavior. That integration will not come about easily, given our deep commitment to a *bureaucratic worldview and way of life*. However, we see the broad umbrella concepts that we have selected from the extraordinary or technical language of the social sciences as giving us the initial tools we require to begin to make the journey toward an *evolutionary way of life*. It is those tools that can help us learn to use the scientific method within our everyday lives. And, as a result, we are convinced that they can enable every single one of us to release his or her infinite potential for learning or evolution.

A fundamental question with respect to any society has to do with the rules governing the society as a whole, as illustrated by the Constitution of the United States, the Supreme Court as the final arbiter on interpreting the Constitution, and the periodic election of the two Houses of Congress. However, a democratic political process, as illustrated by this political system, has only been able to go so far in solving the problems addressed by the different institutions of society, as illustrated by our *growing values-fulfillment gap*. More concretely, we have such problems as war, terrorism with weapons of mass destruction, patterns of stratification—such as the growing gap between the rich and the poor, unemployment and poverty—contradicting our people-oriented values. And we have environmental pollution and global warming, crime, mental and other health problems, and more subtle problems like what sociologists have called the "alienation" of the individual. Also, let us not forget what Stanley Milgram discovered—as presented in chapter 5—about the widespread and abject conformity in democratic societies that have even led to what we see as the greatest crime in human history: the Holocaust.

As Jane Addams has suggested, quoted in chapter 1, "The cure for the ills of Democracy is more Democracy." And she went further in her De- mocracy and Social Ethics to suggest the importance of not merely the practice of voting but the involvement of nothing less than "head," "heart" and "hand." Here, we repeat the quote from her book that we presented in chapter 1:

> A conception of Democracy not merely as a sentiment which desires the well-being of all men, nor yet as a creed which believes in the essential dignity and equality of all men, but as that which affords a rule of living as well as a test of faith. (quoted in Knowles, 2004: 3)

We are convinced that we can actually move toward fulfilling Jane Addams's far-reaching vision of a democratic way of life where individuals throughout society develop "a sentiment which desires the well-being of all men" ("heart"), "a creed which believes in the essential dignity and equality of all men" ("head") and "a rule of living as well as a test of faith" ("hand"). Such movement, we believe, can occur one step at a time as we move toward the "learning individual," "learning group," "learning institution" and "learning society," as discussed throughout this book with its focus on the evolution of the individual and society. In this way Addams's vision of Democracy becomes an evolutionary process based on a society's learning, one step at a time, to use the scientific method in everyday life with the aid of the extraordinary language of social science.

Is it actually possible to measure such movement toward a democratic way of life or an *evolutionary way of life*? Presently, the most influential general statistic used to calculate the development of society as a whole has centered on material development and not on the fulfillment of people-oriented values. This is the calculation by economists and statisticians of the gross domestic product or GDP, performed in the United States. and a great many other countries as well. This measurement was invented during the Great Depression to determine just how much and how quickly the American economy was shrinking, and just how well President Franklin D. Roosevelt's efforts to reverse the economic slump were working.

Although the GDP proved to be a useful measure in helping to determine the success of Roosevelt's New Deal, this measurement is limited in fundamental ways with respect to the range of values that it includes, as indicated by this analysis:

> GDP measures the size of the pie, not the quality of the ingredients—fresh apples or rotten ones are counted the same . . . the sale of an assault rifle and the sale of an antibiotic both contribute equally to the national tally (assuming the sales price is the same). GDP doesn't register, as Robert Kennedy put it, "the beauty of our poetry or the strength of our marriages, or the intelligence of our public debate." GDP measures everything, Kennedy concluded, "except that which makes life worthwhile. . . . Yet we continue to treat economic growth and well-being as one and the same.
>
> But one country does not. Bhutan, a tiny Himalayan nation, has invented a radically new metric: Gross National Happiness. . . . Bhutan, a beautiful land of mountains and temples, has forsaken millions of tourist dollars by, in effect, restricting the number of foreign visitors. It does this by charging a $200 daily fee. And while other developing countries have sold off their natural resources. . .. Bhutan has hardly touched its timber and minerals . . . . Bhutan is no Shangri-La. It has crime and alcoholism and unhappy people, just like other places . . . but alternatives to growth-at-any-cost policies are desperately needed. Bhutan's Gross National Happiness may not be the answer to the problem, but it does re-frame the question—namely, what is a sensible way for a country to achieve the greatest happiness for the greatest number of its citizens? (Uchitelle, 2008: Wk 3)

We submit that we can indeed measure what Robert Kennedy called for, focusing on the measuring the degree of fulfillment of our people-oriented values, as presented in chapter 4. Granting that the validity and accuracy of such measurements have been limited, they can be improved over time, just as any kind of scientific knowledge can develop over time. Specifically, as for his concerns about "the strength of our marriages" and "the intelligence of our public debate," we have cited the value of "intimate or close relationships" For "the intelligence of our public debate" we have cited the value of "understanding the world." As for "the beauty of our poetry," the value of "understanding the world" covers that in part. And the values of "individual personality" and "freedom"—with their attention to the individual's potential for expressing self—also overlaps with that value. Not only can we measure the fulfillment of these values, but we are convinced that we can also learn to move toward fulfilling them, as we have argued throughout this book, by learning to use the scientific method in everyday life so as to move toward an *evolutionary way of life*

Invictus, a film directed by Clint Eastwood that stars Matt Damon and Morgan Freeman, portrays the actual fulfillment of such humanistic values at least to some degree. It focuses on the improvement of relationships between blacks and whites in South Africa after Nelson Mandela took office as president in 1994. Mandela succeeds in convincing blacks to support the nation's almost completely white Rugby team, the Springboks. And Mandela also succeeds in inspiring the Springboks, helping them to win the Rugby World Cup in 1995, leading—we believe—to greater fulfillment of the global value of equality among both whites and blacks. The film presents a sharp contrast with the *Star Trek* episode, "Where No Man Has Gone Before"—presented in chapter 3—with Gary Mitchell illustrating Lord Acton's belief that "power tends to corrupt and absolute power corrupts absolutely." Instead, Mandela demonstrates the idea that great power can yield not great corruption but rather the evolution of society.

As a leader within the African National Congress and as an antiapartheid activist, Mandela was convicted of sabotage in 1962 and spent twenty-seven years in a prison on Robben Island. In the film Mandela inspires the leader of the Springboks by taking him to Robben Island, showing him his prison cell and telling him about the poem that inspired him during those 27 years. It is William Ernest Henley's "Invictus":

> Out of the night that covers me,
> Black as the pit from pole to pole,
> I thank whatever gods may be
> For my unconquerable soul. . . .
>
> In the fell clutch of circumstance,
> I have not winced nor cried aloud:
> Under the bludgeonings of chance
> My head is bloody but unbowed
>
> Beyond this place of wrath and tears
> Looms but the Horror of the shade,
> And yet the measure of the years

Finds, and shall find, me unafraid.

It matters not how straight the gate,
How charged with punishments the scroll,
I am the master of my fate:
I am the captain of my soul.

Henley, a nineteenth-century English poet suffered from tuberculosis of the bone and the amputation of his left leg below the knee. Yet he was extraordinarily optimistic and vital, and was the inspiration for Robert Louis Stevenson's vigorous peg-legged Captain John Silver in *Treasure Island*. We can learn to carry forward his nineteenth century optimism and utopianism into the twenty-first century despite our own escalating world problems that threaten the very survival of the human race. With the aid of such optimism, and realism based on the use of the extraordinary language of social science in everyday life, we can learn to move away from our *bureaucratic way of life* and toward an *evolutionary way of life*.

As we conclude this chapter and this book with our vision of human possibilities, let us not forget the overwhelming importance of an optimistic vision of the future—based on a realistic assessment of the past and present—for actually constructing the future. Fred Polak, a Dutch sociologist, claimed that an image of the future can become the most powerful force that we can develop for actually creating the future (1973). Given the many devastating events of the twentieth and twenty-first centuries it is very easy to become discouraged about the prospects of the human race. Yet we should not allow those events to hide the long march of us humans—building on the interactive nature of our universe and of the process of biological evolution—toward our own continuing development. We might recall from chapter 3, for example, the "respect revolution" discussed by Miller and Savoie with its civil rights movement; women's movement; gay, lesbian and transgender movement; senior movement; and disability movement. These movements—along with new ones like democratic movements throughout the Middle East—suggest the overwhelming power of the people-oriented values discussed in that same chapter, values that these movements are pointing toward fulfilling. They are pushing against the *widening of our values-fulfillment gap* that is a product of our *bureaucratic way of life*.

Just as Robert Fuller is attempting to carry further this "dignitarian revolution" by developing a social movement focusing on the negative impacts of "rankism"—illustrated by "heightism," "weightism" and "beautyism"—so can the rest of us learn to join that movement, which points away from our *bureaucratic way of life* and toward an *evolutionary way of life*. For we humans are already in possession of the tool that sharply distinguishes us from all other organisms throughout the known universe: our complex language. And we can open up to ever more of the infinite power of that tool by learning to integrate it with the aid of umbrella concepts from the extraordinary language of the social sciences.

In that way we can learn, one step at a time, to employ the resulting broad scientific method within our everyday lives. Given the power that has already been demonstrated by the narrow scientific method tied to our *bureaucratic way of life* that has shaped all of us over the past five centuries, we can scarcely imagine the incredible potential of a broad scientific method tied to an *evolutionary way of life* for *narrowing our values-fulfillment gap* and continuing to shape ourselves and the world. By so doing we can learn to say along with William Earnest Henley and Nelson Mandela, "I am the master of my fate: I am the captain of my soul." And we can also learn to take the advice of the Buddha, who said on his deathbed, "Be lamps unto yourselves; be a refuge to yourselves." (quoted in Kaplan, 1961: 244)

References

Abbott, Edwin A. *Flatland: A Romance of Many Dimensions*. New York: Dover, 1884/ 1952.

Addams, Jane. *Democracy and Social Ethics*, 1902. In Elizabeth Knowles (ed.), *The Oxford Dictionary of Quotations*. New York: Oxford University Press, 2004, 3.18

Bardach, Janusz. *Man Is Wolf to Man: Surviving the Gulag*. Berkeley: Univ. of California Press, 1998.

Barry, Ellen. "Study Looks at Loss, Its Role in Depression: Finds Humiliation Triggers Worst Cases," *The Boston Globe*, August 13, 2003, A3.

Baum, L. Frank. *The Wizard of Oz and the Land of Oz*. New York: Random House, 1960.

Blish, James. *Star Trek 8*. New York, Bantam Books, 1972.

Constas, Helen. "Max Weber's Two Conceptions of Bureaucracy," *American Journal of Sociology* 52 (January 1958), 400-409.

Damasio, Antonio. *Descartes' Error: Emotion, Reason, and the Human Brain*. New York: Penguin Books, 1994/2005.

Dewey, John. *Reconstruction in Philosophy*. Boston: Beacon Press, 1920/1948.

Durkheim, Emile. *Suicide*. New York: Free Press, 1897/1951.

Ellison, Ralph. *Invisible Man.*, New York: Vintage, 1947.

Emerson, Ralph Waldo. *The Essential Writings of Ralph Waldo Emerson*. New York: Modern Library, 2000.

Ferguson, Niall. *The War of the World: Twentieth Century Conflict and the Descent of the West*. New York: Penguin Press, 2006.

Forrester, Jay W. *World Dynamics*. Cambridge, Massachusetts: MIT Press, 1971.

Fromm, Erich. *Man for Himself: An Inquiry into the Psychology of Ethics*. New York: Fawcett, 1947.

Fuller, Robert W. *Somebodies and Nobodies: Overcoming the Abuse of Rank*. Gabriola Island, Canada: New Society Publishers, 2003.

Fuller, Robert W. *All Rise: Somebodies, Nobodies, and the Politics of Dignity*. San Francisco: Berrett-Koehler, 2006.

Funakoshi, Gichin, and Genwa Nakasone. *The Twenty Guiding Principles of Karate*. Tokyo: Kodansha International Ltd., 2003.

Gartner, Alan, et al. (eds.). *The New Assault on Equality: I.Q. and Social Stratification*. New York: Harper & Row, 1974.

Goleman, Daniel. *Emotional Intelligence: Why It Can Matter More Than IQ*. New York: Bantam Books, 1995.

Gould, Stephen Jay. *The Mismeasure of Man*. New York: Norton, 1981.

Gouldner, Alvin W. *The Coming Crisis of Western Sociology*. New York: Basic Books, 1970.

Gouldner, Alvin W. "The Politics of the Mind: Reflections on Flack's Review of *The Coming Crisis of Western Sociology*," *Social Policy* 5 (March/April 1972), 13–21, 54–58.

Hayawaka, Samuel I. *Language in Thought and Action*. New York: Harcourt, Brace, & World, 1949.

Hesse, Herman. *The Glass Bead Game (Magister Ludi)*. New York: Bantam Books 1943/ 1969.

Horney, Karen. *The Neurotic Personality of Our Time*. New York: Norton, 1937.

Horney, Karen. *Self-Analysis*. New York: Norton, 1942.

Hornig, Susanna. "Television's NOVA and the Construction of Scientific Truth," *Critical Studies in Mass Communication* (1990), 11-23.

Illich, Ivan. *Deschooling Society*. New York: Harper & Row, 1972.

James, William. *Pragmatism: A New Home for Some Old Ways of Thinking*. New York: Dover, 1907/1995.

Kaplan, Abraham. *The New World of Philosophy*. New York: Random House, 1961.

Kelly, George A. *The Psychology of Personal Constructs*, 2 vols. New York: W. W. Norton, 1955.

Kelly, George A. *A Theory of Personality: The Psychology of Personal Constructs*. New York: W. W. Norton, 1963.

Kincaid, Harold, John Dupre and Alison Wylie (eds.). *Value-Free Science? Ideals and Illusions*. Oxford: Oxford University Press, 2007.

Knottnerus, J. David. *Ritual as a Missing Link: Structural Rationalization Theory, Sociology, and Research*. Boulder, Colorado: Paradigm Publishers, 2011.

Knottnerus, J. David, and Bernard Phillips (eds.). *Bureaucratic Culture and Escalating Problems: Advancing the Sociological Imagination*. Boulder, Colorado: Paradigm Publishers, 2009.

Knowles, Elizabeth (ed.). *The Oxford Dictionary of Quotations*. New York: Oxford University Press, 2004.

Korzybski, Alfred. *Science and Sanity*. Garden City, New York: Country Life Press, 1933.

Kuhn, Thomas S. *The Structure of Scientific Revolutions*. Chicago: Univ. of Chicago Press, 1962.

Lehrer, Jonah. "The Truth Wears Off: Is There Something Wrong With the Scientific Method," *The New Yorker*, December 13, 2010, 52-57.

Leichsenring, Falk, and Sven Rabung. "Effectiveness of Long-Term Psychodynamic Psychotherapy: A Meta-analysis," JAMA, 300 (Oct. 2008), 1551-1565.

Lerner, Daniel. *The Passing of Traditional Society*. New York: Free Press, 1958, 23-25.

Levin, Jack. "The Influence of Social Frame of Reference for Goal Fulfillment on Social Aggression." Ph.D. Dissertation, Boston University, 1968.

Marx, Karl. *Early Writings*. Trans. and ed. by T. B. Bottomore. New York: McGrawHill, 1844/1964.

Maslow, Abraham. *The Further Reaches of Human Nature*. New York: Viking, 1971.

McQuarie, Donald, "Utopia and Transcendence," *Journal of Popular Culture* 14 (Fall 1980), 242-250.

Meadows, Donella H., et al. *The Limits to Growth*. New York: Universe, 1972.

Merton, Robert K. "The Unanticipated Consequences of Purposive Social Action," *American Sociological Review* 1 (December 1936), 894–904.

Milgram, Stanley. *Obedience to Authority*. New York: Harper & Row, 1974.

Miller, S. M., and Anthony J. Savoie. *Respect AND Rights: Class, Race, and Gender Today*. Lanham, Maryland: Rowman & Littlefield, 2002.

Mills, C. Wright. *The Sociological Imagination*. New York: Oxford University Press, 1959.

Mills, C. Wright. "Student Forum: Another Viewpoint." *The Battalion* (Texas A&M University), May 8, 1935. In Keith Kerr, *Postmodern Cowboy: C. Wright Mills and a New 21st-Century Sociology*, 37. Boulder, Colorado: Paradigm Publishers, 2009.

Murray, Donald M. "In Life as in War, Overcoming Fear One Small Step at a Time," *The Boston Globe*, October 30, 2001: 11B.

Nisbett, Richard E. *Intelligence and How to Get It: Why Schools and Culture Count*. New York: W. W. Norton, 2009.

Ouspensky, P. D. *The Fourth Way: A Record of Talks and Answers to Questions Based on the Teaching of G. I. Gurdjieff*. New York: Vintage, 1971.

Parker, Richard, and Katherine Allen. "Turmoil Beyond Elections," *Sarasota Herald-Tribune*, November 9, 2010.

Peirce, Charles S. "The Fixation of Belief," in Peirce, Charles S., *Philosophical Writings of Peirce*. New York: Dover, 1877/1955, 5–22.

Peirce, Charles S. "The Scientific Attitude and Fallibilism," in Peirce, Charles S., *Philosophical Writings of Peirce*. New York: Dover, 1896/1955, 42–59.

Peirce, Charles S. "The Approach to Metaphysics," in Peirce, Charles S., *Philosophical Writings of Peirce*. New York: Dover, 1898/1955, 310–314.

Phillips, Bernard. "When I Begin the Ancient Game of Chess," *Different*. New York: Summer, 1954, 18.

Phillips, Bernard. "A Role Theory Approach to Adjustment in Old Age," *American Sociological Review* 22 (April 1957), 212-217.

Phillips, Bernard. "Expected Value Deprivation and Occupational Preference," *Sociometry*, 27 (June 1964), 151-160.

Phillips, Bernard. *Worlds of the Future: Exercises in the Sociological Imagination*. Columbus, Ohio: Charles E. Merrill, 1972.

Phillips, Bernard. "Paradigmatic Barriers to System Dynamics," *1980 Proceedings of the International Conference on Cybernetics and Society*, Oct. 8-10, 1980, Cambridge, Massachusetts, 682-688.

Phillips, Bernard. *Sociological Research Methods: An Introduction*. Homewood, Illinois: Dorsey Press, 1985.

Phillips, Bernard. *Beyond Sociology's Tower of Babel: Reconstructing the Scientific Method*. New York: Aldine de Gruyter, 2001.

Phillips, Bernard (ed.). *Understanding Terrorism: Building on* The Sociological Imagination. Boulder, Colorado: Paradigm Publishers, 2007.

Phillips, Bernard. *Armageddon or Evolution: The Scientific Method and Escalating World Problems*. Boulder, Colorado: Paradigm Publishers, 2009

Phillips, Bernard and David Christner. *Saving Society: Breaking Out of Our Bureaucratic Way of Life*. Boulder, Colorado: Paradigm Publishers, 2011.

Phillips, Bernard, and Louis C. Johnston. *The Invisible Crisis of Contemporary Society: Reconstructing Sociology's Fundamental Assumptions*. Boulder, Colorado: Paradigm Publishers, 2007.

Phillips, Bernard, Harold Kincaid, and Thomas J. Scheff (Eds.). *Toward a Sociological Imagination: Bridging Specialized Fields*. Lanham, Maryland: University Press of America, 2002.

Plato, *Plato's Republic*, trans. by G. M. A. Grube. Indianapolis: Hackett, 1974.

Polak, Fred. *The Image of the Future*. San Francisco: Jossey-Bass, 1973,

Pope, Alexander. *An Essay in Criticism*, 1711. In Elizabeth Knowles (ed.), *The Oxford Dictionary of Quotations*. New York: Oxford University Press, 2004, 604.2.

Raushenbush, Hilmar S. *Man's Past: Man's Future*. New York: Delacorte, 1969.

Rees, Martin. *Our Final Hour: A Scientist's Warning: How Terror, Error, and Environmental Disaster Threaten Humankind's Future in This Century—On Earth and Beyond*. New York: Basic Books, 2003.

Roberts, Nancy, et al. *Introduction to Computer Simulation: The System Dynamics Approach*. Reading, Massachusetts: Addison-Wesley, 1983.

Rosenthal, Robert, and Lenore Jacobson. *Pygmalion in the Classroom*. New York: Holt, Rinehart and Winston, 1968.

Sarasota Herald-Tribune, "Half of Teenagers Admit to Bullying," Oct. 29, 2010, 9A.

Scheff, Thomas J. *Bloody Revenge: Emotions, Nationalism, and War*. Boulder, Colorado.: Westview, 1994.

Schooler, Jonathan W., and Tonya Y. Engstier-Schooler. "Verbal Overshadowing of Visual Memories: Some Things Are Better Left Unsaid," in *Cognitive Psychology* 22 (January 1990), 36-71.

Schumacher, E. F. *Small Is Beautiful: Economics as if People Mattered*. New York: Harper & Row, 1973.

Senge, Peter M. *The Fifth Discipline: The Art and Practice of the Learning Organization*. New York: Doubleday, 1990.

Shenk, David. *The Genius in All of Us: Why Everything You've Been Told About Genetics, Talent, and IQ Is Wrong*. New York: Doubleday, 2010.

Sociological Imagination Group. www.sociological-imagination.org

Tanay, Emanuel. *American Legal Injustice*. Lanham, Maryland: Rowman & Littlefield, 2010.

Turner, Jonathan H. "The Social Psychology of Terrorism," in Phillips, Bernard (ed.). *Understanding Terrorism: Building on The Sociological Imagination*. Boulder, Colo.: Paradigm Publishers, 2007: 115-145.

Uchitelle, Louis. "GDP Does Not Equal Happiness," *The New York Times*, August 31, 2008: Wk 3.

Uchitelle, Louis. "Irrational Exuberance," *The New York Times Book Review*, April 19, 2009, 18.

Udy, Stanley H., Jr. "'Bureaucracy' and 'Rationality' in Weber's Organization Theory," *American Sociological Review* 24 (1959): 591–595.

Van Vogt, A. E. *The World of Null-A*. New York: Berkley Publishing, 1945/1970.

Van Vogt, A. E. *The Players of Null-A*. New York: Berkley Publishing, 1948.

Vance, Jack. *The Languages of Pao*. New York: Daw Books, 1958.

Vidich, Arthur, and Joseph Bensman. *Small Town in Mass Society: Class, Power, and Religion in a Rural Community*. Garden City, N.Y.: Doubleday, 1960.

Weber, Max. *The Protestant Ethic and the Spirit of Capitalism*. New York: Scribner's, 1905/1958.

Whitman, Walt. "Song of Myself," in *Leaves of Grass*. New York: Random House, 1892/1983, 23-24.

Whorf, Benjamin. *Language, Thought and Reality*. Cambridge , Massachusetts: MIT Press, 1963.

Williams, Robin M., Jr. "Major Value Orientations in America," *American Society*, 3rd ed. New York: Knopf, 1970, 452–500.

Yeats, W. B. "The Second Coming," 1921. In Elizabeth Knowles (ed.), *The Oxford Dictionary of Quotations*. New York: Oxford University Press, 2004, 855.12

Index

About the Authors

Bernard Phillips, a student of C. Wright Mills at Columbia, received a Ph.D. at Cornell and taught at the University of North Carolina and the University of Illinois before teaching at Boston University. He co-founded ASA's Section on Sociological Practice, founded the Sociological Imagination Group, and founded a series of monographs with Paradigm Publishers, "Advancing the Sociological Imagination," which he co-edits with J. David Knottnerus. He resides in Longboat Key, Florida, and can be reached at bernieflps@aol.com.

David Christner has worked closely with Bernard Phillips in an effort to help fulfill the aims of the Sociological Imagination Group. Its work is described and illustrated on its website, www.sociological-imagination.org. He is the founder of World Health Advanced Technology, which focuses on the development and testing of enercel, a substance used for achieving biofunctional health. Its effectiveness for a number of diseases is presently being tested in several countries around the world. For details, see www.enercel.org.

CPSIA information can be obtained at www.ICGtesting.com
Printed in the USA
BVOW011401131111

275951BV00002B/1/P